Creationism Revisited

– 2020 –

A Defense of Recent Creation

by an Agnostic

By James Stroud

Breezeway Books

Requests for permission to make copies of any part of this work should be mailed to Permissions Department, Breezeway Books, 7970 NW 4th Place, Plantation, FL 33324

ISBN: 978-1-62550-6061

Published in the United States of America

A quick note to the reader or reviewer –

This is more of a rough-draft than a finalized book that is a small part of a larger post-graduate project. Breezeway Books was kind enough to put it in book/eBook form for easy distribution as I am needing feedback and critiques of sustenance for this larger project that will be revealed at a later date. I cannot reveal it now or it could skew the critiques like *leading the witness.*

Please critique the information and the easiest way would be through a review on Amazon. Please note it does not matter if this is 1 star or 5 stars as long as it is fairly detailed. For example, I am hoping to hear concrete refutations or support for this work not just "I didn't like it". It is mostly targeting Christians or agnostics with an open mind to be able to see the points for and against the notion of creationism (YEC) in 2020 and beyond.

Again, I am an agnostic on the exact dating, but part of my project is to analyze the credibility or lack thereof concerning the YEC position. I have found the position quite strong if one is a Christian and I would be very grateful for any critique (good/bad/indifferent) posted on Amazon if possible where I can then gather the reviews to add to my project-results.

Please do not get hung-up on grammar, proper citation (APA vs Chicago), my informal tone, etc. as this is mostly in rough-draft form. Moreover, I have given proper citation to any groups I have used their material towards hopefully but please forgive anything I missed. Though this is in book form, it is not commercial, so I am not making money from this work. Instead I asked Breezeway to sell at cost and they were gracious enough to help me by getting it in POD-book form to make it easier to get in your hands for review.

Lastly – I thank all groups that have helped and none of them endorse this work necessarily and the views are my own. Though I may disagree with some elements of these groups (ex: WLC or AIG) I am very thankful for their work and ministry as I am also thankful for the wealth of information they have helped provide both in book, online and in person. Nothing I have written should be out of context or disingenuous but if it is, I apologize in advance as this was not my intention. My hope with this project is to bring the YEC position back into dialog as a robust and intellectually viable position while also helping clear some of the roadblocks out of the way for young Christians growing up in an increasingly hostile environment to their faith.

Thank you –

Comments during the compiling of this work:

I like and accept James' distinction between physics and metaphysics and there is room to believe that the Earth is billions of years old, but that humanity is only tens of thousands of years old. – **Hugh Ross** (noted OEC astronomer and founder of *Reasons to Believe*)

I am always happy to work with James and I'm delighted with what he's doing here to get these questions back onto the table. I think the YEC case is as strong today as ever. – **Walt Brown** (noted engineer MIT, founder of Hydroplate theory)

Congratulations on this book James but I am still a little concerned with you trying to reconcile cosmology with Genesis and the Bible when the fact is that you can't do it and there's certainly no way we can reconcile it with a young earth that I can see. I do however think you bring up some good points that the singularity of the big bang could be very similar with that of a black hole, though the initial conditions are quite different. White holes, time reversed solution of a black hole, are a possibility in principle but how they are created is very unclear and I suspect we will have to have a quantum theory of gravity before we can answer the questions you raise around time dilation modeling. – **Lawrence Krauss**, Noted Theoretical Physicist and atheist (*A Universe from Nothing*)

YEC is a less credible scientific position than OEC today. However, it is a much better fit biblically with several important features such as the Fall, so I broadly agree with you on the points you raise James. – **Stephen Law** (noted atheist philosopher and debater)

YEC is certainly strong enough to share with those who have some inclination to listen. In my assessment, the secular view on the geological record simply has no answers for the to the powerful evidences of catastrophic water processes throughout the rock record. Most educated people in our culture have been conditioned through and through to believe that deep time is an unassailable reality as James alludes to. – **John Baumgardner** (considered one of the world's pre-eminent geophysicists and founder of *Catastrophic Plate Tectonics*)

I appreciate your efforts here James. As you probably know already, hardline inerrantists have been attacking me since 2011 on how I (and other New Testament scholars) interpret a number of biblical texts… I'm presently of the opinion that some brothers and sisters in Christ, though sincere and well-meaning, are not interested in peace, because they view the other position as a threat to orthodoxy. – **Michael Licona** (noted New Testament historian)

I applaud your [James] passion for biblical creationism. William Craig, Norm Geisler, Hugh Ross, William Dembski, etc. are great scholars who will not yield to any YEC model. Most seem to be stuck in some sort of OEC philosophy mainly due the "majority opinion of secular science." I suspect the core reason is pride, sad to say. They are fearful of the persecution they would experience if they publicly committed to YEC. – **Henry Morris IV** (Director of Operations, Institute for Creation Research)

Congratulations on this book James. This specific topic has always intrigued me and I have tried to multiple times myself to put the bible and archaeology together and I know it is really difficult to do James, so I really look forward to this getting published and always remember I'm here for you if you need any further advice on anything. Best of luck! – **Ramy Romany** – Egyptologist, Documentarian (Discovery/History Channels and National Geographic)

I wish you the best with this project James, though I don't envy you. I'm not very optimistic about academia ever becoming more open to biblical-creation. The ID movement was formed specifically to get a foot in the door without the "baggage" of the Bible, and (despite some great research and excellent books, e.g. by Stephen Meyer) hasn't made much progress but I wish you the best with this work. – **Spike Psarris** (founder of CreationAstronomy.com)

You need not agree to every point made by James to gain great insight from this potent book; the concept is unique, the ideas challenging, and the style of writing pleasantly readable. – **Subodh Pandit** (MD, international speaker and philosophy of religion researcher)

Very, very good stuff in here; love what James is doing in this book. We all have points agree and points where we disagree with everyone but that should not hinder our Christian fellowship with each other. – **Kent Hovind** (noted creation speaker)

James - If we have doubting questions such are pointless. To start with we know nothing of the mind asking the questions. It is like a finger trying to point to itself. Instead of being in awe at God's creation, including our power of thinking, in our pride we do not realize that the very doubt is God's miracle of consciousness. God's creation is unfathomable and like Job after 41 chapters of discussion we need come to the conclusion, in our foolishness, we question about things beyond our possible understanding. – **Mikai Wurmbrand** (Romanian author and son of Richard Wurmbrand)

Keep up the great work James. I think it's great you're pursuing another MS in Astronomy and tying it in to this new book. – **Alyssa Carson** (NASA select – one of the first preselected to potentially land on Mars in 2033)

Hey James! I heard you talked to my friend Lawrence Krauss on this book and I'm glad you're talking to us atheists too because we're all looking for truth in all the ways we can and I do love [when someone takes their faith seriously]. Congrats on this and your post-grad work. Peace and love you guys! – **Penn Jillette** – Magician/Speaker/Atheist

Congrats on this book James. Was great having a chance to talk to you about it and maybe we can work something out for a future event together. The age of the earth isn't just a debate at how old a piece of rock is; it's a debate about our origins. God bless and I wish you all the best. – **Kevin Sorbo** – Actor/Documentarian (Andromeda, God's Not Dead, Against the Tide – apologetics tour)

Hey James! Huge congrats on this book I can't wait to read the published copy! Please send a finalized copy; I think it's great that us Christians can work together. Sending you and Gina my love! – **Melissa Joan Hart** – Actress, Spokeswoman (Sabrina, God's Not Dead 2)

James – I love your concept here that science and faith need not be at odds which is a very "Star Trek" idea. Congratulations and may you and this work "live long and prosper". Stay safe James! – **Johnathan Frakes** – Actor/Director (Star Trek, Time Travel Through the Bible)

*Please note – these are snippets of conversations I have had with these individuals about ideas conveyed in the book and are not to be taken as endorsements of my work or the book itself of course. It is also to show I went through opponents not just those who agree with me. (Also the last 4 commenters are from actors/actresses as I have been working with former Hollywood type names that are interested in the role between science and faith and may serve as future emcees for my apologetic meetings to help attract a larger and more diverse crowd).

About the Author

I have grown tired of the constant fighting between young- and old-earth creationists. I'm equally weary of the inconsistences of old-earth creationism (OEC) coupled with the unfair caricatures of young-earth creationism (YEC). My goal for this work is to show why, though I am agnostic on the exact date of creation, I believe YEC is as credible as OEC, if not more so. During seminars, questions often distract the audience and derail my talk on my sympathies towards the YEC position, so I also write this so I could refer seekers here for answers. My credentials are not particularly impressive, though I sometimes wish I had not wasted as much time on academic pursuits as I have. I believe the merits of my work lies in the fact that I have worked diligently with both OEC and YEC while all of my education has been within secular academia; but in as much as credentials matter, here are mine:

- BA in philosophy of religion and MA in ancient history, both from secular universities (magna cum laude); MA in theology, with post-graduate work in the philosophy of history and science; currently a candidate for MS in space studies with a concentration in astronomy
- Member of Collegiate Scholars, the Association of Ancient Historians (AAH), Society for Historical Archaeology (SHA), the Philosophical Research Society (PRS), the National Earth Science Teachers Association (NESTA), Associate of Lunar and Planetary Observers (ALPO), and an active contributor to Francis Schaeffer Studies, as well as a society member of the Discovery Institute (Center for Science and Culture), was a CS Lewis Fellows Program awardee (2016) and am currently a Logos Research Associates ambassador.
- Authored *The Philosophy of History: Naturalism vs. Religion* in 2013 with foreword provided by Discovery Institute (2nd edition 2016). Authored *Mere Christian Apologetics* (2017), an abbreviated version of my previous work and *The Philosophy of Art* (2018)
- Worked at the University of Arkansas microbiology laboratories from 1996–1999 before adjusting my academic career to philosophy and then ancient history. This led me to a more coherent picture of creation history vs. creation science through the philosophy of science and history.
- Owner and operator (with my wife) of Reverie Coffee & Tea Lounge and Art gallery, where we explore the concepts of arts and aesthetics through a post-postmodern vantage point. (www.Post-PostModern.org)
- Owner/director of the Museum of Creation History in Eureka Springs, AR, with *The Great Passion Play*. (www.NWABibleMuseum.org)
- Have held creation think-tank groups from 2008 to today on intelligent design, old-earth creationism, young-earth creationism, and especially the

academic freedom to encourage critical thinking on all sides. I had the privilege of being one of William Lane Craig's Reasonable Faith Chapter founding members and traveling through Italy, Turkey, and Greece with Dr. Craig. I also operated an IDEA Center through Discovery Institute; I'm neither conservative nor liberal, Democrat or Republican, Boomer or Millennial; I'm more of a *Thomas Wolfe* of Generation-X so I do indeed hope to offend those reading this if it will help them to think more critically and reverse the dumbing-down of the West.

Back-cover photo attire: Thank you Tom Wolfe.[1]

Readers/Reviewers: This book is simply a very small part to a much larger *practicum* project I am completing for post-graduate work. Had I opted for a thesis option, this book would have been well over 1000 pages and bored the reader to tears I am sure. Thanks to *New Scientist*, *Christianity Today*, and *Philosophy Now* for advertising so I could get a diverse set of critiques for the practicum (please leave on Amazon if possible and/or email me at CreationHistory@yahoo.com. **Again** – please tear this short work to pieces and show where YEC is not even viable in 2020 but do so based on good/sound reasoning and refutations of what I have written (not semantics, grammar, use of contractions, etc. as this is merely a draft) . More on the heart of this project will be revealed at a later date.   – Thanks in advance

---

[1] https://twitter.com/EsquireClassic/statuses/996807143322988544

Acknowledgements & Dedication:

Special thanks to Drs. Russell Humphreys and Andrew Fabich for providing the foreword to this short work as well as Logos Research Associates (especially John Sanford) and the Discovery Institute. Discovery has invited me to Seattle on several occasions, allowed me to host them numerous times, helped me with my original MA thesis, and provided the foreword when it was published.[2] Logos Research Associates invited me to Utah and Arizona and allowed me to host them at numerous universities. Though both groups represent different mindsets, one predominantly old-earth creationism (OEC) and one young-earth creationism (YEC), they have been instrumental to my work. Also, special thanks to L'Abri and Francis Schaeffer Studies – "Thus saith the LORD, Stand ye in the ways, and see, and ask for the old paths, where is the good way, and walk therein, and ye shall find rest for your souls." (Jeremiah 6:16)

I am set to meet with and host speaking tours with scholars from the Discovery Institute and YEC scholars, such as Russell Humphreys, John Baumgardner, and John Sanford (each of whom are respected within their fields) at universities and churches in the summer of 2020. I am also slated to travel to Mt. St. Helens with a group of researchers in August (Lord willing) as well as continuing elements of this project well into the Fall. Thanks in advance to all past, present, and future associates who have helped to make this work possible, and I pray that it will open a larger, richer, more robust discussion of YEC in the current generation.[3]

This work is dedicated to the persecuted church and those seeking, in the words of Francis Schaeffer, "true truth." I know there will always be skeptics, even skeptical Christians. Brother Yun's stories of miracles sound like fiction to our naturalistically trained ears.[4] Even his miraculous escape from Zhengzhou prison (from which no one else has ever escaped), an escape supposedly orchestrated by the Holy Spirit and the accounting of which has been substantiated by the Chinese government and other prisoners, is always met with attempts to refute the claim by Christians just as often as by the skeptic. I see no reason for a Christian to doubt such stories holistically.[5] It is refreshing to see the West finally catching up with the persecuted church in substantiating such miracles. (Such as Craig Keener in his two-volume work

---

[2] James Stroud, *The Philosophy of History: Naturalism Vs. Biblical Theism.* (Tate Publishing, 1st edition 2013 & 2nd edition 2016)

[3] Though I criticize them heavily, I am thankful for AIG, ICR, Reasonable Faith, and Reasons to Believe.

[4] "Brother Yun," (*The Heavenly Man Tour*) (www.BackToJerusalem.com)

[5] Matthew 18:2-4.

on *Miracles*.[6]) Though I am open to expansion and review of this work, I am quite certain this will be my last academic-based offering. Instead, I wish to further explore reality in such great minds as Yun, Richard Wurmbrand, and others within the persecuted church who, despite their academic shortcomings, could teach me more about being a Christian than another degree ever could.[7] After visiting with more of these underground pastors in January 2020 at our museum, where we were honored to have the first prototype Hologram Bible (used by underground pastors in highly persecuted countries where a printed Bible is not an option) donated to us, I am just as impressed with them than I am with the great minds of the ID/creation movements.[8]

Important – I have tackled why naturalism is false in practically all areas of explanatory scope and plausibility while non-naturalistic hypotheses (such as theism) are superior in my published thesis *The Philosophy of History: Naturalism vs. Biblical Theism*. The work in your hands is more of an appendix to this thesis.[9] I will not be going back through the points made in that work on why naturalism is false since, in the words of Alvin Plantinga, "Naturalism, like logical positivism, should be consigned to the scrap heap of philosophical history."[10] I will instead point you to this previous work if you are an atheist or a skeptic on theism or want an in-depth critique of naturalism and why biblical theism is superior on all fronts, as this book will be presupposing the conclusions from that work. (In *The Philosophy of History*, I largely assume the OEC position, as I was making the case of theism over naturalism at a more macrolevel.)[11]

*Thank you, Breezeway Books for allowing this to premier in pre-book and eBook form for easier critique and revision by the audience. After a year of logically-sound critiques, I hope to come forward with a more formal, non-

---

[6] Craig S Keener, *Miracles: The Credibility of the New Testament Accounts.* (Grand Rapids, MI: Baker Academic, 2011)

[7] See *Tortured for Christ* or *Proofs of God's Existence*, by Richard Wurmbrand. (www.Persecution.com)

[8] I was invited to the intelligent design conference in Dallas to take part in a series of talks and attend a private luncheon to discuss Stephen Meyer's latest book, *The Return of the God Hypothesis*, and then met with ICR at their state-of-the-art creationist facility. I had great talks and fellowship, but it was no more impressive than what poor Chinese preachers and Brother Yun had to tell me.

[9] Physicalism, materialism, reductionism, neo-naturalism, and poetic-naturalism in all their various forms, in which non-naturalism and/or supernaturalism is ruled out *a priori*.

[10] Philosophia Christi, Spring 2012.

[11] This work is mostly geared towards a Christian audience and why the YEC position is stronger intellectually than OEC if one is a Christian. (If I am mistaken, I eagerly look forward to being shown where I am in error).

POD published work. I spend too much time with secularists, OEC and YEC theorists getting hung-up on my noncommitment to the exact dating of Creation, so hopefully this will answer that question, as well as explain why I find YEC theory more intellectually convincing than is usually conveyed by the populace. Moreover instead of just critiquing a group from afar (like many OEC do with YEC and vice-versa) I opted to rollup my sleeves and work diligently over the last 3 years with over 50 doctorates holding to a YEC position to test its viability; not just in the classroom but also the field. I had already done this most of my academic life with the OEC side so before we critique an opposing view, we should do research beyond a few hours on Google in my humble opinion.

**Last, I provided photo citations from various creation sources, Wiki-Commons (https://commons.wikimedia.org/wiki/Main_Page), the public domain (https://en.wikipedia.org/wiki/Public_domain), and NASA, unless otherwise noted. Some pictures were taken by the author at presentations, workshops, or in the field or is properly cited. No source that I reference necessarily endorses any of my work and though I may criticize certain groups, I respect them and am thankful for their continued work in the name of critical thinking and education.

Glossary of Terms:

Old-earth creationism is notated as "OEC" throughout this book and is defined as a variety of creationism that has existed for hundreds of years and encompasses a wide range of beliefs. Like young-earth creationists, old-earth creationists hold that various aspects of living things were created by supernatural intervention. Unlike young-earth creationists, however, old-earth creationists accept the scientific evidence for the age of the earth and the universe; for example, it is held that the earth is around 4.6 billion years old and that the universe is between 11.4 and 13.7 billion years old; OEC accept these secular dates as being compatible with biblical interpretation and exegesis.

Young-earth creationism (or biblical creationism) is notated as "YEC" throughout this book and is defined as: Young Earth Creationists adopt a method of Biblical interpretation which requires that the earth be no more than approximately 10,000 years old, and that the six days of creation described in Genesis each lasted for 24 hours. Young Earth Creationists believe that the origin of the earth, the universe, and various forms of life, etc., are all instances of special creation.[12]

Intelligent design will be notated as "ID" throughout this book and are age neutral. The theory of intelligent design holds that certain features of the universe and of living things are best explained by an intelligent cause, not an undirected process such as natural selection.

The scientific method is commonly described as a four-step process involving observations, hypothesis, experiments, and conclusion. Intelligent design begins with the observation that intelligent agents produce complex and specified information (CSI). Design theorists hypothesize that if a natural object were designed, it would contain high levels of CSI. Scientists then perform tests upon natural objects to determine if they contain complex and specified information. One easily testable form of CSI is irreducible complexity, which can be discovered by reverse-engineering biological structures to see if they require all of their parts to function. When ID researchers find irreducible complexity in biology, cosmology, geology, etc., they conclude that such structures were designed.[13]

Intelligent design agrees that there is a designer, but it does not name who or what this designer is. It is friendly to both OEC and YEC, but it does not use religious texts in its observations or testing methodology.

Theistic evolution is the effort to reconcile Darwin's theory of undirected evolution with belief in God. The term covers a wide array of different approaches and views. For Christians, mainstream theistic evolution raises challenges to traditional doctrines about God's providence, the Fall, and the detectability of God's design in nature. It would accept evolution in all its forms (micro, macro, cosmic, chemical, etc.) but it would posit that God was ultimately the one responsible for the evolution.[14] (See Appendix A)

---

[12] "Young Earth Creationism: National Center for Science Education," (Young Earth Creationism | National Center for Science Education, https://ncse.ngo/young-earth-creationism)

[13] "What Is Intelligent Design?" (What Is Intelligent Design? | Intelligent Design), (https://intelligentdesign.org/whatisid/)

[14] https://faithandevolution.org/topics/theistic-evolution/

CONTENTS

Foreword by Dr. Russell Humphreys   15

Foreword by Dr. Andrew Fabich   17

PREFACE   21

INTRODUCTION   29

PART ONE – YEC vs. Biblical Hermeneutics:
We're all really OEC, right?   43

PART TWO – YEC vs. the Social Sciences:
Natural Science > Social Science, Right?   85

PART THREE – YEC vs. the Natural Sciences:
A New YEC Voice?   135

CONCLUSIONS   251

Appendix A – Theistic Evolution   257

Appendix B – Dinosaurs (just for fun)   260

Appendix C – Theoretical Modeling   267

FOREWORD

By D. Russell Humphreys, Ph.D.

Fellow, Creation Research Society

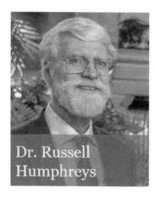

Dr. Russell
Humphreys

Deep time, the idea that the world is billions of years old, came to us so early in life, and so stealthily, that most of us never thought of questioning it. That is true for scientists also. When I worked as a physicist at a national laboratory, I found that most scientists believe the world is old because they believe that most other scientists believe the world is old. They formed that opinion as children, as I did, when parents, schools, books, and media told them the world is billions of years old, usually without offering much evidence. It was just presented as a given, something that everybody believed.

In my case, having been raised in a non-Christian but very science-minded family, deep time became the main reason I came, as a teenager, to believe the Bible was not true. I was vaguely aware that if one takes the Bible at face value, without making modern reinterpretations of it, it presents a young world in which nothing like evolution ever happened. Because deep time and evolution were thoroughly imbedded in my world view by then, I decided that the Bible was wrong, and I began to profess atheism. Of course, another motive in all this was that I felt free to live as I pleased.

A book by Ken Ham and Britt Beemer, *Already Gone*, confirms my impression that many children in conservative Christian homes have rejected the Bible for similar reasons as I did, even though they came from much better surroundings. The authors surveyed 1000 young people in their twenties who had regularly attended a conservative church as children, but now as young adults hardly ever go to church. Among the reasons they had rejected the Bible was their belief in deep time and evolution. Most of them had made up their minds on that as teenagers, as I had, and had simply waited until they were adults to leave the church.

Many churches avoid the issue of deep time altogether, teaching only parts of Scripture which talk about other things. Other churches reinterpret Genesis chapter one and the dozen or so other passages which say or imply, if one reads them straightforwardly, that the earth is young. One such theory suggests that the days of Genesis 1, or Exodus 20:11, etc., should be thought of as long ages of time. Another suggests that there was a time gap of billions of years between the first two verses of Genesis, into which one can put all the alleged geological ages. Another view, increasingly popular these days, is to assert that Genesis 1, and much of the rest of the Bible, is simply ancient near-eastern mythology, not to be taken as meaning what it appears to say.

As a young, atheistic, and rather arrogant, grad student in physics, I was not bothered by any of those theories. I simply ignored the Bible at first. Later however, the Hound of Heaven got on my trail, and I began to read the Gospel of Mark, asking God (whom I had previously denied) to show me if it was true. Within a few weeks, I accepted Jesus Christ as my Savior and Lord.

For the first year after that, I tried to go on believing in deep time and evolution. But those ideas appeared less and less compatible with the Scripture I was learning and trying to take straightforwardly.

At the end of the year, a book by Henry Morris, *Biblical Cosmology and Modern Science*, resolved the tension I was feeling. It offered much scientific evidence that the world is only thousands of years old. Deep time was simply a myth. There was no need to try to reinterpret Scripture to accommodate the alleged billions of years.

This book by James Stroud is your guide to the issue of deep time and how to resolve it. It contains much of the scientific evidence that convinced me the world is young. It also will give you a good idea of the history of the issue, and the context of the controversy surrounding it. I heartily commend it to your attention and reading pleasure.

FOREWORD

Dr. Andrew Fabich

by Dr. Andrew Fabich

Professor of Microbiology, Truett University

I suspect you've received this book because you either outright reject or have honest questions about biblical creationism. I don't want to disappoint you up front, but I've got to tell you that this book won't answer all the questions and issues about biblical creationism that you may have. In fact, it didn't answer mine either!

On top of that, don't expect to agree with 100% of what you read here because I sure didn't (except for the part where he quoted me directly). Flat out, there are some points made by the author that I disagree with (and that's healthy for discussion); yet, I'm still writing this foreword! Unfortunately, you may be accepting an old earth because you've only heard the traditional biblical creationist arguments that were only attacks on evolution rather than also building a biblical model. But the modern biblical creationist movement has come a lot farther than what you probably realize.

If you stop to think of it, no one holding to an old earth has ever built a biblical model either and they're primarily just accepting atheistic science's answer to everything while adding God to the equation. Even though it's important to point out problems with unbiblical philosophies (like Darwinism), blindly accepting secular science is not actually building a biblical model any more than wearing a Christian t-shirt makes you Christian. So why this book? Why now?

Very simply, this book isn't written to prove to you beyond the shadow of a doubt that the author's interpretation of Scripture is the only acceptable interpretation. However, this book's thesis is that biblical creationists have been the brunt of jokes from opponents (believers and non-believers alike) without even considering what biblical creationists are actually saying.

This book should make you stop to pause at several points throughout the book and evaluate your own position and whether there's merit to the biblical creationist position.

I didn't grow up in a Christian home. I received a secular public education from pre-school through Ph.D. Growing up, I bought into evolutionary theory hook, line, and sinker. Even when I became a Christian, I simply adopted the position of baptizing evolution with God. In college, I began the journey of questioning everything that I had ever believed—including the Bible as well as evolution. My then girlfriend (now wife) got some of that creationist propaganda and I decided I'd be open-minded about it and take a look. That was my first step of many towards the position I now hold of being a biblical creationist.

I tell that story because I soaked up everything on that journey but wasn't ever really exposed to the idea of building a biblical model. As thankful as I am for all the material I read (and still draw from to this day), I wish that I had also been educated on the ideas presented in this book to be a more well-rounded biblical creationist (I'm actually just a Johnny-come-lately).

Now my story and current position might not be where you are (I think you're probably not and that's totally cool). I'm guessing you're on a journey that could potentially end up where I am (if you're open-minded about it). For *at least* that reason, I hope this book could supplement your journey (wherever it leads) towards becoming a more well-rounded person.

One of the things I like about this book is that he names names throughout. I'd encourage you to formulate your own opinion about each of these having weighed the reasoning provided for you as well as checking all the terrific references. Even my favorite organization is named here, but I encourage you to find yours and then support it.

While this isn't my book, I strongly hope you walk away with a better appreciation that your grandpa's biblical creationism doesn't compare with today's biblical creationism. I'm honored to be quoted among such a great number of other credentialed Ph.D. scientists. I never dreamt I'd ever call some of these people my friends—including James.

Lastly, I'd be remiss if I didn't mention that the points in this book aren't ultimately made to win an argument. The goal of a book like this is for you to come to a saving knowledge of the Creator of the cosmos. Once finishing this book, I challenge you to ask yourself whether you truly know Jesus as

Savior or if it's just a mental game you're playing with yourself. Use this book as a springboard into finding out what it means to having a saving relationship with the Lord Jesus Christ. As Jesus said Himself, "for what shall it profit a man, if he shall gain the whole world [i.e., win the argument], and lose his own soul?" (Mark 8:36)

Sincerely,

Andrew J. Fabich, Ph.D.

PREFACE

"Men of science never talk that way..."[15]

New York Times, November 20, 1924

I had just moved back from NYC and received word that my master's thesis would be published when I sat down to watch a 2013 debate between agnostic philosopher Michael Ruse and old-earth creationist Fazale Rana at Biola University. Rana is a biochemist and serves with Hugh Ross at Reasons to Believe. It was painful to watch. Rana was completely caught off guard during this exchange:

Ruse: What's going on here? [on Rana's view of Genesis] I'm staying at a hotel here, so [Ruse holds up a Bible] I borrowed a Gideon Bible for the evening. I want to know what your position is. Are you saying that we have an earth that is suspended in space and then the sun comes along, or what exactly?

Rana: Um, our view is that, uh, the Genesis 1 creation account is a natural history of life... sorry, the earth and life on earth. And we would argue that, uh, if this text is inspired by a creator, then it should be essentially a text that corresponds to, uh, the scientific record. And so, we would argue that the appropriate frame of reference when you're looking at the Genesis 1 account, we take the days in Genesis to be long period of time, so I'm an old-earth creationist. I think the earth is 4.5 billion years old. Life has been present on earth 3.8 billion years or so, uh, so we take "day" to be a long period of time, but the frame of reference for the Genesis 1 account is not a hypothetical observer looking down on the planet but a hypothetical observer on the surface of the earth looking upwards, because Genesis 1:2 tells us that the Spirit is hovering above the waters, and so the text is telling us that initially there is darkness everywhere, and so it means the sun is not visible. On the first day of creation there is a transformation that allows light to penetrate to the surface of the planet and day four, um, the text in the original Hebrew does not say the sun/moon/stars are created but to let them appear. And so, it is not describing the creation but instead the appearance. And in fact, there is a parenthetical statement that reminds the reader that the sun/moon/stars were

---

[15] The headline of the *New York Times* article criticizing African American scientist George Washington Carver, who was also a firm believer in Christianity and creation science. In the article, Carver is heavily criticized for crediting God, Christ, and the Bible as the source of all his science. (The article goes on to bring up Carver's race, as well as saying real scientists don't evoke God or the Bible, showing their ignorance and racism.) Some things never change as many used the same attacks in 2016 against Ben Carson for being a YEC theorist.

created by God, but their first appearance was on day 4, but that doesn't mean that's when they were created.

Ruse [Looking perplexed]: Then what you're saying is that as most of us read Genesis, it is profoundly misleading?

Rana: No, I don't think so, um…

Ruse: Look, it says [he quotes from his Gideon Bible], "God made two great lights, the greater to rule the day and the lesser to rule the night." I mean God made the sun and the moon on the fourth day? He made the light earlier.

Rana: No, um… The text isn't saying that, because that is making a statement about a past activity so, uh, the text in the original Hebrew is giving the impression that the sun/moon/stars appeared but were not created. So, I don't think the Genesis account is misleading at all, but keep in mind it was written in biblical Hebrew and then translated into English. And the message of Genesis 1 is quite clear, I think.

Ruse: Just to go back to Genesis 1:2, and I don't mean to spend the evening cutting this, but this is your position in your book and [when Genesis says] "the Spirit of God was hovering over the water" I don't see anything about organisms here? Is that in the original Hebrew, too?

Rana: No.

Ruse: Okay.

Rana: Okay… That's a… [he looks around nervously] We only have a few minutes left here. We actually explain how we arrive to that position in the book *Origins of Life*, but basically it is not a direct statement but an inference that we're drawing from the text how it relates to another passage of scripture, uh, called the Song of Moses in Deuteronomy 32. So when you take that imagery and transpose it to Genesis 1:2, you can make a reasonable inference that there was something on the surface of the earth that was a great value to the creator and so in the book we draw the inference that that was perhaps something akin to the origin of life, but arguably that is essentially an interpretation but based on that we then develop a model.

These hermeneutical gymnastics made me think how obvious it was that a clear reading of Scripture would almost never let one conclude independently that billions of years were needed (eisegesis vs. perspicuity). I have talked to many atheists who have said the same thing. For example, in the fall of 2019, I had a brief discussion with Stephen Law, who said, "YEC is a much better fit with several important features, such as the Fall. If you watch Ken Ham debating OEC Christians, he often seems to get the better of them when it comes to giving a broadly consistent worldview. He exposes all sorts of problems with the OEC position."[16]

Ironically, this seems to be the position of many prominent atheists over the last century:

> In a 1909 lecture in Los Angeles entitled, "Breakdown of Protestantism," Edward Adams Cantrell (later part of the pro-evolution Science League of America, formed in 1925 and associated in later years with the American Civil Liberties Union) said, "All this is fundamental, for on the genetic story is based the entire Christian system. Without Adam's fall there is no need of Christ or the vicarious atonement. With the removal of the foundation the superstructure falls."[17]

Similarly, in 1978, the atheist Richard Bozarth declared in *American Atheist* magazine:

> Christianity is – must be – totally committed to the special creation as described in Genesis, and Christianity must fight with its full might, fair or foul, against the theory of evolution.... It becomes clear now that the whole justification of Jesus' life and death is predicated on the existence of Adam and the forbidden fruit he and Eve ate. Without the original sin, who needs to be redeemed? Without Adam's fall into a life of constant sin terminated by death, what purpose is there to Christianity? None.[18]

In 1996, the year I graduated high school, Frank Zindler, then president of the American Atheists, in a debate with evangelical philosopher William Lane Craig (a progressive OEC theorist), remarked:

> The most devastating thing though that biology did to Christianity was the discovery of biological evolution. Now that we know that Adam and Eve never were real people, the central myth of Christianity is destroyed. If there never was an Adam and Eve, there never was an original sin.... If there was never an original sin, there is no need of salvation. If there is no need of salvation, there is no need of a savior. And

---

[16] Personal correspondence available upon request.

[17] "Modern Science and Theology Compared," *Los Angeles Herald*, February 15, 1909. (https://cdnc.ucr.edu/cgi-bin/cdnc?a=d&d=LAH19090215.2.83)

[18] G. Richard Bozarth, "The Meaning of Evolution," *American Atheist*. (Feb. 1978, p. 19)

I submit that puts Jesus, historical or otherwise, into the ranks of the unemployed. I think that evolution is absolutely the death knell of Christianity.[19]

In 2006, Richard Dawkins, one of the world's most famous and widely read atheists said, "Oh, but of course, the story of Adam and Eve was only ever symbolic, wasn't it? Symbolic? Jesus had himself tortured and executed for a symbolic sin by a non-existent individual? Nobody not brought up in the faith could reach any verdict other than — barking mad!"[20]

In a 2011, posting on the *American Atheist* website just before Christmas, we read, "No Adam and Eve means no need for a savior. It also means that the Bible cannot be trusted as a source of unambiguous, literal truth. It is completely unreliable, because it all begins with a myth, and builds on that as a basis. No fall of man means no need for atonement and no need for a redeemer."[21]

Now, perhaps these atheists are naïve, but it does seem, as was evident in the debate between Rana and Ruse, that the more evident level of perspicuity of Genesis would not equate to an immediate inference of billions of years. At the same time, if you are a Christian, to jettison a historical narrative surrounding Adam and Eve, the Fall, Noah's Flood, and Babel does cut the foundation out from under the Old Testament and the New Testament.[22]

I am and will remain agnostic when it comes to the exact dating of creation, but YEC is no more or less an "embarrassment," as William Lane Craig has called it, than OEC. I am not a young-earth creationist per se, if you mean 4004 BC-at-midnight dogmatism. I fall more into the Francis Schaeffer camp of agnosticism on exact dating, so what am I doing defending the credibility of young-earth creationism? Having worked directly with many of the greats of OEC and YEC theory and within the framework of the intelligent design movement while it was coming to fruition, I feel that my experiences studying the philosophy of history help in separating fact from fiction in YEC theory

---

[19] Frank Zindler, in a debate at Willow Creek Community Church with Dr. William Lane Craig. *Atheism vs Christianity* (video), Zondervan, 1996.

[20] Dawkins, Richard. "The Root of All Evil?" Channel 4 (UK), (January 16, 2006)

[21] "You KNOW It's a Myth: This Season, Celebrate REASON!" American Atheists, accessed June 1, 2011 (https://atheists.org/atheism/Christmas)

[22] Terry Mortenson, "Adam, Morality, the Gospel, and the Authority of Scripture," (Answers in Genesis, March 1, 2017), (https://answersingenesis.org/bible-characters/adam-and-eve/adam-morality-gospel-and-authority-of-scripture/)

while distancing myself from groups like Answers in Genesis (AIG) or Institute for Creation Research (ICR).[23]

All sides have asked me, "How will this work add to the debate?" To answer, I use both a fictional and non-fictional analogy. Recently, I re-watched the entire series of *Star Trek: The Next Generation*, and the episode "Peak Performance" (S2E21, July 10, 1989) really resonated. It featured the android Data and a highly intelligent alien known as Kolrami, who was a master of the game strategema (think of chess on steroids). Data challenged Kolrami to a game of strategema, assuming that with his greater reflexes and computational ability it would be an easy victory; however, Data is soundly beaten, convincing him that he has malfunctioned. At the end of the episode, the two rematch and Data is able to hold Kolrami in check. Kolrami grew more frustrated as the match progressed until he realized he couldn't win and stormed off. Data explained that he altered his strategy, giving up opportunities for victory to maintain a stalemate. Data initially regarded the results as a draw, but after further contemplation, he admitted it was a win.

A scene from Star Trek: Next Generation where Data wins a game of Strategema by playing for a draw instead of a win.[24]

---

[23] I am thankful for both AIG and ICR and the work they have done. Criticism of them is not the same as throwing them out completely; I still use much of their material, and I am thankful for their ministries.

[24] Data and Kolrami playing the game strategema. "Peak Performance," *Star Trek: the Next Generation*, (July 10,1989)). To serve as a means of visual identification within the article dedicated to the work in question. It provides an illustration of the entity that the image represents. The image is being used in an informational capacity to the article as a whole.

Similarly, YEC theory has many strengths, but it constantly tries for an "all-out" win against OEC theory, which causes extrapolations that are not always warranted and thereby cause it to appear to lose, when if they had played for a draw, they could have potentially won the cumulative case for their position.

I wish to play for a draw, to maintain the viability of YEC theory. I have worked with big names on both sides of the debate for almost twenty years, and I will be supportive yet critical of my colleagues when they make faulty or weak inferences. I argue for the intellectual viability of YEC theory, not for its truth, and thus I am like Data in his second match with Kolrami. (I feel this a good analogy and one that my counterparts can relate to, as *Star Trek* continues to be a bridge upon which atheist and theist can find commonality). By arguing for a stalemate, the mere viability of YEC theory, I have discovered YEC is more tenable for the Christian than OEC, as we will see.

In 2009, William Lane Craig and Francisco J. Ayala debate:
Is Intelligent Design Viable?[25]

My analogy in support of YEC theory is mirrored by the 2012 debate "Viability of Intelligent Design," where William Lane Craig defended the concept of intelligent design against Francis Ayala as a "worthy and

---

[25] Brian Auten et al., "William Lane Craig vs. Francisco J. Ayala – Is Intelligent Design Viable?" (Apologetics315, March 18, 2020), (https://apologetics315.com/2009/11/william-lane-craig-vs-francisco-j-ayala-is-intelligent-design-viable/)

legitimate scientific endeavor, even if it ended up being false."[26] This moderate position usually makes enemies on both fronts, which historically speaking, tells me I am probably on the right path. Similar to how Craig argued for only the viability of intelligent design, if I can show that YEC is viable, then a thinking Christian should not dismiss it prematurely, as I am arguing from a stronger position intellectually than Answers in Genesis or The Institute for Creation Research.

Important – As mentioned earlier, my published works on the philosophy of history deal with the almost-certain falsity of naturalism and the credibility of non-naturalistic hypotheses (such as Christian theism) and after six years, it has held up to debates and dialogs here in the United States as well as the United Kingdom with graduates and professors. If this is still true, then I see no reason a non-naturalistic hypothesis like YEC theory cannot be on the table. Afterall, as I outline in *The Philosophy of History,* any non-naturalistic theory is stronger than naturalism. This by necessity would include YEC. Since my original MA thesis in 2013, I have only become more convinced of my conclusions. This current book is meant for Christians specifically or for skeptics who want to know why I give so much credit to YEC theory. So, for example, if I presuppose the law of biogenesis (that life comes only from life) in this current work and a skeptic wishes to challenge this, I will reference them to my earlier work, where I breakdown naturalistic and atheistic claims as this is not the purpose of this current book.[27]

We will also discuss the inconsistencies and ad hoc assertions leveled at YEC theory by some OEC theorists, like Hank Hanegraaff, Stephen Meyer, Hugh Ross as well as philosopher William Lane Craig and why I felt it necessary to end our working relationship. They attempt to disqualify YEC *a priori* and then equivocate on their own positions. It is important, however, to mention that my disagreements with AIG or ICR are just as heavy in some ways as my misgivings with Craig and Hugh Ross, of Reasons to Believe (RTB). So, while I champion AIG or ICR's work, I feel that they take too much of a dogmatic approach that leaves YEC theorists inflexible and at a middle-

---

[26] "Is Intelligent Design Viable? The Craig-Ayala Debate," Reasonable Faith, (https://www.reasonablefaith.org/media/debates/is-intelligent-design-viable-craig-ayala-debate/)
[27] I refer you to my prior work if you still think naturalism is tenable. (https://www.amazon.com/Philosophy-History-Naturalism-Religion/dp/1544771460)

school level, academically.[28,29] Similarly, many of these groups spend too much energy attacking the Discovery Institute, intelligent design, and one another. I hope this work will bring the YEC approach out of these caricatures and the shadows of AIG to be taken seriously. If I offend someone, good. That means both camps are being forced to think. I am more than happy to engage in dialog or friendly debate but encourage both sides to read through this informal work with their biases in check.

Sincerely,
James Stroud

Summer 2020

---

[28] "Kicked Out of Two Homeschool Conferences," Answers in Genesis, (March 22, 2011), (https://answersingenesis.org/ministry-news/core-ministry/kicked-out-of-two-homeschool-conferences/)

[29] "A Setback for the ICR in Texas: National Center for Science Education," (A Setback for the ICR in Texas | National Center for Science Education), (https://ncse.com/library-resource/setback-icr-texas)

INTRODUCTION

"Although our conclusions are tentative, at this point in our understanding, Scriptures seem to be more easily understood to suggest a young earth view, while the observable facts of creationism seem increasingly to favor an old earth view. Both views are possible, but neither one is certain."

Wayne Grudem, *Systematic Theology*

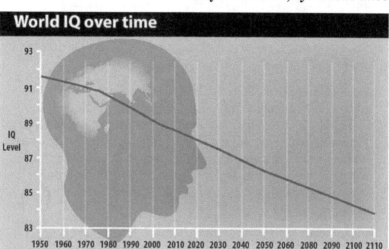

What about peer-reviews?

I recently compiled a historiography of science journals from 150-175 years ago and guess what? Most scientific ideas taught as factual then are now known to be wrong. Moreover, fewer, and fewer hold scientism as accurate, so why do we place so much emphasis on the natural sciences over the social sciences (or the Bible) if you are a Christian especially? I think asking why there aren't more creation (non-naturalistic) articles in peer reviewed (naturalistic) journals is amusing. If the journal's prerequisite is a naturalistic ontology, then a non-naturalistic ontology would be disqualified at the onset. See my point?

For some time, I have studied the failure rate of science, century after century. I have a collection of 19th- and 20th-century textbooks and the inaccuracies would be laughable if they were not so tragic. I understand that at one point in history, Aristotle might have believed fish came from mud, and that science works through trial and error.[30] And I understand that we learn more as our ability to attain knowledge grows. Nonetheless, the realization that most

---

[30] Aristotle, *History of the Animals.*

29

science since the time of Darwin has been falsified yet secularists continue to support these *icons of evolution* is appalling.[31] Could it be that many OEC proponents have conspired similarly to keep their own worldview alive? We will look at that later, but for now it is interesting to compare the accuracy of the social sciences to the natural sciences. We are told that natural sciences are objective, while social sciences are subjective. But is this accurate? After all, even the most skeptical secularists know that scientific theories are found false in some capacity every year, so why put so much emphasis on the natural sciences over other modes of knowledge?

In *But What If We're Wrong?* Cluck Klosterman makes an interesting and obvious point:

> I am interested in the possibility that we are going to be wrong in the same way that history has indicated that mankind always is. It seems as though the history of ideas is the history of being wrong. It's a continual path that shows we don't always know something, but we're always sifting to a path that makes us feel more comfortable in the moment, even if that shift is wrong, and new shift is destined to happen again.[32]

Similarly, one only need do the briefest internet research to see "10 most famous scientific theories that were later debunked," symptomatic of a growing list of what was taught as fact being completely overturned.[33] On the other hand, for a 2000-year-old book, the Bible has held up incredibly well. Not even the secularists can deny that it is the best qualitative and quantitative source of ancient philosophical history and science in existence. It has yet to be shown significantly fallacious in any point, as I painstakingly explained in my published MA thesis *The Philosophy of History: Naturalism vs. Biblical Theism.*

With the advent of the science textbook, we systemized certain truths in history, science, literature, but it also helped incapsulate indoctrination and

---

[31] See my friend and colleague Johnathan Wells's works *Icons of Evolution* 2000 and *Zombie Science* 2017 on lies still in textbooks that promote a worldview, not science. (https://www.discovery.org/store/a/authors/jwells/)

[32] Jim McLauchlin and Chuck Klosterman, "What If We're Wrong? History Suggests Everything Will Be Disproved," LiveScience (Purch, August 15, 2016), (https://www.livescience.com/55729-klosterman-what-if-we-are-wrong.html)

[33] Scientist, "Home," Famous Scientists, (https://www.famousscientists.org/10-most-famous-scientific-theories-that-were-later-debunked/)

teach false doctrines.[34] My concern has always been academic freedom, critical thinking, and reversing the dumbing-down of the educational system.[35] There is a fine line between an honest mistake and *zombie science*, as I discovered during my third year of employment at the University of Arkansas' microbiology laboratory, when I was first handed a copy of *Icons of Evolution*, by Johnathan Wells.[36]

> Zombies are the walking dead. In science, a theory or image is dead when it doesn't fit the evidence. I wrote a book in 2000 about ten images, ten *icons of evolution*, that did not fit the evidence and were empirically dead (though still be taught as fact in the majority of school textbooks). They should have been buried, but they are still with us, haunting our science classrooms and stalking our children. They are part of what I call zombie-science. The icons of evolution are not simply textbook mistakes. They are used to promote a grand materialistic story even after scientists have shown that these icons misrepresent the evidence. They are tools of zombie science.[37]

People are inclined to respect science and trust its authority. But science can mean different things. In one sense, science is the enterprise of seeking truth through formulating and testing hypotheses (empirical science), and in another, science can refer to the scientific establishment, which consists of people who are trained and employed to conduct research (establishment science); the majority opinion of this group is sometimes referred to as "the scientific consensus," which is at times expressed as "science says," or "all scientists agree," even though many sometimes don't.

> Throughout history, the scientific consensus has often proven to be unreliable. In 1500, the scientific consensus held that the sun revolved around the Earth, a view that as overturned by Nicolaus Copernicus and Galileo Galilei. In 1750, the consensus held that some living things (such as maggots) originate by spontaneous generation, a view that was

[34] "The Invention of the Science Textbook," ETEC540 Text Technologies Community Weblog, (https://blogs.ubc.ca/etec540sept12/2012/10/27/1494/)

[35] Peter Dockrill, "IQ Scores Are Falling in 'Worrying' Reversal of 20th Century Intelligence Boom," ScienceAlert, (https://www.sciencealert.com/iq-scores-falling-in-worrying-reversal-20th-century-intelligence-boom-flynn-effect-intelligence)

[36] *Zombie Science* (2017) and *Icons of Evolution* (2000) – Johnathan Wells. (https://www.discovery.org/store/a/authors/jwells/)

[37] Johnathon Wells. *Zombie Science*: *More Icons of Evolution*. (Seattle, Wa: Discovery Institute Press, 2017, p. 169)

overturned by Francesco Redi and Louis Pasteur. There are many such examples in the history of science. Whenever people persist in defending a position after it has been shown to be inconsistent with the evidence, and is thus empirically dead, they are practicing *zombie science*.[38]

Could zombie science be like the attacks leveled against YEC theory?

Think about Dr. Wells' following statement, but replace "evolution" with "OEC," so we can leave our presuppositions at the door: "When it comes to evolution [old-earth creationism], it seems, establishment science is less interested in evidence and critical thinking than it is in promoting the doctrine that all life can be explained naturalistically [billions of years ago]."[39]

In like manner, think about the following quote from Harvard geneticist and evolutionary biologist Richard Lewontin employing neo-Darwinian thought and considering old-earth creationism:

> Our willingness to accept scientific claims that are against common sense is the key to an understanding of the real struggle between science and the supernatural. We take the side of science in spite of the patent absurdity of some of its constructs, in spite of its failure to fulfill many of its extravagant promise of health and life, in spite of the tolerance of the scientific community for unsubstantiated 'just-so' stories, because we have a prior commitment to naturalism [OEC]. It is not that the methods and institutions of science somehow compel us to accept a material [OEC] explanation of the phenomenal world, but, on the contrary, that we are forced by our *a priori* adherence to material [OEC] causes to create an apparatus of investigation and set of concepts that produce material [OEC] explanations, no matter how counter-intuitive, no matter how mystifying to the uninitiated. Moreover, that naturalism [OEC] is absolute, for we cannot allow a Divine-Foot [YEC] foot in the door.[40]

Before Darwin and Lyell, YEC theory and science got along quite well, despite what many people think. Indeed, the founders of most modern scientific disciplines were Christians and had no problems with YEC. Were

---

[38] Ibid., 17-18.
[39] Ibid., 169.
[40] Richard Lewontin, "Billions and Billions of Demons." *New York Review of Books*, (January 9, 1997)

they not *evolved* enough to know better? Ignorant? Perhaps. Either way, this alleged controversy was post-Enlightenment, and since we now know that this period of alleged *science* and *reason* was anything but, why are we so insistent that they were right? Indoctrination into zombie science begins well before college. In 2004, child psychologist Deborah Kelemen wrote that young children are "intuitive theists" who are "disposed to view natural phenomena as resulting from nonhuman design.[41] Replace "intuitive theists" with YEC, and you catch my drift. Of course, this indoctrination into zombie science continues into high school with the icons of evolution [OEC]. Even so, political science professors Michael Berkman and Eric Plutzer lament the success of "evolution [OEC] deniers" and lay the blame at the feet of high school teachers, whom they call "enablers of doubt" because of their own uncertainty about evolution [OEC].[42]

So, am I an enabler of doubt, or a supporter of critical thinking?

Most OEC proponents seem unfamiliar with their own history of science. They ask, "How could the majority of scientists be wrong about the age of the universe?" in the same way atheists ask how scientists could be wrong about there being no god. Quite ironically for both camps, it was Darwin who, when asked how scientists in his day (who were largely creationists) could be wrong, said, "Why, it may be asked, have the most eminent living naturalists and geologists rejected my view on the mutability of species? I by no means expect to convince experienced naturalists whose minds are already made up by a lifetime of having a point of view directly opposite to mine."[43] Between 1859 and 1869, Darwin went from laughable to highly respected, so I would caution OEC proponents (like naturalists) not to throw too many stones at the glass house that is academia.

Good Education Necessitates an OEC viewpoint?

Many of my OEC colleagues are disingenuous towards YEC thinkers. You would think that being looked down upon by atheists would give them a sense of empathy, but this is not the case. When I push OEC theorists to tell me where YEC is wrong, I am usually answered with a question. "Are you YEC now?" Rarely do they give any answer other than a caricature of YEC as being on the level of *flat-earth* theory. Tim Chaffey, of Midwest Apologetics, mentions this same anger, ridicule, and hubris in the article "Rabid Opposition to a Literal Genesis – From Christians":

---

[41] Ibid., 226.
[42] Ibid., 174.
[43] Paraphrase end of *Origin of Species* (1859).

Sadly, much of the persecution comes from within the church. Even worse, it seems that many Christians reserve their harshest criticism for fellow believers. Nowhere is this more evident than in the old earth creationist (OEC) vs. young earth creationist (YEC) debate. To demonstrate this concept, I started a thread at www.theologyweb.com entitled "Roses are Red, Violets are Blue." In this article, I demonstrate how these two flowers topple every one of the views that attempt to blend the "billions of years" with the Genesis account of creation. In the first week on Theology Web, there were more than 1,150 views and over 120 posts. In all, there are about eight major contributors to the thread. Only one other person is a young earth creationist. The rest are either old earth creationists or atheists. For the most part, the atheists have been very cordial in their debate. While I certainly don't agree with them, I have enjoyed discussing this topic with them. Sadly, it is the old earth creationists (not all of them) who have resorted to ad hominem attacks on my character and view. Here is just a sampling of some of the quotes aimed at YECs by OECs:

- "You are a fool. I mean that sincerely."
- "a handful of slimy [sic] fearful liars at AIG and ICR who ignore the plain evidence of creation itself and seek to mislead the scientifically ignorant layperson for the sake of who knows what (profit? pride?... I dunno...)"
- "you despicable ignoramus"
- "you are a reprehensible person"
- "so what Adam was meant to do with his genitals before God realized that Adam didn't have a 'suitable helper' just doesn't bear thinking about"
- "This is a typical despicable rhetorical trick of YEC apologists. I can understand why they do it, since rhetoric and hot air is all they have.'
- "arrogant ignoramus"[44]

Similarly, I have heard Bill Dembski, of the Discovery Institute, explain that YEC proponents "damage Christian apologetics," rather than assist it, yet Dembski credits noted young-earth creationist A.E. Wilder-Smith for being

---

[44] Tim Chaffey, Rabid Opposition to a Literal Genesis - from Christians, (http://www.midwestapologetics.org/articles/creation/rabidopposition.htm#_ftn3)

one of the most important scientists in his life and influencing the intelligent design movement.[45] Christian commentator and member of the Geological Society of America Greg Neyman agrees, explaining that because of YEC, "Religion becomes to seekers and critics as the equivalent of folly, fools blindly ignoring scientific facts in favor of a book, which they now believe to be nothing more than a collection of fairy tales." Neyman notes, "YEC has become a 'stumbling block' to belief in Jesus and the Bible. While a person can believe in YEC and be a fruitful Christian, their belief in YEC can also hinder people from coming to Christ."[46]

Is this a fair assessment? Of the more than fifty PhDs holding to YEC that I engaged with while compiling this work, most were humble and strong in their Christian convictions. I am humble and knowledgeable enough on the topics to have a conversation with someone of differing views without fear of being brainwashed, which OEC thinkers seem to believe possible if they mingle too long with a YEC supporter. I did wonder what it would look like if OEC thinkers and atheists' fears were realized and a school taught a robust YEC curriculum. I did not have to look far before I had answers from a secular source:

> Education reform has taken center stage lately as Americans struggle to close the oft-condemned achievement gap. But quietly in our midst, the second largest Christian school system in the world has been steadily outperforming the national average – across all demographics. We are not advocating for religious instruction to be included in school curricula, but we were very surprised by the results. My colleagues and I analyzed test scores of 51,706 students, based on the Iowa Test of Basic Skills for Grades 3-8, the Iowa Test of Educational Development for Grades 9 and 11, and the Cognitive Abilities Test for all grades, as well as surveys completed by students, parents, teachers, and school administrators. In each subject category, students attending Adventist schools scored higher than the national average. They also scored higher than their expected achievement based on assessment of individual ability – a factor few other schools measure. One of our most dramatic findings is that students who transferred to Adventist schools saw a marked improvement in academic achievement. The more years a

[45] David F Coppedge, "A. E. Wilder-Smith," CEH, (https://crev.info/scientists/a-e-wilder-smith/)
[46] https://jamesbishopblog.com/2016/08/28/young-earth-creationism-damages-christianity/

student attended an Adventist school, the more his or her performance improved. A skeptic might argue that private schools such as those run by the Adventists are made up primarily of wealthy, white, upper-middle-class students, hence the reason for higher achievement. Not so. Our research shows the demographics of Adventist schools are closer to those of public schools, with high economic and socioeconomic diversity. Enrollment is open, meaning students are admitted without the kind of screening for ability that many other private schools employ. In North America, the Adventist Church runs almost 1,000 schools, many of which are small and rural. We found no relationship between the size of the school that students attended and achievement. Significantly, in this time of decreasing budgets for public schools, we found no link between per-pupil spending and student achievement. Research by Dave Lawrence, a graduate student at La Sierra University in Riverside, Calif., indicates that students at Adventist schools that spend as little as $2,000 to $4,000 per pupil are roughly at the same achievement level as students in schools that spend as much as $12,000 per student. We found no significant correlation between a school's budget and student achievement.[47]

The article does not mention that every level of Adventist education holds to a YEC viewpoint.

"Recent" means that life on Earth began over the relatively short time period suggested by a strictly literal reading of the Bible, "probably 7,000 to 10,000 years," though some Adventists think the planet itself could be billions of years old, explains Angel Rodriguez, director of the church's Biblical Research Institute. And six days means just that — "literal 24-hour days forming a week identical in time to what we now experience as a week," the Adventist decree says.[48]

---

[47] Elissa Kido, "For Real Education Reform, Take a Cue from the Adventists," *The Christian Science Monitor* (The Christian Science Monitor, November 15, 2010), (https://www.csmonitor.com/Commentary/Opinion/2010/1115/For-real-education-reform-take-a-cue-from-the-Adventists)

[48] Associated Press, "Adventists Stick to Belief in a Literal 6-Day Creation," *Deseret News* (Deseret News, November 27, 2004),

Most Adventist homeschool programs maintain a YEC viewpoint and almost always get the same successful results, so the claims of OEC thinkers and atheists that a YEC view will stunt one's educational growth while weakening one's faith is demonstrably false. If anything, it is the opposite. A point to be taken notice of during this Coronavirus season that has forced many public schools into a homeschool infrastructure for 2020.

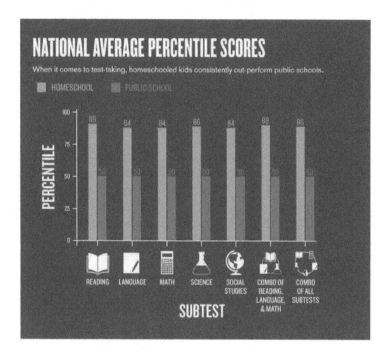

https://www.home-school.com/

Creationism Doesn't Really Matter!

The Guardian, no friend to Christianity, ran an article on "Why creationism matters – and irks so many people," in 2014 and acknowledged the need for freedom of inquiry in our age of socio-relativism.[49] More importantly, however, is that since naturalism is almost certainly false, it seems plausible that recent creation should be on the list of potential non-naturalistic hypotheses until someone can defeat its consideration.

(https://www.deseret.com/2004/11/27/19863433/adventists-stick-to-belief-in-a-literal-6-day-creation)

[49] Andrew Brown, "Why Creationism Matters – and Irks so Many People," *The Guardian*, (September 2014)

The more I worked with atheist groups, the more I realized they have no serious arguments in favor of naturalism and no serious opposition to YEC. More surprising was that most old-earth creationists really had no sound case against YEC, either.

This doesn't mean YEC groups have it all right. These groups are often as egocentric and dogmatic as are the OEC groups, nonetheless all sides must acknowledge:

1) Humans are finite.

2) God is infinite.

3) Humans thus cannot comprehend God's ways fully.

4) Therefore, YEC is possibly true.

The fact of the matter is that both groups (YEC/OEC) have contributed greatly to apologetics, but each are equally mistaken or over-extended in many instances.[50] While I agree with the late philosopher of science Karl Popper that history is a singular process that occurs once, making it impossible to formulate and test either theory holistically, I see both positions as viable and think we should be able to make a logical inference as to which provides the best explanation of biblical Christianity. Therefore, my two intentions, after twenty years of research, are:

1. **To show that YEC is viable, rational, plausible, and intellectually strong, now more than ever.**
    a. To look at YEC theory outside of groups like Answers in Genesis, which has stagnated YEC in many instances.

2. **To show that OEC is inconsistent, ad hoc, and has no greater intellectual vigor than YEC.**
    a. To encourage OEC advocates to better articulate their viewpoints and decrease their dependency on secular theories (e.g., concordism, scientism, logical positivism) and to abandon *gurus* like William Lane Craig and instead think on their own to a greater extent.[51]

---

[50] If I am wrong, I'd love a point-by-point rebuttal of what I have written and a replacement theory. E.g., "James you're wrong on these points and this is why."

[51] Apologetics YouTube channel *Capturing Christianity* by Cameron Bertuzzi is a good example of whom I am addressing.

I intend to show that young-earth creationism is on the same playing field or superior to old-earth creationism. I hope to encourage critical thinking coupled with a greater partnership and ecumenical dialog for Christians while helping to re-define YEC outside of the often-limited scope brought by groups like AIG or ICR. I hope old-earth creationists will provide strong arguments against this book instead of hand-waving and *a priori* assertions. Hugh Ross has generally acknowledged many of these points while William Craig has mostly broken off dialog with me as he has drifted more *Barthian* and liberal in his theology based largely on his *post-foundational realism*.

To measure viability for these points we will use:

1) **Common science/intuition** – see *Undeniable*, by Douglas Axe[52]
   - Highly esteemed molecular biologist, Douglas Axe argues for the notion of common science and intuition, in which we don't need to rely slavishly on scientists' interpretations because, in an important sense, we are all scientists, capable of judging a scientific idea, like evolution, though perhaps not the technical details, for ourselves. We are all capable of making an informed decision without "checking our brains at the door" and allowing theories from the elders of academia, who often contrive conclusions without facts.

2) **Utilization of standard steps in establishing historicity and truth**
   - A good theory should serve as the best inference in explanatory scope and power and be less contrived than competing theories; if a theory succeeds in this way, it should be considered viable and possibly true.[53]

3) **Occam's Razor**
   - This principle, attributed to William of Occam, suggests that in explaining a thing, no more assumptions should be made than are necessary. (If two competing theories are equally plausible, then the simpler and less contrived theory is probably true.)

Therefore, if I say, "The social and natural sciences have long maintained that Noah's Flood is global and historic," I should be able to make a case for this

---

[52] Douglas Axe, *Undeniable: How Biology Confirms Our Intuition that Life Is Designed* (NYC, NY: HarperCollins, 2016)

[53] Christopher B McCullagh, *Justifying Historical Descriptions* (Cambridge, NY: Cambridge University Press, 1984, P. 51–52)

statement that, upon review, should be more likely true (or not), according to these three points. If it succeeds, the view should be held as viable and probably true.

Anyone saying my argument is not viable should be able to refute my claim and replace it with an OEC theory from biblical theology/historiography, the social sciences, and the natural sciences (depending on the section). If we are Christians, let us all have the humility to leave the question of divine agency open and avoid thinking that God's actions must be within a naturalistic framework or understanding. God's ways are not our ways; however, I believe YEC is not only viable, but stronger than my OEC colleagues realize.

I had the privilege of hosting the first Academic Freedom Day with the Discovery Institute at the University of Arkansas in 2009 before relocating to New York City.[54] A January 2020 study from Arizona State University concluded that the biases against Christians in the scientific realm are enormous. So, what about YEC discrimination?[55]

[54] Telos, "Academic Freedom Day," Free Science,
(https://freescience.today/organize/academic-freedom-day/)
[55] M. Elizabeth Barnes et al., "Are Scientists Biased against Christians? Exploring Real and Perceived Bias against Christians in Academic Biology," PLOS ONE (Public Library of Science, January 29, 2020),
(https://journals.plos.org/plosone/article?id=10.1371/journal.pone.0226826)

Viewpoint discrimination and academic freedom & integrity: I have had peers and colleagues from every side of the debate read through this work, and for the most part, they have agreed with my message, though obviously not with every detail, word, or conclusion. I welcome robust debate, because we are thinking through these issues, but I wish to avoid the growing discrimination against YEC. As I touch on in *The Philosophy of History*, this is still a problem in public education, which knowingly teaches fallacious ideas favoring a naturalistic philosophy. This has contributed to the dumbing-down of academia and the church. My friend and former colleague, Casey Luskin, represented the Discovery Institute when California's Science Center blatantly committed viewpoint discrimination against Discovery's theory of intelligent design and critique of Darwinism in 2010.[56] I hope OEC's supporters are not falling into the trap of viewpoint discrimination against the YEC; moreover, I hope there will never need to be a book like Johnathan Well's *Icons of Evolution* against OEC theory for the same fallacies.[57]

Grab a pen and paper – I encourage you to have a notepad handy and read the various points I make, and if you agree with my argument, put a checkmark on the side of agreement. If you give my arguments even one check as potentially true or the best explanation, then we must conclude that YEC warrants being in the field of credible scientific and historic options.[58]

---

[56] Casey Luskin, "The California Science Center's Convenient Excuses: 'Contractual Issues' or Viewpoint Discrimination?" Evolution News, (September 20, 2010), (https://evolutionnews.org/2010/09/the_california_science_centers/)
[57] *Icons of Old Earth Creationism?*
[58] If no checkmarks are allotted to this side, contact me or leave an Amazon review detailing why the YEC position fails. It would be a great service. And again, I feel I must reiterate that this is not to get Creation into the schools nor is it to even argue for the truth of YEC; instead it is to show that **if** one is a Christian then YEC is viably true while OEC not only requires more "naturalism + God" but truly does seem to be a case of the emperor having no (or at least very few) clothes.

PART ONE

We're all really OEC, right?

"Time is in fact the hero of the plot... What we regard as impossible on the basis of human experience is meaningless here. Given so much time, the "impossible" becomes possible, the possible probable, and the probable virtually certain. One has only to wait: time itself performs the miracles."

George Wald, biochemist/Nobel Prize recipient

I had the privilege of spending almost two weeks in Seattle in 2016 with the Discovery Institute and a group of approximately fifty undergraduates and graduates from around the world speaking on the merits of intelligent design. We were honored to spend time with molecular biologist and the director of Biologic Institute, Douglas Axe, as well as attend his book release for *Undeniable: How Biology Confirms Our Intuition that Life Is Designed*. I had the opportunity to discuss these concepts with Dr. Axe, and he felt that the merits of common science found in his book could and should be applied to the concepts I am now discussing here.

Starting with the hallowed halls of academic science, Axe dismantles the belief that Darwin's theory of evolution is indisputably true, showing instead that a gaping hole has been at its center from the beginning. He explains the science that proves our design intuition scientifically valid, and he uses everyday experiences to empower ordinary people to defend their design intuition, giving them the confidence, courage, and vision to imagine what biology will become when people stand up for truth. Our intuition was right all along, Axe argues beautifully.[59] When I asked if this same concept could be applied to a YEC viewpoint, Axe said, "I don't see why not."

I want us to keep this perspective in mind throughout this book. Ask yourself if it is plausible, coherent, consistent, and a stronger explanation (both in power and scope) than what OEC theory offers. If so, then we should welcome YEC to the debate arena specifically if you are a Christian reading this. Otherwise, we are guilty of the same *zombie science* that naturalism has forced upon us all for a century.

I commented on YEC/OEC in the first edition of *Mere Christian Apologetics*, in 2013, while living in New York City, and it seems to hold true today:

> So, what about the age of the universe or earth? I fall more into the Francis Schaeffer camp of agnosticism on the topic, I do, however, personally feel that historically and theologically speaking, the creation of all life only seems to be logical within a relatively young creation (perhaps 4,000–10,000 BC). In all my studies in ancient history, I do find it ironic that all of history seems to start around 3000 BC, with anything much before Gilgamesh (2700 BC) being simply assertions (we really only have good history as far back as Hammurabi around 1750 BC). The only reason we have begun assuming such long periods of time in the nineteenth and especially the twentieth century is because we assume Darwinism (and naturalism) is true and requires the long periods of time; thus, the assumption of these massive ages are very circular. The historians, as well as the Bible, seem to suggest (but not require) a relative recent creation. It is only modern science that necessitates billions of years because it presupposes that the Bible is false, and naturalism is true, though it cannot defend either of these views. (Example: It was only a century ago that the proposed age of the universe was around 100 million years compared to today's 13.7 billion years.) Therefore, I will simply encourage the reader to search this out on their own and just say that we must not sacrifice or placate the heart of the Christian message for the sake of man's everchanging theories. In other words, if we say death was all around us before Adam or that Adam may not have really existed, then

---

[59] *Undeniable.* Douglas Axe. 2017. Inside cover (https://undeniabledesign.com)

that automatically begs the question "Then what did Christ save us from exactly?" (See Rom. 5:12.) Moreover, if Adam was created an adult and not a baby, is it not possible the earth may appear old just as Adam appeared old? And this is not "god of the gaps" reasoning any more than it would be to assume virgins do not normally give birth naturally.[60]

The Philosophy of History was published in 2013, revised in 2017, and has been put through a plethora of critiques and reviews in the UK and US, and I am more convinced of its truth and plausibility today than ever before. I half-jokingly asked Dr. Craig in 2013 if he'd be willing to hold a YEC/OEC debate on the topic in the same way he debated Francisco Ayala on intelligent design. He said he would rather focus on *Mere Christianity*, though his version of "mere" is not mine or CS Lewis's. If he doesn't feel comfortable defending his views of OEC theory, he probably shouldn't refer to its antithesis as an "embarrassment." I do not see where theologian Wayne Grudem is wrong:

> Although our conclusions are tentative, at this point in our understanding, Scriptures seem to be more easily understood to suggest a young earth view, while the observable facts of creationism seem increasingly to favor an old earth view. Both views are possible, but neither one is certain. And we must say very clearly that the age of the earth is a matter that is not directly taught in Scripture but is something we can think about only by drawing more or less probable inferences from Scripture. Given this situation, it would seem best to admit that God may not allow us to find a clear solution to this question before Christ returns, and to encourage evangelical scientists and theologians who fall in both the young earth and old earth camps to begin to work together with much less arrogance, much more humility, and a much greater sense of cooperation in a common purpose.[61]

Both sides study the same evidence. Young-earth creationists take issue with the OEC interpretation. YEC theorists are not anti-science, as evidenced by the number of young-earth creationists that hold advanced degrees in science. Many of these scientists became believers as a result of their research, as discussed in the book *In Six Days*. Young-earth creationists are not alone in

---

[60] An abbreviated version of my more secular work, *The Philosophy of History*, into a more digestible overview that showed why this tied in beautifully with Christianity: https://www.amazon.com/Mere-Christian-Apologetics-Bible-Simple/dp/1544288662.

[61] Wayne Grudem, *Systematic Theology* (Downers Grove: IV Press, 1994, P. 307)

their rejection of popular scientific theories. While most secular scientists hold an old-earth viewpoint, many disagree on how the universe came about. A growing group of secular scientists continue to call for research into alternative cosmogonies because they believe a naturalistic big-bang model is fraught with too many insurmountable problems.[62] At present, over five hundred scientists have signed on, affirming their agreement. Once you begin to peel back the layers, you find that the scientific evidence does not lend as much support for OEC as implied.[63]

> The interpretation that takes into account the widest array of factors in a coherent fashion is likely the best reading. A text cannot mean just anything that a reader can construe it to mean. This does not suggest that we always agree on which potential meaning is most likely. This is why it is necessary to discuss why we support a given reading – to make the case that it is the most likely possibility. This is known as validation. Nevertheless, often only a handful of candidates will possibly reflect what the text means. It is important to be reflective about how we observe meaning in the text because no one is a perfect interpreter. Interpretation within community, in dialogue with others, is an important check for understanding the text.[64]

I agree with above quote from New Testament scholar and textualist Dr. Bock. The YEC position not only passes as sound interpretation of scripture, it is supported by the vast majority of past historians, theologians, church fathers, apostles, and prophets. It also passes the smell check of Occam's Razor for being the best interpretation of the text. I'm willing to be convinced otherwise, but if it requires the hermeneutical gymnastics that Rana, Craig, Hanegraaff, and others play at, then I see why they don't want to debate the topics outside of their own carefully contrived sandboxes.

YEC and biblical exegesis

It is important to touch on a few points of biblical interpretation so we can compare and contrast YEC and OEC viewpoints to establish whether we have enough information to say that an exegetical reading of Scripture fits better

---

[62] *New Scientist Magazine*, 2004, p. 20.
[63] Ibid., 22.
[64] Darrell L Bock, *CSB Worldview Study Bible*, ed. David S Dockery and Trevin Wax (Nashville, TN: Holman Bible Publishers, 2017, p.30)

theologically with a particular understanding. I leave it to readers to reach their own conclusions as to the virtue of each argument.[65]

Young-earth creationists believe that the creation days of Genesis 1 were six literal (24-hour) days, which occurred 6,000–12,000 years ago. They believe that about 2,300–3,300 years before Christ, the surface of the earth was radically rearranged by Noah's Flood. All land animals and birds not in Noah's Ark (along with many sea creatures) perished, many of which were subsequently buried in the Flood sediments. Therefore, creationists believe that the global, catastrophic Flood was responsible for *most* (but not all) of the rock layers and fossils (i.e., some rock layers and possibly some fossils were deposited before the Flood, while other layers and fossils were produced in postdiluvian localized catastrophic sedimentation events or processes). The biblical arguments in support of this view can be briefly summarized as follows:

1. Genesis is history, not poetry, parable, prophetic vision, or mythology. This is seen in the Hebrew verbs used in Genesis 1, the fact that Genesis 1–11 has the same characteristics of historical narrative as in Genesis 12–50, most of Exodus, much of Numbers, Joshua, 1 and 2 Kings, etc. (which are discernibly distinct from the characteristics of Hebrew poetry, parable, or prophetic vision), and the way the other biblical authors and Jesus treat Genesis 1–11 (as literal history).
2. The dominant meaning of *yôm* [Day] in the Old Testament is a literal day, and the context of Genesis 1 confirms that meaning there. *Yôm* is defined in its two literal senses in verse 5. It is repeatedly used with a number (one day, second day, etc.) and with evening and morning, which elsewhere in the OT always means a literal day. It is defined again literally in verse 14 in relation to the movement of the heavenly bodies.
3. God created the first animate and inanimate things supernaturally and instantly. They were fully formed and fully functioning. For example, plants, animals, and people were mature adults ready to reproduce naturally "after their kinds." When God said "let there be..." He did not have to wait millions of years for things to come into existence. He spoke, and things happened immediately (Psalm 33:6–9) ....
4. Exodus 20:8–11 resists all attempts to add millions of years anywhere in or before Genesis 1 because Exodus 20:11

---

[65] Most of these points are well defended, including refutation of the most common objections to the young-earth view, in Tim Chaffey and Dr. Jason Lisle, *Old Earth Creationism on Trial* (Green Forest, AR: Master Books, 2008) and Johnathon Sarfati, *Refuting Compromise*, 2nd ed. (Green Forest, AR: Creation Book Publishers, 2011)

says that God created everything in six days. The day-age view is ruled out because the plural form of the Hebrew word for day (yôm) is used in both parts of the commandment. The days of the Jewish work-week are the same as the days of Creation Week. God could have used several other words or phrases, here or in Genesis 1, if He meant to say "work six days because I created in six long, indefinite periods." But He didn't. These verses also rule out the gap theory or any attempt to add millions of years before Genesis 1:1 because God says He created the heavens, the earth, the sea, and all that is in them during the six days described in Genesis 1. He made nothing before those six days. It should also be noted that the fourth commandment is one of only a few of the Ten Commandments that contains a reason for the commandment. If God created over millions of years, He could have not given a reason for Sabbath-keeping or He could have given a theological or redemptive reason as He did elsewhere.

5. In Jesus' comments about Adam and Eve, Cain and Abel, Noah and the Flood, Sodom and Gomorrah, etc., He clearly took the events recorded in Genesis as literal history, just as did all the New Testament writers. Several passages show that Jesus believed that man was created at the beginning of creation, not billions of years after the beginning (as all old-earth views imply), which confirms the young-earth creationist view (Mark 10:6 and 13:19 and Luke 11:50–51). His miracles also confirm the young-earth view. From His first miracle of turning water into wine (which revealed his glory as the Creator, cf. John 2:11 and John 1:1–5) to all His other miracles (e.g., Matthew 8:23–27, Mark 1:40–42), His spoken word brought an immediate, instantaneous result, just as God's word did in Creation Week.

6. The Bible seems to teach that there was no animal or human death before the Fall of Adam and Eve. If this is true, the geological record of rock layers and fossils could not have been millions of years before the Fall otherwise there was millions of years of death before the Fall....

7. The global catastrophic Flood of Noah was responsible for producing most (but not all) of the geological record of rock layers and fossils. Both a casual reading and careful exegesis show that this was not a local flood in Mesopotamia. It is most unreasonable to believe in a global, year-long Flood that left no geological evidence (or that it only left evidence in the lowlands of the Fertile Crescent, as some suppose). The global evidence of sedimentary rock layers filled with land and marine fossils is exactly the kind of evidence we would expect from Noah's Flood. If most of the rock record is the evidence

of the Flood, then there really is no geological evidence for millions of years. But the secular geologists deny the global Flood of Noah's day because they deny that there is any geological evidence for such a flood. So, the fossiliferous rock record is either the evidence of Noah's Flood or the evidence of millions of years of geological change. It cannot be evidence of both. If we do not accept the geological establishment's view of Noah's Flood, then we cannot accept their view of the age of the earth. So, it is logically inconsistent to believe in both a global Noachian Flood and millions of years. [In other words, you can have millions of years or Noah's non-local Flood, but you cannot have both]....

8. The genealogies of Genesis 5 and 11 give us the years from Adam to Abraham, who virtually all scholars agree lived about 2000 BC. This sets the date of creation at approximately 6,000 to 8000 years ago. Some young-earth creationists say the creation may be 10,000–12,000 years old [but there is simply no way of getting millions or billions of years from what the bible gives us]....

9. For eighteen centuries the almost universal belief of the Church was that the creation began 4,000–5,500 years before Christ. So, young-earth creationism is historic Christian orthodoxy. It was also Jewish orthodoxy at least up to the end of the first century of church history. In light of this fact, it seems inconsistent with the truth-loving nature of God revealed in Scripture to think that for about 3,000 years God let faithful Jews and Christians (especially the writers of Scripture) believe that Genesis teaches a literal six-day creation about 6,000 to 8,000 years ago but that in the early nineteenth century He used godless men (scientists who rejected the Bible as God's inerrant Word) to correct the Church's understanding of Genesis.[66]

Thousands of pages have been dedicated to this topic. Some OEC proponents, such as William Lane Craig, disagree, so let's make sure we give all parties a seat at the table.

---

[66] Terry Mortenson, "Young-Earth Creationist View Summarized & Defended," Answers in Genesis, n.d., (https://assets.answersingenesis.org/doc/articles/pdf-versions/YEC-summary-defense.pdf)

William Lane Craig, Hugh Ross, and Ken Ham[67]

William Lane Craig – Reasonable Faith

I have had the pleasure of working with many great minds (Christian and non-Christian alike) over the last twenty years, most of whom believed in a traditional 13.7 billion-year-old universe and a 4.6 billion-year-old earth; however, very few could properly or consistently defend it. Similarly, behind closed doors, my OEC colleagues acknowledged inconsistences within their worldview. J.P. Moreland has acknowledged on several occasions that he is YEC two days per week and that he thinks the YEC position might end up being right.[68] Gary Habermas went one further by saying he was YEC three days of the week. There are a slew of others I have worked with from various think-tank organizations that recognized their own OEC inconsistencies while still ridiculing YEC theory.

I helped William Lane Craig set up and oversee some of his early Reasonable Faith chapters in the Midwest and New York areas (2008–2013), and my wife and I accompanied him to the Mediterranean, "retracing the footsteps of Paul," in which we visited Italy, Greece, and Turkey. During this trip and afterwards, I confronted Dr. Craig on some of his own inconsistencies, and instead of denying them, he embraced them. I told him he was being pejorative when he said, "YEC is an embarrassment," and my comments were later transposed to his "Question of the Week." A summary of our discussion:

---

[67] www.ReasonableFaith.org, www.Reasons.org, www.AnswersInGenesis.org
[68] John M Reynolds et al., *Three Views on Creation and Evolution*, ed. James P Moreland, Counterpoints (Grand Rapids, MI: Zondervan Publishing House, 1999)

James Stroud: Dr. Craig, over and over again you use terminology such as "modern science tells us" when dealing with the age of the earth, but you do not use this same methodology when discussing the virgin birth of Christ. I am in the Francis Schaeffer camp on the issue – humble openness. Perhaps you are right, but until you can defend your position without using ad hoc and circular assertions, perhaps we shouldn't go so far as calling YEC theory an embarrassment.

Dr. Craig: Are you open to Henri Blocher's literary framework interpretation? Or Walton's functional interpretation? Or are you open only to YEC views? As for the origin of life and the development of biological complexity, I have no strong views on the subject. Perhaps the lack of clarity in my views that you mention is because I am undecided on these topics and genuinely open to alternatives. Progressive creationism is perhaps the view that best integrates biblical and scientific data.

JS: Like I said, I'm agnostic on the exact age of the earth, but I cannot rule YEC out based on modern science. You repeatedly say you are not an evidentialist, but that our theology should be molded by modern-day science. For example, you specify the biblical account of creation *ex nihilo* as an accurate and historical conjecture recorded with Genesis because that is what modern, "secular" cosmology tells us. While I agree mostly with you, if we use the same logic based on modern biology, shouldn't we conclude that the biblical text of the Virgin Birth was a symbol of Jesus's purity but not an actual birth, since modern science necessitates that virgins don't give birth? Do you see what I am getting at? I again agree with Schaeffer and Grudem that there is nothing wrong with saying, "I don't know," on such topics. To cherry-pick when Genesis is historical and when it is a myth or allegory seem disingenuous.

Dr. Craig: I am not an evidentialist in that I do not think faith needs to be based upon argument and evidence in order to be rational. I reject the view that exegesis should be guided by evolutionary theory or any other scientific theory. That's just bad hermeneutics. I think we should try to understand what the biblical text teaches and integrate that teaching with what we learn from modern science to create a coherent worldview that takes both theology and science seriously. How should we apply this approach to the virgin birth of Jesus? We begin by ignoring what biology has to say about conception and ask what these narratives teach about Jesus's birth. When we examine these narratives and their literary genre, we find that the Virgin Birth is not intended to be a symbol of Jesus's purity but factual. Turning to modern science, we find that like the Resurrection, such an event is naturally impossible. Therefore, if such an event took place, it had to be a miracle – i.e., an event with a supernatural cause. That will be a thorn in the eye to any naturalist, but for the theist, it is hardly problematic.[69]

I hope the reader can see the inconsistency here. While I respect and love Craig as a friend, he says we must follow modern science and at the same time says we "ignore what modern science has to say" on the Virgin Birth because that was a supernatural event. So the Virgin Birth, the Resurrection, the walls of Jericho, etc. are no problem, but when it comes to recent creation, that is just too much for God? This position is self-refuting, as you cannot have your proverbial cake and eat it, too. Since then, Craig has gone on to say that if God created what "appeared" to be an old universe to our eyes and it really was young, then God would be a deceiver. I asked him if the tale of the Virgin Birth made God a deceiver since virgins don't normally give birth. Needless to say, though we are still cordial, we no longer work together. Fast-forward to 2020 and we find Craig on the fence about giving up a historical Adam and Eve altogether as well as a historical Fall, which we will look at later. This is a great example of just one of the many inconsistencies held by OEC groups and individuals as intelligent as William Lane Craig based partially on a type of *post-foundational realism* which equates to a type of deistic-Christianity (which is not biblical Christianity at all).[70]

Noted atheist and Darwinist Jerry Coyne has rightly recognized many of Dr. Craig's inconsistencies in an article titled *William Lane Craig waffles on Adam and Eve*:

> I'm both amused and bemused by William Lane Craig's latest "Monthly Report" on his Reasonable Doubts website, a report that deals with a "Creation Project" conference he attended. So, what does William Lane Craig think? 'The New Testament's claims about Adam and Eve, and the meaning of their existence, might be literary conceits.' Craig's penultimate redoubt is this: 'Well, even if the geneticists are right, and Adam and Eve didn't exist as the Bible says, we can still confect a story from Genesis, even if the Bible be metaphorical.' Craig clearly is an odd duck (sorry for the insult to ducks) in so explicitly claiming that the Fall, and perhaps the Resurrection, aren't so important at all. My questions are three: Dr. Craig, how do you discern what the Bible truly means given that you think that at least some of

---

[69] www.ReasonableFaith.org (Questions of the week and personal correspondence paraphrased)
[70] Robert C. Greer. *Mapping Postmodernism: A Survey of Christian Options.* IVP Academic. 2003.

its claims are fictional? Second, why couldn't the story of Jesus, his crucifixion, and his resurrection be just as fictional as the story of Adam and Eve which you appear to see as myth? Finally, why isn't the claim that we can be saved only through God's grace also a myth?[71]

While I have always been critical of Coyne's antiquated and 20th century notion on the feasibility of Darwinism, I couldn't agree with him more on Dr. Craig's utter impotence in his recent retreat from what Francis Schaeffer called the "historical core" recorded in *Genesis in Space and Time*.[72]

So, what about the framework hypothesis that Craig referenced?

This view is rather hard to understand. The late Meredith Kline from Westminster Theological Seminary was the view's major spokesperson. Andrew Kulikovsky did a good job breaking it down in *Creation Technical Journal*:

> The framework [hypothesis]…takes the Genesis account of Creation as a theological framework rather than a strictly historical, chronological account. It is important to note that proponents of the framework view do not deny that the people and events alluded to in the Creation account are essentially historical. It should be obvious, however, that in denying the historical and chrono-logical nature of the account, they have very little basis for this acceptance.[73]

The reason this view is confusing due to the amount of doublespeak utilized by supporters such as Craig. Often, Genesis 1–11 is described as a myth. When asked if this means that this is not true, they respond with an emphatic, "No! It's a myth!" As you can see, this can be rather confusing. The term myth usually implies that something is fictional or made up. Nevertheless, the framework hypothesis suffers from many of the problems inherent in gap theory, day-age theory, and theistic theory, in which they attempt to combine

[71] https://whyevolutionistrue.wordpress.com/2018/07/12/william-lane-craig-waffles-on-adam-and-eve/ (I predict Bill Craig will become increasingly more Barthian in his theology going forward)

[72] Frances Schaeffer. *Genesis in Space and Time*. Intervarsity Press. 1972.

[73] *Creation Technical Journal*, vol. 16. Issue 1 p. 40 (2002) Andrew Kulikovsky, "Sizing the Day," *Journal of Creation*, (April 2002, p. 40), quoted in Chaffey and Lisle, *Old Earth Creationism*, 167, 168.

elements of naturalism with non-naturalism, a combination as compatible as oil and water.[74]

This is why the late R.C. Sproul abandoned the frame-work hypothesis in favor of YEC:

> For most of my teaching career, I considered the framework hypothesis to be a possibility. But I have now changed my mind. I now hold to a literal six-day creation, the fourth alternative and the traditional one. Genesis says that God created the universe and everything in it in six twenty-four-hour periods. According to the Reformation hermeneutic, the first option is to follow the plain sense of the text. One must do a great deal of hermeneutical gymnastics to escape the plain meaning of Genesis 1-2. The confession makes it a point of faith that God created the world *in the space of six days*.[75]

I would dare to say that Craig would not think R.C. Sproul an embarrassment for his YEC understanding of Scripture. Before we go on, we should look at the two strongest OEC theories leading up to the framework hypothesis to see if a framework-type understanding of Genesis might give us a more holistically plausible view of science and scripture. Gap theory, which was one of the first OEC theories to have a large following during Charles Lyell and Charles Darwin's time, postulates that there were large "gaps" of time between the first two verses of Genesis 1. It was proposed in 1814 by Thomas Chalmers but popularized by G.H. Pember in 1876. The acceptance and popularity of gap theory may be attributed in large part to the influence of Cyrus Scofield, best known for promoting this view in the *Scofield Reference Bible* (1917). Gap theory has mostly been abandoned because there is no good reason to believe it is accurate exegetically or scientifically, as even the *Christian Research Journal* and Hank Hanegraaff acknowledge; in their words, "Gap theory is not only false but it's self-refuting."[76]

To salvage an OEC worldview,

---

[74] Chaffey and Lisle, *Old Earth* Creationism, 167, 168.

[75] Karisa Schlehr, "What Is R.C. Sproul's Position on Creation?" Ligonier Ministries, February 9, 2011, (https://www.ligonier.org/blog/what-rc-sprouls-position-creation/)

[76] Hank Hanegraaf, "The Gap Theory of Genesis 1:2 By Lee Irons," The Gap Theory of Genesis 1:2 By Lee Irons - Bible Answer Man with Hank Hanegraaff, (https://www.oneplace.com/ministries/bible-answer-man/read/articles/the-gap-theory-of-genesis-12-by-lee-irons-16836.html)

...a second model, known as day-age theory rose to prominence in the late nineteenth and early twentieth century. In the late nineteenth century, Arnold Guyot sought to harmonize science and Scripture by interpreting "days" as "epochs in cosmic history" to "correlate the earth's physical, geological, and biological development with the sequence of creative events sketched by Moses." In his book *Creation; or, The Biblical Cosmogony in the Light of Modern Science* (1884), he insisted on the special creation of "matter, life, and humans" but allowed for development, for which he might be described today as a progressive creationist."[77] His scheme was popularized by a Canadian geologist, John William Dawson, who became the most frequently cited anti-evolutionist in the late nineteenth century.[78]

He used an OEC starting point to keep up with modern science but added that the Genesis Flood was only universal from the narrator's limited perspective, and that it was only humanity, not the Earth itself.[79] Though largely abandoned in the mid-20th century, Hugh Ross re-popularized a combination of day-age and progressive views of Genesis in the 1980s and they continue to fascinate many in the OEC camp.

Hugh Ross, with whom I have had continued correspondence over the years, is probably the most recognized name of the OEC movement. Ross and those connected with the ministry Reasons to Believe (RTB) hold to a progressive view of creation and Genesis that aligns closely with the *Day Age Theory*. Ross earned his Doctor of Philosophy in Astronomy from the University of Toronto and founded RTB in 1986. He has written dozens of books and articles on this topic and most recently, in 2017, was one of four contributors to the book *Four Views on Creation, Evolution, and Intelligent Design*. He has made many appearances on media outlets and written numerous news articles. He best represents progressive days of creation, (PDAC) which affirms that "evidence of a cosmic beginning in the finite

---

[77] Ibid., 22.
[78] Ibid.
[79] Ronald L. Numbers, *Creationism in Twentieth-Century America* (Hamden, CT: Garland Publishing, 1995, p.21-23)

past—only 13.8 billion years ago" agrees with Genesis 1.[80] This means the days of creation in Genesis 1 must be long, indefinite periods of time.[81]

The PDAC view insists that there are sound reasons and reliable evidence that the universe is billions of years old. First, there are two inerrant sources of revelation—the Bible and nature. Both are reliable and will not contradict each other. Second, the Hebrew word *yôm* (translated as day) can mean a definite, long period of time, and the nouns *ereb* (translated as sunset) and *boqer* (translated as sunrise) have a limited bearing upon understanding the definition of *yôm*. Day in Genesis 1 does not mean a 24-hour period of time. Third, the seventh day in Genesis does not end with the same "evening and morning phrase" as Day 1 through Day 6 do, thus there is the possibility that the unending aspect of Day 7 could apply to Days 1 through 6. Fourth, the second law of thermodynamics requires the decay and death of plants (Adam and Eve ate plant-based food), which would mean Romans 5:12 only addresses the spiritual death of humans. These reasons (and more) lead Hugh Ross to conclude that he is warranted to claim that the universe is certainly not thousands of years old, but billions of years old.

> The division between PDAC and YEC is vast. The debate is about more than just interpreting scientific evidence. In fact, the most important part of the debate is about the presuppositions of each group and their biblical hermeneutics. The PDAC view affirms the equality of general and special revelation in theory, while in practice they elevate their understanding of general revelation above special revelation, which means prevailing scientific discovery will be preferred to the theological teachings of the Bible. They believe Scripture is consistent with the prevailing view that the universe is billions of years old. The creation event did not happen over six twenty-four-hour periods of time, rather over billions of years. Genesis is not read consistently as historical narrative and is often

---

[80] Ross, Hugh. 2014. *Navigating Genesis: A Scientist's Journey through Genesis 1–11* (Covina, California: RTB Press, p.15), quoted in David McGee, "Critical Analysis of Hugh Ross' Progressive Day-Age Creationism Through the Framework of Young-Earth Creationism," Answers in Genesis, February 13, 2019, (https://answersingenesis.org/creationism/old-earth/critical-analysis-hugh-ross-progressive-day-age-creationism/)

[81] Ross, Hugh. 1994. *Creation and Time: A Biblical and Scientific Perspective on the Creation-Date Controversy* (Colorado Springs, Colorado: NavPress, p. 36), quoted in McGee, "Critical Analysis," (https://answersingenesis.org/creationism/old-earth/critical-analysis-hugh-ross-progressive-day-age-creationism/)

influenced and then interpreted according the consensus of scientists whose worldview conflicts with biblical worldview. The theological significance of each view affects the story of the gospel and the perception of the trustworthiness of the Bible.[82]

The question remains not whether one of these OEC views are right or wrong, but whether they are so "right" that the YEC view is unviable.

13.7 billion or 11.7 billion?

As of September 2019, the universe is potentially 2.3 billion years younger than conventional estimates, taking it from 13.7 to 11.4 billion years old. As I worked on this book, *Popular Mechanics, Astronomy, Science*, and several other publications began running the same story, which began, "The universe is looking younger every day, it seems."

> New calculations suggest the universe could be a couple billion years younger than scientists now estimate, and even younger than suggested by two other calculations published this year that trimmed hundreds of millions of years from the age of the cosmos. The huge swings in scientists' estimates— even this new calculation could be off by billions of years— reflect different approaches to the tricky problem of figuring the universe's real age.

> "We have large uncertainty for how the stars are moving in the galaxy," said Inh Jee, of the Max Plank Institute in Germany, lead author of the study in Thursday's journal *Science*. Scientists estimate the age of the universe by using the movement of stars to measure how fast it is expanding. If the universe is expanding faster, that means it got to its current size more quickly, and therefore must be relatively younger.[83]

I realize that trial and error is how science works, but in the words of my old director, "We don't learn what is true from our mistakes. We just learn what

[82] David McGee, "Critical Analysis of Hugh Ross' Progressive Day-Age Creationism Through the Framework of Young-Earth Creationism," Answers in Genesis, February 13, 2019, (https://answersingenesis.org/creationism/old-earth/critical-analysis-hugh-ross-progressive-day-age-creationism/)
[83] Seth Borenstein, "Study Finds the Universe Might Be 2 Billion Years Younger," Phys.org (Phys.org, September 12, 2019, (https://phys.org/news/2019-09-universe-billion-years-younger.html)

is wrong." A two-billion-year swing is significant, and the methods used for dating the distant past are arbitrary and problematic as we see in more detail as secular scientists challenge conventional dating.

Before we look at natural and social science reasons for the tenability of YEC, it is important to properly summarize the dominant OEC positions. To William Craig, Gary Habermas, JP Moreland, and others we can add Hank Hanegraaff (the Bible Answer Man). I have had conversations with Hank in the past, and much like Craig, he said we should turn to modern science for cosmology, but jettison modern science when investigating the Virgin Birth and Resurrection. When I pushed Hank towards an agnostic view on the age of the universe and pointed out that people he had hosted on his show, such as Paul Nelson, were sympathetic to YEC theory, he still said that we must hold to an OEC interpretation. Hank is surprisingly skeptical of miracles, refusing to answer when I asked about the validity of the two-volume *Miracles* set, by Craig Keener, but when it came to the presence of Christ in the Eucharist, Hank had no problem accepting it as within our apprehension, but beyond comprehension. I love and respect Hank, but his OEC viewpoint, like Craig's, is seemingly inconsistent.

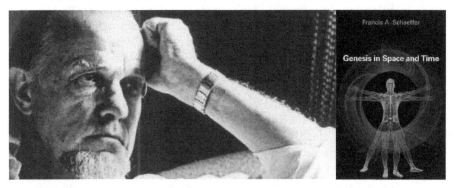

GENESIS IN SPACE AND TIME

Someone might say the topic is of secondary importance and that it doesn't really matter, but obviously, it matters to those like Craig or Ross for a reason, so let's look at a different viewpoint to see why. Whenever anyone asks how I align from an apologetics' standpoint, I usually refer them to the late Francis Schaeffer.[84] Schaeffer, like me, was agnostic when it came to the age of the earth, but he noted where we must be careful, both as Christians and good philosophers of history, not to jettison more than we realize:

---

[84] www.FrancisSchaefferStudies.org

We must leave open the exact length of time indicated at creation. In the light of the word [day] used in Genesis and the lack of finality of science concerning the problem of dating, in a sense there is no debate because there are no clearly defined terms upon which to debate. However, we have a strong testimony to the unity of Genesis 1 and 2 and to the historicity of Adam and Eve. They bear the weight of the authority of Paul and Luke as well as that of Jesus; the objective, historic existence of Adam and the objective existence of God himself. If we take away the historicity of Adam, we are left rather breathless. Christianity as a system does not begin with Christ as Savior, but with the infinite-personal God who created the world in the beginning and who made man significant in the flow of history. Similarly, it's interesting to note that no other story is as widespread historically as the flood [of Noah]. The New and Old Testaments speak clearly of the historicity of the flood and it sounds universal. The concept of catastrophe in general [in regard to a global flood] was thrown away, especially in geology. And with it the creation account and the flood account were rejected. Likewise, Genesis 9:19 indicates that the entire human race as it now stands came specifically from the three sons of Noah. <u>If we tamper with the ordinary way of understanding what is written in the Bible, the structure of Christianity is reduced to only an existential leap.</u> Genesis 1-11 sets in perspective all the history we now have in our secular studies. These chapters tell us "why" of all history man knows through his studies, including "why" of each man's personal history. For this, Genesis 1-11 is more important than anything else one could have.[85]

While Schaeffer remained agnostic on the precise dating of the age of the earth and universe, he was quick to point out the historicity of all the other events of Genesis 1–11 and warned future generations that the Bible and secular history equally fall apart (ontologically) if we deny a historic Adam and Eve, Fall, Flood, and Tower of Babel. Yet, William Lane Craig and many OEC have denied all of these or taken an agnostic mindset towards them. Perhaps we should just bury our heads in the sand on the issue and follow a

---

[85] Francis A. Schaeffer, *Genesis in Space and Time: the Flow of Biblical History* (London: Hodder and Stoughton, 1973, p.57, 58)

John Piper type of **eisegesis**: "That the earth is billions of years old if it wants to be—whatever science says it is."[86] Whatever science says it is? Seriously?

Is this good exegesis, let alone good science or history? While the majority of OEC faithful deny a recent creation, I find those that deny all of Genesis 1–11 more consistent because they realize that if you take a naturalistic stance on "billions of years," you can't coherently work in a biblical acceptance of a Fall, Adam and Eve, the Flood, Babel, etc. If these are all false, then the patriarchs, prophets, apostles, and Jesus are mistaken about their historicity. What did Jesus save us from if there was no Fall to begin with? A naturalistic "super-naturalist" is an oxymoron and logically fallacious (like a married bachelor), which is what Schaeffer beautifully outlined in *Genesis in Space and Time.*[87]

Dr. William Lane Craig has a quite serious problem on his hands. He's painted himself into a corner. Dr. Craig has built a career and made and name for himself in apologetics and is well respected in the field. He now faces a problem that could undo all the good work he has done in defending the faith. What problem could possibly be so severe you wonder? Like the man cutting off the branch he's sitting on, Craig is heading in the direction of undermining most if not all the work he has done in defending the existence of God and the resurrection of Jesus Christ. He appears ready to embrace the creation account as "mytho-historical."[88]

---

[86] https://www.desiringgod.org/interviews/what-should-we-teach-about-creation
[87] It was refreshing that in a private luncheon in Dallas, Texas, Stephen Meyer acknowledged that he is more aligned with Schaeffer and myself on natural and social sciences supporting a recent, historical Adam and Eve, though he does support an old universe. (January 2020)
[88] http://rationalfaith.com/2019/11/creation-craig-and-the-myth/

Old-earth creation has been around forever, right?

While there is no way to do justice to this topic, it is undeniable that OEC theory is relatively recent and based on naturalistic presuppositions found largely within the Enlightenment period and exponentially grown after Charles Lyell and Darwin.

> Prior to the 1700s, few persons believed in an old earth [one greatly over 10,000 years old]. The approximate 6,000-year age for the earth was challenged only rather recently, beginning in the late 18th century. These opponents of the biblical chronology essentially left God out of the picture. Three of the old-earth advocates included Comte de Buffon, who thought the earth was at least 75,000 years old. Pièrre LaPlace imagined an indefinite but very long history. And Jean Lamarck also proposed long ages. [89]

However, the idea of millions of years really took hold in geology when men like Abraham Werner, James Hutton, William Smith, Georges Cuvier, and Lyell used their interpretations of geology as the standard, rather than the Bible. Werner estimated the age of the earth at about one million years. Smith and Cuvier believed untold ages were needed for the formation of rock layers. Hutton said he could see no geological evidence of a beginning of the earth; and building on Hutton's thinking, Lyell advocated millions of years. From these men and others came the consensus view that the geologic layers were laid down slowly, over long periods of time, based on the rates at which we see them accumulating today. Hutton said, "The past history of our globe must be explained by what can be seen to be happening now.... No powers are to be employed that are not natural to the globe, no action to be admitted except those of which we know the principle."[90]

> This viewpoint is called naturalistic uniformitarianism, and it excludes any major catastrophes, such as Noah's flood. Though some, such as Cuvier and Smith, believed in multiple catastrophes separated by long periods of time, the uniformitarian concept became the ruling dogma in

---

[89] Terry Mortenson, "The Origin of Old-earth Geology and its Ramifications for Life in the 21st Century," (*TJ*, 2004, 22–26), quoted in Bodie Hodge, "How Old Is the Earth?" Answers in Genesis, May 30, 2007, (https://answersingenesis.org/age-of-the-earth/how-old-is-the-earth/)

[90] James Hutton, *Theory of the Earth* (Trans. of Roy. Soc. of Edinburgh, 1785); quoted in A. Holmes, *Principles of Physical Geology* (UK: Thomas Nelson & Sons Ltd., 1965, p. 43–44), quoted in Bodie Hodge, "How Old Is the Earth?" Answers in Genesis, May 30, 2007, (https://answersingenesis.org/age-of-the-earth/how-old-is-the-earth/)

geology.... After Lyell, in 1899, Lord Kelvin (William Thomson) calculated the age of the earth, based on the cooling rate of a molten sphere, at a maximum of about 20–40 million years (this was revised from his earlier calculation of 100 million years in 1862).[91] With the development of radiometric dating in the early 20th century, the age of the earth expanded radically. In 1913, Arthur Holmes's book, *The Age of the Earth*, gave an age of 1.6 billion years.[92] Since then, the age of the earth has expanded to its present estimate of about 4.5 billion years (and about 14 billion years for the universe). [The point is to show the evolution of OEC theory and that it coincides with the concepts surrounding naturalism.][93]

Who?	Age of the Earth	When Was This?
Comte de Buffon	78 thousand years old	1779
Abraham Werner	1 million years	1786
Charles Lyell	Millions of years	1830–1833
Lord Kelvin	20–100 million years	1862–1899
Arthur Holmes	1.6 billion years	1913
Clair Patterson	4.5 billion years	1956

Perhaps these long dates are accurate, and perhaps they will greatly increase in the future; nonetheless, there are many (not just Christians) that question

[91] Mark McCartney, "William Thompson: King of Victorian Physics," *Physics World*, December 2002, quoted in Hodge, "How Old Is the Earth?" (https://answersingenesis.org/age-of-the-earth/how-old-is-the-earth/)
[92] Terry Mortenson, "The History of the Development of the Geological Column," in *The Geologic Column*, eds. Michael Oard and John Reed (Chino Valley, AZ: Creation Research Society, 2006), quoted in Hodge, "How Old Is the Earth?" (https://answersingenesis.org/age-of-the-earth/how-old-is-the-earth/)
[93] Bodie Hodge, "How Old Is the Earth?" Answers in Genesis, May 30, 2007, (https://answersingenesis.org/age-of-the-earth/how-old-is-the-earth/)

current dating methods.[94] Either way, one must acknowledge that the idea of billions of years is a phenomenon arising in the last two hundred years. Perhaps all the generations before were inept and did not understand how science works, and perhaps the same will be said about our own generation a century from now. We should at least look back at what these pre-20th-century voices had to say on the topic.

Historiography and science?

A beautifully poignant work, *Inventing the Flat Earth* is "historian Jeffrey Russell's attempt to set the record straight". He begins with a discussion of geographical knowledge in the Middle Ages, examining what Columbus and his contemporaries actually did believe, and then moves to a look at how the error was first propagated in the 1820s and 1830s—including how noted writers Washington Irving and Antoinne-Jean Letronne were among those responsible. He shows how later day historians followed these original mistakes, and how this snowball effect grew to outrageous proportions in the late nineteenth century, when Christians opposed to Darwinism were labelled as similar to Medieval Christians who (allegedly) thought the earth was flat. But perhaps the most intriguing focus of the book is the reason why we allow this error to persist. Do we prefer to languish in a comfortable and familiar error rather than exert the effort necessary to discover the truth? This uncomfortable question is engagingly answered and includes a discussion about the implications for historical knowledge and scholarly honesty.[95]

Why is this relevant to our discussion? Because I have seen this same sloppy and inaccurate thought process applied to YEC theory. Similarly, most of these historians and philosophers know better, yet as Russell shows, they allow these errors against YEC to persist, so I must ask my OEC colleagues the same question Russell asks when they falsely equate YEC with flat-earth theory: "Do we prefer to languish in a comfortable and familiar error rather than exert the effort necessary to discover the truth?" What is the truth surrounding the historiography of YEC?

I was excited and then shocked with the 2014 Neil deGrasse Tyson reboot of the classic TV series *Cosmos: A Spacetime Odyssey.* It was immensely popular, "garnered twelve Emmy Award nominations and headed straight into

---

[94] "Half-Life Heresy: Accelerating Radioactive Decay," *New Scientist Magazine,* (October 21, 2006, pp. 36-39), abstract online
at (www.newscientist.com/channel/fundamentals/mg19225741.100-halflife-heresy-acceleratingradioactive-decay.html)
[95] Jeffrey B. Russell, *Inventing the Flat Earth: Columbus and Modern Historians* (New York, NY: Praeger, 1997)

schools as a science teacher's instructional aid." Why would I be shocked? Because it not only was a notably "agenda-driven vehicle for scientific materialism, casting religion as an arch foe of the search for truth about nature" and in so doing, falsified several points in history along the way.[96] The one positive was that several groups, both pro and anti-Christian, spoke up on the falsities throughout: Why believe the science if other parts of the show are inaccurate?[97] Similarly, my colleagues at the Discovery Institute wrote a fantastic rebuttal of each and every point where *Cosmos* got it wrong.[98] In *The Unofficial Guide to Cosmos: Fact and Fiction*, Casey Luskin describes why it is not justifiable for anyone to lie about science in the hopes of helping science, and he is not alone. Historian of science Michael Newton Keas has helped set the record straight on how modern-day science has been a friend to biblical theism while exposing the outright lies of naturalists like deGrasse.[99] Likewise, historian of science Joseph Martin commented:

> I've been watching with interest as the history of science community, particularly on Twitter, has reacted with consternation to the historical components of Neil deGrasse Tyson's *Cosmos* reboot. To a large extent I agree with these criticisms. It is troubling that the forums in which the public gets the most exposure to history of science also tend to be those in which it is the least responsibly represented. If we grant *Cosmos* the artistic license to lie, the question is then whether it is doing so in service of a greater truth and if so, what is it?[100]

While most of the claims made by *Cosmos* or any other materialistic interpretation of truth is easy to show as fallacious, less noticeable is the irony that almost all these same claims can be laid at the feet of OEC. It's dubious that OEC colleagues, characterized as flat-earth believers and science deniers by the naturalistic side, are often guilty of the same characterizing of YEC as being flat-earth believers and science deniers. Equally ironic is that when the OEC side correctly calls the founders of science "Christian," they usually omit the fact they were also YEC believers.

---

[96] David Klinghoffer, *The Unofficial Guide to Cosmos: Fact and Fiction in Neil DeGrasse Tysons Landmark Science Series* (Seattle, WA: Discovery Institute Press, 2014, back cover)
[97] Klinghoffer, *The Unofficial Guide*. Laurel Brown, "Cosmos Review." p 35.
[98] Klinghoffer, *The Unofficial Guide*.
[99] Michael Newton Keas, *Unbelievable: 7 Myths about the History and Future of Science and Religion* (Wilmington, DE: ISI Books, 2019)
[100] Joseph Martin, "H-Net: Humanities and Social Sciences Online," *H-Net: Humanities and Social Sciences Online* (blog), May 14, 2014, (https://networks.h-net.org/node/25318/discussions/26537/we-need-talk-about-cosmos)

My friend William Dembski, an important person in the ID movement, has rightly said, "Our critics have, in effect, adopted a zero-concession policy toward intelligent design. According to this policy, absolutely nothing is to be conceded to intelligent design and its proponents. It is therefore futile to hope for concessions from critics."[101] On the flip side, Dembski has said, "YEC and the Noah theme park in Kentucky is an embarrassment and waste of money."[102] Is Dembski double-talking? Is he guilty of adopting the zero-concession attitude that many naturalists have against ID or OEC theory? Dembski does seem to recognize a certain fluidity in the YEC position: "The YEC solution to reconciling the order of creation with natural history makes good exegetical sense. Indeed, the overwhelming consensus of theologians up through the Reformation held to this view. I would adopt it in a heartbeat except that nature seems to present such a strong evidence against it. I'm hardly alone in my reluctance to accept YEC."[103]

Is the above accurate? *Francis Schaeffer Studies* colleague and YEC advocate, Nancy Pearcey, in the *Soul of Science*, champions what many Christians already know and many OEC theorists use—most of the great scientific minds of the past were Christian; but by this same logic, many of them were YEC, so I think it is inconsistent to assert that our greatest past scientists were Christian, but then ridicule YEC theories, since these same scientists were by and large YEC.

> Our main purpose in this book is to reintroduce Christians to a part of our rich intellectual heritage. By acquainting ourselves with forerunners in the faith, however, we discover a different model. We learn that until comparatively recent times, Christians have actively worked out the implications of their faith in all areas of life and scholarship – from philosophy to mathematics to physics to biology. Christian faith has not been a purely private matter. Nor has it been shut off in a separate part of life, as though it were relevant to worship but not to work. In this book we introduce readers to people whose "secular" accomplishments flowed from a

---

[101] William A. Dembski, "Dealing with the Backlash Against Intelligent Design," Discovery Institute, April 14, 2004, (https://www.discovery.org/a/dealing-with-the-backlash-against-intelligent-design/)

[102] Scott Buchanan, "Whatever Happened to Intelligent Design Theorist William Dembski?" Letters to Creationists, March 19, 2017, (https://letterstocreationists.wordpress.com/2017/03/19/whatever-happened-to-intelligent-design-theorist-william-dembski/)

[103] William Dembski, *End of Christianity* (Erscheinungsort nicht ermittelbar: B & H Publishing Group, 2014)

deep commitment to their faith, who understood that Christianity is meant to be developed into a complete worldview. May their example rekindle the same vision in us and inspire us to go and do likewise.[104]

This is not to say they were right or wrong in their views, only to show that modern science was built on a Christian understanding, specifically a YEC worldview. YEC has a loud, distinct voice in the past as well as the present, if we put our preconceptions behind us and listen before making dogmatic or condescending judgements.

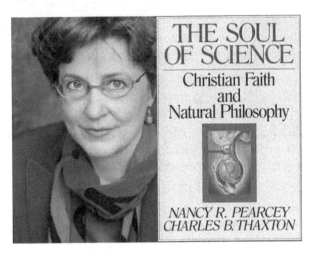

Author and FSS colleague Nancy Pearcey[105]

These scientists are sorted by birth year and supported a recent earth or YEC perspective:

Early Scientific Period:

- Francis Bacon (1561–1626) scientific method

- Galileo Galilei (1564–1642) (WOH) physics, astronomy (see also: "The

Galileo affair: history or heroic hagiography?")

- Johann Kepler (1571–1630) (WOH) scientific astronomy

---

[104] Nancy R Pearcy and Charles B Thaxton, *The Soul of Science: Christian Faith and Natural Philosophy*, (Wheaton, IL: Crossway Books, 1994, p. xiii)
[105] www.NancyPearcey.com

- Athanasius Kircher (1601–1680) inventor

- John Wilkins (1614–1672)

- Walter Charleton (1619–1707) president of the Royal College of Physicians

- Blaise Pascal (biography page) and article from Creation magazine (1623–1662) hydrostatics, barometer

- Sir William Petty (1623–1687) statistics, scientific economics

- Robert Boyle (1627–1691) (WOH) chemistry, gas dynamics

- John Ray (1627–1705) natural history

- Isaac Barrow (1630–1677) professor of mathematics

- Nicolas Steno (1638–1686) stratigraphy

- Thomas Burnet (1635–1715) geology

- Increase Mather (1639–1723) astronomy

- Nehemiah Grew (1641–1712) medical doctor, botany

The Age of Newton:

- Isaac Newton (1642–1727) (WOH) dynamics, calculus, gravitation law, reflecting telescope, spectrum of light

- Gottfried Wilhelm Leibnitz (1646–1716) mathematician

- John Flamsteed (1646–1719) Greenwich Observatory founder, astronomy

- William Derham (1657–1735) ecology

- Cotton Mather (1662–1727) physician

- John Harris (1666–1719) mathematician

- John Woodward (1665–1728) paleontology

- William Whiston (1667–1752) physics, geology

- John Hutchinson (1674–1737) paleontology

- Johnathan Edwards (1703–1758) physics, meteorology

- Carolus Linneaus (1707–1778) taxonomy, biological classification system

- Jean Deluc (1727–1817) geology

- Richard Kirwan (1733–1812) mineralogy

- William Herschel (1738–1822) galactic astronomy, Uranus (probably believed in an old earth)

- John Dalton (1766–1844) atomic theory, gas law

Just before Darwin's Time:

- The 19th-Century Scriptural Geologists, by Dr. Terry Mortenson

- Timothy Dwight (1752–1817) educator

- William Kirby (1759–1850) entomologist

- Jedidiah Morse (1761–1826) geographer

- Benjamin Barton (1766–1815) botanist, zoologist

- Samuel Miller (1769–1850) clergy

- Charles Bell (1774–1842) anatomist

- Humphrey Davy (1778–1829) thermokinetics, safety lamp

- Peter Mark Roget (1779–1869) physician, physiologist

- David Brewster (1781–1868) optical mineralogy, kaleidoscope (probably believed in an old earth)

- William Prout (1785–1850) food chemistry (probably believed in an old earth)

- Michael Faraday (1791–1867) (WOH) electro-

- magnetics, field theory, generator

- Samuel F. B. Morse (1791–1872) telegraph

- Joseph Henry (1797–1878) electric motor, galvanomete

Just after Darwin:

- Matthew Maury (1806–1873) oceanography, hydrography (probably believed in an old earth*)

- Henry Rogers (1808–1866) geology

- James Glaisher (1809–1903) meteorology

- Philip H. Gosse (1810–1888) ornithologist, zoology

- Sir Henry Rawlinson (1810–1895) archaeologist

- James Simpson (1811–1870) gynecology, anesthesiology

- Sir Joseph Henry Gilbert (1817–1901) agricultural chemist

- James Joule (1818–1889) thermodynamics

- Thomas Anderson (1819–1874) chemist

- Charles Piazzi Smyth (1819–1900) astronomy

- George Stokes (1819–1903) fluid mechanics

- Rudolph Virchow (1821–1902) Pathology

- Gregor Mendel (1822–1884) (WOH) genetics

- Louis Pasteur (1822–1895) (WOH) bacteriology, biochemistry, sterilization, immunization

- Henri Fabre (1823–1915) entomology of living insects

- William Thompson, Lord Kelvin (1824–1907) energetics, absolute temperatures, Atlantic cable (believed in an older earth than the Bible indicates, but far younger than evolutionists wanted*)

- William Huggins (1824–1910) astral spectrometry

- Bernhard Riemann (1826–1866) non-Euclidean geometries

- Joseph Lister (1827–1912) antiseptic surgery

- Balfour Stewart (1828–1887) ionospheric electricity

- James Clerk Maxwell (1831–1879) (WOH) electrodynamics, statistical thermodynamics

- P. G. Tait (1831–1901) vector analysis

- John Bell Pettigrew (1834–1908) anatomist, physiologist

- John Strutt, Lord Rayleigh (1842–1919) similitude, model analysis, inert gases

- Sir William Abney (1843–1920) astronomy

- Alexander MacAlister (1844–1919) anatomy

- A.H. Sayce (1845–1933) archeologist

- John Ambrose Fleming (1849–1945)

Early Modern Period

- George Washington Carver (1864–1943) inventor

- L. Merson Davies (1890–1960) geology, paleontology

- Douglas Dewar (1875–1957) ornithologist

- Howard A. Kelly (1858–1943) gynecology

- Paul Lemoine (1878–1940) geology

- Dr. Frank Marsh (1899–1992) biology

- Dr. John Mann: agriculturist, biological control pioneer

- Edward H. Maunder (1851–1928): astronomy

- William Mitchell Ramsay (1851–1939): archeologist

- William Ramsay (1852–1916): isotopic chemistry, element transmutation

- Charles Stine (1882–1954): organic chemist

- Dr. Arthur Rendle-Short (1885–1953): surgeon

- Dr. Larry Butler (1933–1997): biochemist

- Sir Cecil P. G. Wakeley (1892–1979): surgery

- Dr. Clifford Burdick (1919–2005): geologist

Modern Period

- Dr. Thomas Barnes (1911–2011): physics

- Arthur E. Wilder-Smith (1915–1995): three science doctorates, a creation science pioneer

- Dr. John W. Klotz (1918–1996): biology

- Dr. Henry M. Morris (1918–2006): hydrology

- Dr. Charles Taylor (1918–2009): linguistics

- Dr. William Arion (1940–2010: biology, molecular neurogiology

- Dr. Duane Gish (1921–2013): biochemistry, chemistry[105]

- Dr. Clifford Wilson (1923–2012): psycholinguistics and archaeology

- Prof. Verna Wright (1928–1998): rheumatology

- Dr. Leonid Korochkin (1935–2006): genetics

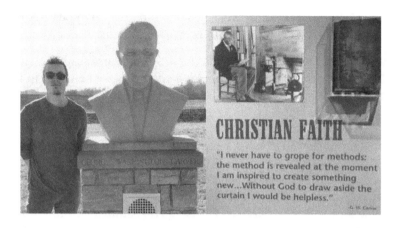

CHRISTIAN FAITH

"I never have to grope for methods: the method is revealed at the moment I am inspired to create something new...Without God to draw aside the curtain I would be helpless."

-G. W. Carver

Author at George Washington Carver Memorial (December 2019)

YEC theory has a rich history, a history that might be able to help us develop a more robust version of YEC or serve to critique elements of OEC. Even if all of these scientists were wrong in their belief in YEC, it should be undisputed that YEC has served as a catalyst for natural and social sciences through the Enlightenment era. As I discussed in detail in *The Philosophy of History*, the advance of science from the Enlightenment through the modern age, based on naturalism and logical positivism, has been exaggerated. So now the question is whether OEC has been a catalyst for the advancement of knowledge while YEC has been a stumbling block to *real* science.

Church fathers: YEC vs OEC?

What about the church fathers?[106] I sometimes hear OEC theorists assert that many were OEC, but this seems demonstrably false even from a superficial reading of ancient commentaries. I accept that past church and bible historians and interpreters could have been wrong, but while a few wrote in favor of OEC or a non-literal creation account, the vast majority of early church fathers and interpreters viewed the creation as relatively early and the days of Genesis as literal. I have heard Dr. Hugh Ross and Dr. William Craig imply that many church historians and fathers support an older creation. Ross cites "Philo, Josephus, Justin Martyr, Irenaeus, Hippolytus, Ambrose, Origen,

---

[106] GotQuestions.org, "Who Were the Early Church Fathers?" GotQuestions.org, May 17, 2009, (https://www.gotquestions.org/early-church-fathers.html)

Lactantius, Victorinus of Pettau, Methodius of Olympus, Augustine, Eusebius, and Basil the Great" to support his assertions.[107]

There are several problems with this. First, Ross overstates his claim, since Josephus, Ambrose, Lactantius, and Methodius clearly believed in a recent creation in their writings. Only Philo, Origen, and Augustine questioned the recent creation account. The others Ross referenced are too unclear to form a conclusion one way or the other.[108] Craig often cites Augustine, as does Ross, but they do so impartially. Even a superficial reading of St. Augustine's work on the six days of Creation will show that his understanding of the word "day" is different from, for instance, his mentor, Ambrose of Milan, who holds day to mean a twenty-four-hour period.[109] But can we go as far as to say that Augustine was an OEC theorist? We have Augustine's writings, so we can reference them ourselves.[110]

> Let us, then, omit the conjectures of men who know not what they say, when they speak of the nature and origin of the human race... They are deceived, too, by those highly mendacious documents which profess to give the history of many thousand years, though, reckoning, by the sacred writings, we find that not 6,000 years have yet passed.[111]

In Book Four, chapter 33, page 142 (The Literal Meaning of Genesis) he writes:

> In this narrative of creation Holy Scripture has said of the Creator that He completed His works in six days; and elsewhere, without contradicting this, it has been written of the same Creator that He created all things together. It follows, therefore, that He, who created all things together, simultaneously created these six days, or seven, or rather the one day six or seven times repeated. Thus, in all the days of

---

[107] Tim Chaffey and Jason Lisle, *Old Earth Creationism on Trial: the Verdict Is In* (Green Forest, AR: Master Books, 2008, p.167, 168)

[108] Robert Bradshaw, "Chapter 3: The Days of Genesis I," Creationism and the Early Church, 1998, (https://www.robibradshaw.com/chapter3.htm)

[109] Saint Ambrose of Milan, op. cit, 42, 43.

[110] Jonathan Sarfati, "William Lane Craig's Intellectually Dishonest Attack on Biblical Creationists," Creation.com | Creation Ministries International, September 17, 2013, (https://creation.com/william-lane-craig-vs-creation)

[111] Augustine Healey, *The City of God*, trans. John Healey, vol. 10, 12, 15 (Harvard: JM Dent and Company, 1903)

creation there is one day, and it is not to be taken in the sense of our day.[112]

It seems Augustine believed everything was created in one day (or perhaps in a split second). Most scholars agree Augustine was undecided or agnostic on the timing of creation. Augustine commented on Genesis 1 at three points in his life; he remained unsure of the time of creation or the exact use of the word *yom*. To assert that Augustine believed in true OEC is false and a distortion of his writings. Augustine clearly believed in Noah's global flood.[113] Indeed, in *The City of God*, he indicates a belief that the world from Adam to the Flood consisted of 2,262 years.[114] When I asked Craig why he cites one account of Augustine's interpretation but not the others, and breaks from Augustine on his belief in a global flood or historical Adam and Eve, he remained aloof.[115]

From Basil of Caesarea (329–379), Ambrose (339–397), Bede (672–735), Peter Lombard (1096–1164), Bonaventure (1221–1274) to reformers like William Tyndale (1494–1536), Martin Luther (1483–1546), John Calvin (1509–1564), Wolfgang Musculus (1497–1563), Peter Vermigli (1499–1562), and Henry Bullinger (1504–1575), many have agreed with a YEC interpretation of the world. "The Westminster Confession, Larger Catechism, and Shorter Catechism teach us to regard Genesis 1 as a real week of time."[116]

> Therefore, as the proverb has it, he calls "a spade a spade," i.e., he employs the terms "day" and "evening" without allegory, just as we customarily do.... Moses spoke in the literal sense, not the allegorical or figurative, i.e., that the world, with all its creatures, was created within six days, as the words read. If we do not comprehend the reason for this,

[112] Ibid.

[113] Douglas F Kelly, *Creation and Change* (Tain: Christian Focus Publications, 2017, p. 127-8)

[114] Augustine Healey, *The City of God*, trans. John Healey, vol. 10, 12, 15 (Harvard: JM Dent and Company, 1903)

[115] William L Craig, "Should OT Difficulties Be an Obstacle to Christian Belief?" Reasonable Faith, April 16, 2017, (https://www.reasonablefaith.org/writings/question-answer/should-ot-difficulties-be-an-obstacle-to-christian-belief/)

[116] Ken Ham, *The New Answers Book*, vol. 4 (Green Forest, AR: Master Books, 2013, p.109)

let us remain pupils and leave the job of teacher to the Holy Spirit.[117]

While much more could be written, it is sufficient to say that the vast majority of church fathers endorsed a literal reading of Genesis as regards the days of Creation and a historical Adam and Eve, Fall, Flood, and Tower of Babel, but so too did most of the Reformers. All of them could be wrong of course, but nonetheless, YEC seems to be on firm footing as a coherent theory long maintained by the Church. So perhaps we should all reassess what OEC William Dembski stated on the coherency of a YEC worldview considering his allusion to *nature* being strongly against it: "The YEC solution to reconciling the order of creation with natural history makes good exegetical sense. Indeed, the overwhelming consensus of theologians up through the Reformation held to this view. <u>I myself would adopt it in a heartbeat except that **nature** seems to present such a strong evidence against it.</u> I'm hardly alone in my reluctance to accept YEC."[118]

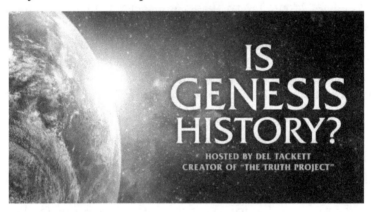

So, is Genesis history?

I was honored to spend a few days touring the Grand Staircase and talking with Thomas Purifoy, the director of the film *Is Genesis History?* In this film, not only did Dr. Del Tackett come out as a YEC (since which he has suffered much ridicule), but the YEC movement holistically made a strong, history-based claim based on its plausibility.

> *Is Genesis History?* features over a dozen scientists and scholars explaining how the world intersects with the history

---

[117] Luther, *Lectures on Genesis*, in *Works*, 1:5. See also John A. Maxfield, *Luther's Lectures on Genesis and the Formation of Evangelical Identity* (Kirksville, MO: Truman State University Press, 2008), p. 41.
[118] Dembski, *End of Christianity*.

recorded in Genesis.... The film's goal is to provide a reasonable case for Creation in six normal days, a real Adam and Eve, a historical Fall, a global flood, and a tower of Babel.... Many people don't realize just how many scientists and scholars see Genesis as the key to understanding the world around us. Each of these experts has spent decades working in his respective field to better understand how it relates to the history recorded in the Bible.

- Kevin Anderson, PhD – microbiologist
- Steve Austin, PhD – geologist
- Steven Boyd, PhD – Hebraist
- Robert Carter, PhD – marine biologist
- Arthur Chadwick, PhD – taphonomist
- Danny Faulkner, PhD – astronomer
- George Grant, PhD – pastor
- Paul Nelson, PhD – philosopher of science
- Douglas Petrovich, PhD – archeologist
- Marcus Ross, PhD – paleontologist
- Andrew Snelling, PhD – geologist
- Kurt Wise, PhD – paleontologist
- Todd Wood, PhD – biologist
- Stuart Burgess, PhD – mechanical engineer (bonus features)
- Douglas Kelly, PhD – theologian (bonus features)
- Larry Vardiman, PhD – atmospheric physicist (bonus features)[119]

Many OEC theorists cannot conceive of the possibility of a global flood as described in Genesis and focused on in *Is Genesis History?* One need only look back to the mid-20th century to see the blunders of naturalism and OEC when geologist J Harlen Bretz took Socrates's adage to heart and took the evidence where it led. His positing has come to be known as *The Spokane Floods: An Outrageous Hypothesis.* Bretz published his first paper in 1922, arguing that the geologic evidence around the Missoula Floods all pointed to massive and catastrophic flooding. This was seen as an argument against the prevailing view of uniformitarianism, so Bretz was initially discredited. Bretz was a noted atheist, but his theory implied a Biblical flood, which the scientific community strongly rejected, no matter the evidence.[120] The

---

[119] Del Tackett, "A Brief Overview of 'Is Genesis History?'" December 11, 2019, (https://isgenesishistory.com/a-brief-overview/)

[120] John Soennichsen, *Bretz's Flood: the Remarkable Story of a Rebel Geologist and the World's Greatest Flood* (Seattle, WA: Sasquatch Books, 2009)

Geological Society of Washington, D.C., invited Bretz to present his published research at a 1927 meeting, where other geologists planned to ambush and discredit him; Bretz referred to the group as six "challenging elders" that, due to their commitment to uniformitarianism, were not interested in facts. By the 1950s, however, his views were vindicated, and by the 1970s, it was universally accepted that catastrophic flooding over a short amount of time indeed caused the Missoula Flood.[121]

The history of science since the Enlightenment, especially in the last century, is full of similar stories, whether it be on the origins of the universe and life or the beginnings of civilization, where the evidence has been tampered with or ignored when it aligned too closely with a biblical narrative, especially when it seemed to align with YEC theory. If OEC theorists wish to remain on the side of good science, then they should take the evidence where it leads instead of holding to antiquated methods (such as with Bretz). YEC scientists and philosophers I interviewed were malleable when looking at the floods of Missoula, Mt. St. Helens, and the 1996 flooding in Iceland, and adjusted their theories accordingly, so I found *Is Genesis History?* a step in the right direction. As Dr. Marcus Ross notes, one can be academically inclined and maintain a YEC perspective; he thinks that his YEC beliefs help him do better science and from my experience I tend to agree.

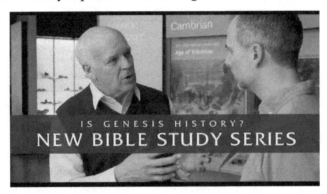

Host Dr. Del Tackett and Dr. Marcus Ross (Is Genesis History?).[122]

Liberty University students [had] the opportunity to see one of their professors, Dr. Marcus Ross, present the case for young-earth creationism (YEC) on the big screen, using his expertise in geology to show how scientific

---

[121] John Soennichsen, "Legacy: J Harlen Bretz (1882-1981)," University of Chicago Magazine, 2009, (http://magazine.uchicago.edu/0912/features/legacy.shtml)
[122] www.IsGenesisHistory.com

evidence supports this view…. The film explores a number of scientific topics in the context of the Bible. Thirteen scientists and scholars share their expertise, making a positive argument for biblical creation and Noah's flood. From rock layers to fossils, and from lions to stars, the film challenges the way viewers see the world. "A lot of it comes down to what the sources of evidence are," said Ross, director of Liberty's Center for Creation Studies and an associate professor of geology in the Department of Biology & Chemistry. "If you are going to say that the rules of science exclude any forms of evidence that aren't derived from a naturalistic set of experiments or observations, then something like evolution is going to have to be true — you are deciding ahead of time that there is only a certain path out there. There might be lots of different ways in that path, but the reality is that there is only one system. I never felt that was logically necessitated, and there is no way that I would say that the Bible is irrelevant to this discussion."[123]

Ross serves as an expert on the fossil record in the film, and his segment takes place at Discovery Park of America in Tennessee. Ross is no stranger to the YEC-evolution debate. He garnered attention from the *New York Times* when he completed his Ph.D., publishing research through an evolutionary perspective while maintaining his YEC beliefs. He has appeared in three documentary projects on the topic ("Is Genesis History?" is the first to show in theaters). He also manages Corner-stone Educational Supply, a company that provides engaging, hands-on educational materials and curriculum from a YEC perspective for homeschoolers.

In paleontology, unlike other areas of science, the age of the earth and evolution are at the forefront of discussion every day. Since declaring himself a creationist, he said he is often met with criticism when presenting research. Still, Ross has the credentials to prove his proficiency in the field: he holds a bachelor's degree in earth science from Pennsylvania State University, a Master of Science in paleontology from South Dakota School of Mines and Technology, and a Ph.D. in geosciences from the University of Rhode Island.

> Most colleagues (in paleontology) think that a creationist is an uneducated individual. Those I've met know that I am versed in the topics of paleontology. They may not understand why I think the Bible is relevant to this debate, but they can't dismiss me as someone who does not understand geology or the fossil record. Even though I have

[123] "Geology Professor Defends Creationism in Documentary Showing in Theaters This Week: Liberty University," Liberty University, February 20, 2017, (https://www.liberty.edu/news/index.cfm?PID=18495&MID=222937)

big differences with them, when I think of an evolutionist, I think of a real person that I know. These names and these terms have real people associated with them. I think God used (my state school education) to soften my heart toward those who don't agree with me.[124]

This carries over into how he teaches at Liberty. In his science classes, Ross teaches students how the greater scientific community interprets evidence while also sharing how they can be viewed from a YEC perspective. Ross also teaches creation studies, an apologetics course that is part of Liberty's general education curriculum. He realizes that in a large class, not every student is a young-earth creationist.

His educational experience has given him an empathy for those whom he disagrees with and has helped him to inject love into what can oftentimes be a hot-button debate filled with hostility.

I want to be a passionate advocate for YEC, but I want to be a respectful advocate and a respectful communicator to those that disagree," he said, noting that he doesn't like it when issues are used to polarize people. "My goal is to present YE creationism in a fresh way that is academically rigorous, that is spiritually deep, theologically sound and robust, and appealing to those who have not considered it before. I want students to be in a place where they can be challenged and feel safe to come to me with questions, even if their views are not in line with mine. God has a way of putting His people where they need to be," Ross said. "I am where I need to be. There are a whole bunch of students here who sooner or later will be out where God wants them. All they need is the confidence to hear God and act. If I can help instill some of that through the story that I have to tell, all the better.[125]

Christianity is an historical religion. Its teachings are rooted and grounded in history. It is not just a collection of ethical teachings. The Bible records the actions of God in history, and repeatedly points to these real, historical events, showing who God is, what He is like and what He is doing. These events include Creation, the Fall, the Flood, the confusion of Babel, the call of Abraham, the deliverance from Egypt, and many other events in the history of Israel, and, of course, the birth, life, death and Resurrection of Jesus. If the Resurrection account is no more than a story, what does it achieve and what

---

[124] Ibid.
[125] Ibid.

does it prove? If the deliverance from Egypt never happened, what does the story prove? Why does the Bible repeatedly point to these and other episodes as crucially important historical events which achieved God's purposes and demonstrated His mighty, saving power?[126]

Again, this is not dogmatism but just a reasonable question anyone (YEC or OEC) should ask and be asked.

Miracles and the Christian in 2020?

I recently finished a series of online meetings with historian Gary Habermas about the philosophy of history, the notion of miracles, and how with the demise of naturalism they have regained credibility within academia. Specifically, CS Lewis's book *Miracles*, Eric Metaxas's *Miracles*, Geivett's *In Defense of Miracles*, and Craig Keener's two-volume *Miracles*. During this discussion, Dr. Habermas discussed the renaissance of New Testament studies regarding the Resurrection of Christ, now predominantly accepted by historians, a renaissance that has occurred since he first began his PhD work.[127] We may have also been premature in our dismissal of supernatural claims made by past historians—e.g., Herodotus, Plutarch, Caesar, etc.

This conversation led to me asking Dr. Habermas about YEC theory. He said that he was OEC four days per week and YEC three days per week, and he hoped YEC theorists would polish their arguments in the future. He agreed that YEC has been the primary position of the church and history and that it is in no way an embarrassment, even if it ends up being inaccurate. While one could almost classify Dr. Habermas as agnostic on the age of the earth, let's compare him to William Lane Craig, Hugh Ross, and countless other staunch OEC theorists. It seems ironic that in a day when naturalism is collapsing and miracles are regaining credibility, that the miracle of a recent creation is too much to ask for. Again, this antiquated and logically fallacious endorsement of a case against miracles and a recent creation, while at the same time recognizing David Hume's view as self-refuting when it comes to the Resurrection seems too convenient to be taken seriously. It is thus logical to conclude that:

1) The Bible favors a YEC interpretation theologically and textually.

---

[126] Robert Gurney, "History and Pseudo History," Creation.com | Creation Ministries International, July 2010, (https://creation.com/history-and-pseudo-history)
[127] Habermas has currently 3400 sources compiled in his bibliography (www.GaryHabermas.com)

a. Eisegesis and concordism are poor replacements textually for perspicuity and exegesis unless strong and logically sound reasons for doing so exist.

2) The Bible has mostly been read and interpreted through a YEC understanding (historiographically).

3) OEC is a relatively new interpretation of the Bible based on changes within science.[128]

4) Most scientists and philosophers pre-1850 have been YEC.

Based on the above four points, from a theological and historiographical interpretation, we should conclude that YEC is a viable position. Moreover, it seems to be a stronger position than OEC theologically speaking based on these same four points.[129]

The purpose of this chapter is to explore why OEC is a weaker theory than YEC biblically and theologically, and to reiterate that OEC is a relatively new position. OEC is in several ways self-refuting, in that it attempts to adopt naturalistic premises, link them with a super-naturalistic conclusion, and then call it biblically sound.

Once we measure the points in this chapter against our consistency checklist and Occam's Razor, as well as the criterion for establishing historicity, we see why YEC theory remains a strong player. While science changes as often as the weather, the Bible remains the same and gains plausibility with each passing decade. Have we been too quick to put YEC on the same intellectual level as flat earth theory? From a strictly biblical and theological understanding of Genesis, it seems we have grounds for determining the theological and historiographical truth of my original points:

1. YEC is a viable, rational, and plausible academic option on theological grounds now, more than perhaps ever before with our added insight into textual criticism, biblical historiography and the inevitable fall of naturalistic hypotheses.
2. OEC is often inconsistent and ad hoc, with no more intellectual vigor than YEC, regarding biblical perspicuity and interpretation as it is often forced to replace sound exegesis with eisegesis and concordism.

---

[128] This does not mean exclusively new, but that before 1800 AD, the OEC camp was the minority. After 1800, and especially after 1900 AD, OEC theory spread rapidly.

[129] I would welcome a rebuttal of my 4 premises but if they stand then my conclusions would be inductively true.

Approximately 70% of critics will agree that the two above points, based strictly on biblical perspicuity when interpreting Genesis, lie strongly on the side of YEC. Similarly, this same majority agree that historically, the YEC interpretation of Genesis 1–11 has been the majority position until the late 19th and early 20th centuries. We also see Occam's Razor falling strongly on the YEC side based on even moderate take of biblical perspicuity would make it difficult to read into the text billions of years. Similarly, we find McCullagh's steps for establishing truth to be strong on the YEC side for the same reasons. The notion of a recent creation satisfies explanatory scope and power and is less ad hoc or contrived than the eisegesis of billions of years (from a strictly biblical history standpoint).

Please keep in mind that I am hardly alone in my critiques of OEC methodology and inconsistencies. As already mentioned, OEC William Lane Craig recognizes that the days of Genesis (yom) are best represented as a literal 24-hour period just as YEC would advocate. What he will disagree with is that these are anything more than a simple literary invention to describe a "framework" around creation. On the flip side, OEC Hugh Ross very much disagrees with Craig on the framework theory because he believes you can get around yom meaning a literal-day while he also feels Craig downplays the effort put forth by the author of Genesis to write real history:

> I have many friends in the framework camp. They all agree that there is some chronology in Genesis 1 but are unwilling to read the entire account of the creation days as chronological because as non-scientists they cannot see how to reconcile such an interpretation with the established scientific record. I think if Bill [Craig] were to apply the scientific method to interpreting Genesis 1, he would have no problem with our complete chronological view of Genesis 1. I am impressed with all the effort Moses uses in writing Genesis 1 to communicate that the creation days account is fully chronological.[130]

Similarly, OEC Lydia McGrew (analytical philosopher and prolific writer) disagrees with both Craig and Ross:

> I believe that theologically and historically Adam and Eve are very important. Important to anthropology as well. The idea of physically indistinguishable beings that are subhuman is actually pretty troublesome for natural law [Ross' view].

---

[130] Personal correspondence with Ross available upon request.

The 'days' of creation might not be literal days. On the other hand, as you reference, well before Genesis 11 we get to specific names and statements about what appears to be physical begetting and so forth. I think an old-earther probably has to insert a lot of unstated generations/time into those genealogies. If that's what we have to do in order to accommodate all the evidence, we can do that, but I think we should not go any further on that than absolutely necessary. The author [of Genesis] certainly seems to be stating that these were real people who lived and literally did the things attributed to them. ...It's a great shame that Bill [William] Craig has chosen to associate his own views so closely with those of Joshua Swamidass. Swamidass is by his own account a methodological naturalist of science.[131]

These three OEC bring up good critiques of one another and I believe force us to reconsider the simplicity and cohesiveness of the YEC interpretation of Genesis. Of these three I find Lydia not only the most open-minded but the best equipped to supply a literary critique of Genesis. Though an analytical philosopher, her work, *The Mirror or the Mask: liberating the Gospels from literary devices*, is ingenious. In this work Lydia breaks down why, before we simply assert notions that the Gospel authors may have simply invented or carelessly edited their own stories, we need to have convincing reasons for thinking this.[132] In like manner I discussed with Lydia that I do not find sufficiently good reasons to conclude the author(s) of Genesis were doing anything other than reporting a straight-forward chronological account of creation. In addition to her comments above, she reminded me of the words of G.K. Chesterton when someone references: "the consensus of scholars today". We must not forget the "democracy of the dead". Point being, just because some scholars happen to be alive today, it does not follow that they are most likely to be the ones that are right let alone the consensus when we add past scholars into this *democracy*. As we have seen in this chapter, when we do this the consensus is overwhelmingly on the side of YEC.

Of course, YEC theory could still fail so badly within the social and natural sciences that we must jettison the points of biblical exegesis and the historic church understanding. So, before we proclaim the Genesis account as real history based on the Bible alone, let's look at what history is in the first place

---

[131] Personal correspondence with Lydia available upon request.
[132] Bill Craig, Mike Licona, Craig Hazen are a few evangelicals that presuppose the authors may have invented or coerced (or simply gotten confused) on certain elements of the Gospels

and decide whether history and social sciences can add clarity and plausibility to YEC or not.

PART TWO

Natural Science > Social Science, Right?

"Historical events illustrate more clearly than anything the injunction against eating of the Tree of Knowledge. The only activity that bears any fruit is subconscious activity, and no one who takes part in any historical drama can ever understand its significance. If he so much as tries to understand it, his efforts are fruitless."

— **Leo Tolstoy,** *War and Peace*

I have been reminded over the years that the natural sciences are superior to the social sciences, but is that really the case? The success rate of the natural sciences decade to decade and century to century are quite low. If we look millennia to millennia, they are less than ten percent successful, which means they are more than ninety percent wrong; what was believed true scientifically in the year ten thousand AD is now understood to be mostly false. That is hardly a "good rate of success." We now know that logical positivism (that we can only be sure of things directly perceived by the senses) is demonstrably false by its own measures.[133] We also know that scientism (the notion that the natural sciences have superiority over other modes of knowledge and inquiry) is similarly a growingly antiquated concept.[134] There is little empirical reason to not believe that much of what we believe today scientifically will be found false in the future.

What about the social sciences? Overall, the social sciences including history, anthropology, sociology, archeology, economics, geography, politics/law, linguistics, and to a lesser degree, psychology, have held up much better than the natural sciences. For example, we still believe most of what Plutarch and Arrian wrote concerning Alexander the Great is true. Similarly, the epic of Gilgamesh was considered good literature three thousand years ago and still is today. Arts and aesthetics of five thousand years ago are still considered worthy of study, and though there may have been some tweaks to how a certain artist's philosophy might have been portrayed a century ago, overall,

---

[133] GotQuestions.org, "What Is Positivism?" GotQuestions.org, April 5, 2018, (https://www.gotquestions.org/positivism.html)
[134] J.P. Moreland, "The Deep Cultural Impact of Scientism," JP Morelands Web, October 9, 2018, (http://www.jpmoreland.com/2018/10/09/the-deep-cultural-impact-of-scientism/)

they remain holistically accurate. Likewise, the Bible has grown in credibility year over year with the help of archaeology and literary criticism and research. In my twenty years of research in the natural and social sciences, I found many reasons to believe the social sciences and the arts are superior to the natural sciences, and modern academia is beginning to agree with the recognition that scientism is false. So, what can the social sciences tell us about OEC and YEC?

The Philosophy of History

The author at a university book signing in 2014 for the
1ˢᵗ edition of The Philosophy of History.

The following excerpt is taken straight from my previous work, *The Philosophy of History*; however, it works perfectly to open this chapter on the social vs. the natural sciences. It serves as an equally good challenge to an OEC position by the same criterion, it would seem. I have again added the word "OEC" to be read in place of "naturalism," and I think you will begin to see my point:

> The vast majority of historians since the mid-nineteenth century through today have endorsed a level of naturalism [OEC] when dealing with the ancient past, though when cornered, these historians have in my personal experiences admitted that they have often accepted naturalism [OEC] as the primer of ancient history though they really could not explain to me why to the slightest degree. This is a perfect example of naturalism [OEC] retarding our social sciences;

if a PhD historian cannot explain what he or she has written on the ancient past, then they have no business writing about it in my opinion. Sadly, many of these historians have said that their departments, universities, or publishers have oftentimes insisted on at least a few pages of support to a naturalistic [OEC] worldview leading up to the ancient appearances of the first civilizations in Mesopotamia and Sumer. For example, the late Norman F. Cantor (emeritus professor of history, sociology, and comparative literature at New York University) dedicated approximately *five* pages for all history before 3000 BC in which he too infers a rehashed naturalistic [OEC] viewpoint in his book *Antiquity*. On a much more extensive viewpoint, historian Dr. J. M. Roberts (previously of Oxford University) provides us with thirty-four pages on history "before" Sumer in his work *A History of the World*.[135]

I am not attacking historians who use OEC philosophy to begin their discourse as I used the same philosophy for much of my academic career. I do however, want to show that if there is no good reason to believe OEC to be true within the confines of history, then why should as accomplished an historian as J.M. Roberts punt to the natural sciences to tell him what is ancient history: "Traditionally, what happened before writing is called prehistory, and historians have left it to other scholars."[136] The term prehistory is a definitional misnomer in many ways, since it alludes to before-history, so as a historian, I am aghast that Roberts tells us "we must leave this topic to other scholars" and accept what they tell us *a priori*. History and the social sciences are permeated with these type introductions, which only begs the question *why*? We could seriously be retarding the way we do history, science, and education. Dr. Roberts makes vague assertions that man discovered fire around 100,000 BC and began working with crops and domesticated animals between 15,000-7,000 BC, presupposing naturalism and an evolutionary timeline. Dr. Roberts admits that there is no real evidence for language or writing evolving over time, but that Sumerian language seemed to rapidly arise at approximately 4000 BC. Written language appeared by 3500 BC. This philosophy of history, endorsed by OEC, seems to force inferences that have no data to back them up, as Roberts admits:

---

[135] Stroud, *Philosophy*, 33-5.
[136] J. M. Roberts, *A Short History of the World* (New York, NY: Oxford University Press, 1997, p. 2,3)

In prehistory much was settled to ensure that one day humans would know how to write—as well as engineer, build, organize and many other things. Though so much has happened so recently in the last 5,000 years or so, it does not start happening without any preparation. In sheer weight of years most of the story of human beings lies in prehistoric times, and that is why we have begun there. In looking at the beginnings of civilized life, we have to start with what lies behind it.[137]

It is ironic that Roberts is amazed that so much history seems to have happened recently. What is driving these undirected processes in prehistory to ensure the preparation that Roberts mentions? Alas, it is not open to debate, and it is left to non-historians to fill in the blanks. I ask colleagues and peers what happened around 10,000 BC, and when they give me a spoon-fed response like the above, I push for details on how we know these things historically. Most eventually admit the assertion is unprovable and, like Roberts, assume the natural sciences have it covered. Do you see the problem? So, if we look at what we know concerning recorded history without presupposing naturalism, YEC seems more fact-based than OEC, which often assumes assertions with little to no evidence.

The Shell-Game: OEC evidence – who has it?

---

[137] Ibid.

But perhaps I am being disingenuous towards OEC, but I think not.[138] It is important to remember that unlike most religions, Christianity rests its finality on the life, death, and Resurrection of Jesus. If these events are not true, then Christianity is false.[139] Yet if biblical claims can be established through historical methodologies, then we have a compelling reason to believe Christianity is true. In this chapter, we utilize historic and philosophical inquiries to see if YEC is credible per the social sciences, and in the next chapter, we will do the same through the lens of the natural sciences. John Warwick Montgomery presents a definition of the historical method we will use:

> History...will be defined as: An inquiry focusing on past human experience, both individual and societal, with a view towards the production of significant and comprehensive narratives, embracing men's actions and reactions in respect to the whole range of natural, rational, and spiritual powers.[140]

Moreover, we will continue to use C. Behan McCullagh's criteria, to weigh these evidences across the social and natural sciences. When deciding on the best explanation, a credible hypothesis must:

1) Be as plausible as possible. (The data must imply something like the hypothesis)
2) Have great explanatory scope. (The hypothesis must explain quantity and variety of the data)
3) Have great explanatory power. (The hypothesis must explain the data with a high degree of probability)
4) Not be disconfirmed by other reasonable belief. (There must not be data that implies the hypothesis is improbable)
5) Not include additional ad hoc components. (The data must not be twisted to fit the theory)[141]

In my previous works, I have shown why age-neutral biblical theism fulfills these five points better than any of the naturalistic theories.[142] Does YEC hold its own against OEC within the social sciences? In the previous chapter, we looked at OEC's lack of consistency theologically and at the hermeneutical

---

[138] This is no false dichotomy or straw man.

[139] 1 Corinthians 15:14, 17.

[140] John W Montgomery, *The Shape of the Past: A Christian Response to Secular Philosophies of History* (Eugene, OR: Wipf and Stock Publishers, 1975, p.13)

[141] Christopher B McCullagh, *Justifying Historical Descriptions* (New York: Cambridge University Press, 1984, p. 51, 52)

[142] I assumed the standard 13.7B-year-old universe in *The Philosophy of History*.

gymnastics needed to relegate the early chapters of Genesis to myth, fable, and allegory. Let's take a moment to review how these two square up from a historiographical approach.

Young-earth creation – a short historiography

Let's do a rough calculation to show how the YEC gets to a date of less than 10,000 years ago. The age of the earth can be estimated by taking the first five days of creation (from earth's creation to Adam), then following the genealogies from Adam to Abraham in Genesis 5 and 11, then adding in the time from Abraham to today. Adam was created on day 6, so there were five days before him. If we add up the dates from Adam to Abraham, we get about 3500 years, using the pre-Masoretic Hebrew (see the Septuagint, Josephus, Samaritan Pentateuch) text of Genesis 5 and 11.[143] Christian or secular, most scholars agree that Abraham lived in about 2,000 B.C. (4,000 years ago).

So, a simple calculation is:

+~3,500 years (Adam to Abraham)
+~4,000 years (Abraham to today)

~7,500 years...

Quite a few people have done this calculation using the Masoretic text (which is what most English translations are based on) and...have arrived at...about 6,000 years, or about 4000 BC.[144]

The 4000 BC date is problematic for the traditional YEC position.[145] For one, you must allow room for when these persons' birthdates fell, which allows for a +300 year-swing. "Two of the most popular [defenses] of the 4000 BC

---

[143] Russell Grigg, "Meeting the Ancestors," *Creation*, (March 2003, p. 13–15), quoted in Chris Hardy and Robert Carter, "The Biblical Minimum and Maximum Age of the Earth," Creation.com | Creation Ministries International, August 2014, (https://creation.com/biblical-age-of-the-earth)

[144] Chris Hardy and Robert Carter, "The Biblical Minimum and Maximum Age of the Earth," Creation.com | Creation Ministries International, August 2014, (https://creation.com/biblical-age-of-the-earth)

[145] Henry B Smith, "The Case for the Septuagint's Chronology in Genesis 5 And 11," Bible Archaeology, 2018, https://biblearchaeology.org/images/Genesis-5-and-11/Smith-Henry-The-Case-for-the-Septuagints-Chronology-in-Gen-5-and-11-ICC.pdf)

position are a recent work by Dr. Floyd Jones and a much earlier book by Archbishop James Ussher (1581–1656)."[146,147]

This is what groups like Answers in Genesis, Kent Hovind, and to a degree, Institute for Creation Research will tell you. The truth is that these dates must be given +/- 300 years, even if Ussher was correct. Groups like AIG do a great disservice to the YEC cause by rarely admitting their limited scope and not humbly acknowledging their own ignorance. There is no way, biblically or historically, to provide exact dating for the Creation using the Bible other than saying, "less than 10,000 years ago." Fellow Logos research associate Dr. Rob Carter writes:[148]

> From creation to the Babylonian Captivity, we calculated a per-link imprecision of 219 years (including the 50-yr ambiguity concerning how long Abram remained in Haran), plus an overall systemic imprecision of 89 years. It is not possible to date creation with any more accuracy using just the genealogical data. We should allow for the possibility of ±10 years of imprecision from calendar system changes, and the possibility of up to 3% less solar years before the Exodus if the ancients used 12-lunar-month years or longer blocks of lunar months which would later be converted to 12-lunar-month years. We must also consider the possibility of 1326 additional years if the LXX chrono-genealogies represent the original wording, 301 additional years if the Samaritan Pentateuch is correct, 215 less years for the 'Short Sojourn' view, and 46 fewer or 8 more years due to the ambiguities in the king lists of Judah and Israel. This yields an outside range of 3236 to 5078 years from Creation to the Babylonian Captivity. If the traditional historic date of 587 BC or 586 BC for the Captivity is correct, the earth cannot be more than 7,680 years old, having been created between 5665 BC and 3822 BC. The date of the Flood is more significant to the evaluation of extra-biblical history than is the date of creation. The Flood probably occurred between

---

[146] Hardy and Carter, "Biblical Minimum and Maximum," (https://creation.com/biblical-age-of-the-earth)

[147] James Ussher, *The Annals of the World*, transl. Larry and Marion Pierce (Green Forest, AR: Master Books, 2003), as quoted in Hardy and Carter, "Biblical Minimum and Maximum," (https://creation.com/biblical-age-of-the-earth)

[148] Hardy and Carter, "Biblical Minimum and Maximum," (https://creation.com/biblical-age-of-the-earth)

2600 BC and 2300 BC, but certainly between 3386 BC and 2256 BC.[149]

Ironically, secular historical dating gets us to the same range of creation as the following list of cultures and times shows us:[150]

	Chronologist	When Calculated?	Date B.C.
1	Julius Africanus	c. 240	5501
2	George Syncellus	c. 810	5492
3	John Jackson	1752	5426
4	Dr. William Hales	c. 1830	5411
5	Eusebius	c. 330	5199
6	Marianus Scotus	c. 1070	4192
7	L. Condomanus	n/a	4141
8	Thomas Lydiat	c. 1600	4103
9	M. Michael Maestlinus	c. 1600	4079
10	J. Ricciolus	n/a	4062
11	Jacob Salianus	c. 1600	4053
12	H. Spondanus	c. 1600	4051
13	Martin Anstey	1913	4042

---

[149] Ibid.
[150] Dr. Floyd Jones's chronologist calculations, "How Old Is the Earth?" Answers in Genesis, May 30, 2007, (https://answersingenesis.org/age-of-the-earth/how-old-is-the-earth/)

14	W. Lange	n/a	4041
15	E. Reinholt	n/a	4021
16	J. Cappellus	c. 1600	4005
17	E. Greswell	1830	4004
18	E. Faulstich	1986	4001
19	D. Petavius	c. 1627	3983
20	Frank Klassen	1975	3975
21	Becke	n/a	3974
22	Krentzeim	n/a	3971
23	W. Dolen	2003	3971
24	E. Reusnerus	n/a	3970
25	J. Claverius	n/a	3968
26	C. Longomontanus	c. 1600	3966
27	P. Melanchthon	c. 1550	3964
28	J. Haynlinus	n/a	3963
29	A. Salmeron	d. 1585	3958
30	J. Scaliger	d. 1609	3949
31	M. Beroaldus	c. 1575	3927

As you will likely note from [the above], the dates are not all 4004 B.C. There are several reasons chronologists have different dates, but two primary reasons:

1. Some used the Septuagint or another early translation instead of the Hebrew Masoretic text. The Septuagint is a Greek translation of the Hebrew Old Testament, done about 250 B.C. by about 70 Jewish scholars (hence it is often cited as the LXX, which is the Roman numeral for 70).

2. Several points in the biblical timeline are not straightforward to calculate. They require very careful study of more than one passage. These include exactly how much time the Israelites were in Egypt and what Terah's age was when Abraham was born....

The first four [above] are calculated from the Septuagint, which gives ages for the patriarchs' firstborn much higher than the Masoretic text or the Samarian Pentateuch.... Because of this, the Septuagint adds in extra time [that would have been in the pre-Masoretic Hebrew]. Though the Samarian and Masoretic texts are much closer, they still have a few differences.[151]

Name	Masoretic	Samarian Pentateuch	Septuagint
Adam	130	130	230
Seth	105	105	205
Enosh	90	90	190
Cainan	70	70	170
Mahalaleel	65	65	165
Jared	162	62	162
Enoch	65	65	165

---

[151] Hodge, "How Old," (https://answersingenesis.org/age-of-the-earth/how-old-is-the-earth/)

Methuselah	187	67	167
Lamech	182	53	188
Noah	500	500	500

Cultures throughout the world have kept track of history as well. From a biblical perspective, we would expect the dates given for creation of the earth to align more closely to the biblical date than billions of years.

This is expected since everyone was descended from Noah and scattered from the Tower of Babel. Another expectation is that there should be some discrepancies about the age of the earth among people as they scattered throughout the world, taking their uninspired records or oral history to different parts of the globe and this is exactly what we see.

Under the entry "creation," *Young's Analytical Concordance of the Bible* lists William Hales's accumulation of dates of creation from many cultures, and in most cases Hales says which authority gave the date....[152]

Historian Bill Cooper's research in *After the Flood* provides intriguing dates from several ancient cultures.[153] The first is that of the Anglo-Saxons, whose history has 5,200 years from creation to Christ, according to the Laud and Parker Chronicles. Cooper's research also indicated that Nennius's record of the ancient British history has 5,228 years from creation to Christ. The Irish chronology has a date of about 4000 B.C. for creation...The Mayans have a date for the Flood of 3113 B.C. which aligns very close with the same Flood dating of Gilgamesh, the Sumerian Kings List and the Septuagint dating of the Flood of Noah.[154]

This meticulous work of these various historians should not be dismissed for being primitive. Their dates of only thousands of years are good support for

---

[152] Robert Young, *Young's Analytical Concordance to the Bible* (Peabody, MA: Hendrickson, 1996), referring to William Hales, *A New Analysis of Chronology and Geography, History and Prophecy*, vol. 1 (1830, p. 210), as quoted in Hodge, "How Old" (https://answersingenesis.org/age-of-the-earth/how-old-is-the-earth/)
[153] Bill Cooper, *After the Flood* (UK: New Wine Press, 1995, p. 122–129), as quoted in Hodge, "How Old" (https://answersingenesis.org/age-of-the-earth/how-old-is-the-earth/)
[154] Ibid.

[the YEC position], but not for billions of years from a social science perspective.[155]

Below Table: Dates for the Age of the Earth by Various Cultures: [156, 157]

Culture	Age, BC	Authority listed by Hales
Spain by Alfonso X	6984	Muller
Spain by Alfonso X	6484	Strauchius
India	6204	Gentil
India	6174	Arab records
Babylon	6158	Bailly
Chinese	6157	Bailly
Greece by Diogenes Laertius	6138	Playfair

---

[155] Most laypersons will not understand how important is the understanding that we do not have any real Sumerian history before about 4,000 BC. If human history had been much older, as OEC theorists and secularists assert, we should have a huge array of evolving and developing history in a plethora of forms, and we simply do not. Simply calling it prehistory does nothing to explain it.

[156] Hodge, "How Old" (https://answersingenesis.org/age-of-the-earth/how-old-is-the-earth/)

[157] "Historical Creation Scientists," Answers in Genesis, (https://answersingenesis.org/creation-scientists/historical/), as quoted in Hodge, "How Old Is the Earth?" (https://answersingenesis.org/age-of-the-earth/how-old-is-the-earth/)

Egypt	6081	B
Persia	5507	Bailly
Israel/Judea by Josephus	5555	Playfair
Israel/Judea by Josephus	5481	Jackson
Israel/Judea by Josephus	5402	Hales
Israel/Judea by Josephus	4698	University history
India	5369	Megasthenes
Babylon (Talmud)	5344	Petrus Alliacens
Vatican (Catholic using the Septuagint)	5270	N/A
Samaria	4427	Scaliger
German, Holy Roman Empire by Johannes Kepler*	3993	Playfair
German, reformer by Martin Luther*	3961	N/A
Israel/Judea by computation	3760	Strauchius
Israel/Judea by Rabbi Lipman*	3616	University history

One of the first rules of history is to avoid **presentism** ("uncritical adherence to present-day attitudes, especially the tendency to interpret past events in terms of modern values and concepts"[158]). That said, the overwhelming consensus of both religious and secular sources across cultures is that Creation was historical and not earlier than 7000 BC. This does not mean it is accurate, of course, but neither can we rule it out without having a **defeater**,[159] which I do not believe OEC proponents have. Adhering to natural sciences will not do the trick; even if natural sciences are on the OEC side, the Bible and theology are seemingly not, and neither do the social sciences appear to be.

After careful research, I find the pre-Masoretic dating of the Septuagint to coincide best with biblical textual criticisms and secular data. Walt Brown, Brian Thomas, Henry Smith, and a growing number of others agree, as these dates align with biblical exegetes and secular timelines for Noah's Flood and the Tower of Babel, as well as similar events across cultures.[160,161] While we will not be going into these subtle differences, we need to train our minds not to look at Answers in Genesis as the definitive YEC voice, but simply a starting point.

---

[158] Chip Hughes, "Presentism: Don't Judge Our Ancestors' Actions by Today's Standards," Voices and Images, August 10, 2018, (https://www.voicesandimages.com/presentism-dont-judge-ancestors-actions-by-todays-standards/)
[159] https://iep.utm.edu/ep-defea/
[160] "Two Date Range Options for Noah's Flood," Creation.com | Creation Ministries International, 2017, https://creation.com/images/pdfs/tj/j31_1/J31_1_120-127.pdf)
[161] Steve Rudd, "Septuagint (LXX) vs. Corrupted Masoretic," Bible Chronology Charts, November 2017, (http://www.bible.ca/manuscripts/Bible-chronology-charts-age-of-earth-date-Genesis-5-11-Septuagint-text-LXX-original-autograph-corrupted-Masoretic-MT-primeval-5554BC.htm)

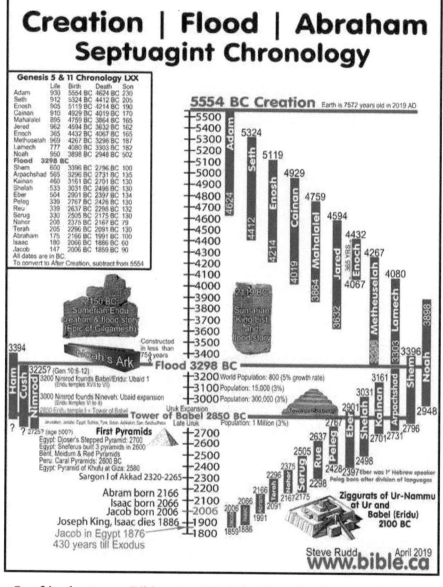

Our friends at www.Bible.ca provided the above timeline that aligns well with modern scholarship and biblical dating so you that can get a better idea of what a YEC time-frame might look like.[162]

---

[162] Steve Rudd, "The Septuagint LXX And Other Manuscripts of the Old Testament (Tanakh)," The Septuagint, LXX, origin, textual transmission 282 BC, November 2017, (https://www.bible.ca/manuscripts/septuagint.htm)

A Historical Adam and Eve:

The Bible is the story of God's creative work, of humanity's rebellion against God, and of God's work to redeem fallen humanity. Adam and Eve are central to Genesis's account of Creation and humanity's Fall, and the church has historically viewed them as real persons. This view has come under attack in recent years. While doubts are hardly surprising from a secular society that largely rejects the authority of the Bible, it has surprised some to see these doubts rise in Christians of OEC and theistic evolution viewpoints.[163]

> The cover story in *Christianity Today* on June 2011 was, "The Search for the Historical Adam." The subtitle read, "Some scholars believe genome science casts doubt on the existence of the first man and woman. Others say the integrity of the faith requires it." The number of professing evangelical scholars doubting or denying a literal Adam and Eve has continued to grow. Some say the account of Adam and Eve is a myth, a symbolic story to teach us theological and moral truth. Others say that Adam and Eve were the first two humans but that they evolved from ape-like creatures and became human when God breathed into them. Others say they really existed, but that Adam was merely the head of a clan or tribe: Adam and Eve weren't the only humans at that time but were chosen by God for His purposes. Still others take Genesis 1–3 as literal history: the first man, Adam, was made from dust, and the first woman, Eve, was made from his rib. So, what is the truth, and does it really matter as long as you believe in Jesus Christ as Lord?[164]

While there is no way to do justice to every OEC theory concerning Adam and Eve, we can summarize the major points of OEC and YEC from a social science perspective. In a nutshell, OEC theorists often argue for Adam and Eve as being archetypes of humans, and thus Jesus was simply mistaken when referencing Adam as a historical figure. Old Testament scholar John Walton asserts, "Adam and Eve are historical figures but I am persuaded that the biblical text is more interested in them as archetypal figures who represent all of humanity."[165] A similar view would be that of Old Testament professor

---

[163] Josh McDowell and Sean McDowell, *Evidence that Demands a Verdict: Life-Changing Truth for a Skeptical World* (Nashville, TN: Thomas Nelson, 2017, p.423)

[164] Terry Mortenson, "In Defense of the Historical Adam," Answers in Genesis, July 28, 2015, (https://answersingenesis.org/adam-and-eve/defense-of-historical-adam/)

[165] Ardel B Caneday and Matthew Barrett, eds., *Four Views on the Historical Adam* (Grand Rapids, MI: Zondervan, 2013, p.89)

John Collins, who looks at Adam and Eve as historical, insofar as "they were *real* persons as the headwaters of humankind but don't read them as literally *literal*."[166] On the flip side, many OEC theorists wish to believe in a historical Adam and Eve (as well as a historical flood) but also wish to believe in billions of years of history, in keeping with the most up-to-date cosmologies.

So, the extremes of OEC are:

1) Adam and Eve didn't exist.
2) Adam and Eve might have been part of a larger, ape-like population.
3) Adam and Eve were archetypes of humanity.
4) Adam and Eve were historical, but we must jettison concordist and naturalistic assumptions to maintain them and a historic Fall but still keep a standard 13.7B-year dating of Creation.

We will review these from a social scientific viewpoint against the YEC position that simply posits:

- Adam and Eve were real/historical persons, just as the Bible suggests.

Do we really need to jettison all of history to maintain a pseudo-naturalistic viewpoint? We are growingly becoming confident that naturalism is false today, so why must we maintain a naturalistic type understanding when it comes to Adam and Eve? Is the OEC perspective really so palatable that we must adhere to a concordist view and force our biblical meta-narrative to conform to a modern, ever-changing science-exegete of scripture and reality?

> The Name "Adam" is from the Hebrew word meaning either "humanity" or individual "man"; or a proper name. The creation of Adam in Genesis 1:26, 27 describes the creation of humanity in general, while the accounts in Genesis 2:7 and 2:21, 22 refer to the creation of two individuals: a man and woman. These individuals are subsequently identified as Adam and Eve (Gen. 2:20; 3:20). Theologians from Patristic to modern times have recognized the importance of Adam to Christian doctrine, in particular the doctrines of man, sin and salvation.[167]

---

[166] Ibid. p.143.
[167] William VanDoodewaard, *The Quest for the Historical Adam: Genesis, Hermeneutics, and Human Origins* (Grand Rapids, MI: Reformation Heritage Books, 2015)

The biblical genealogies (Genesis 5:1 vs Jude 1:14, 1 Chronicles 1:1 vs Luke 3:38); Second Temple Literature; Teachings of Jesus (Matthew 19:3–12, Mark 10:2–12); the teachings of Paul (Romans 5 and 1 Corinthians 15, Acts 17:26); the Prophets (Isaiah 43:27, Hosea 6:7, Job 31:33); and the church fathers all treat Adam and Eve as actual people. In addition to affirming a historical Adam, scriptural evidence seems to support the traditional view that Adam and Eve were the first humans, created by God, and from whom the entire human race descended.[168]

What is funny but ironic is that even Bio-Logos (the extreme version that adopts a form of naturalistic Darwinism and Christian theism) agrees that:

> Part of the challenge this subject generates for Evangelicals is due to confusion over exactly what the science can and cannot say about human origins in general, or the historicity of Adam and Eve in particular.... In addition to these scientific questions, however, Evangelicals are also strongly interested in the question of Adam and Eve's historicity: were they a literal couple that lived about 6,000 – 10,000 years ago? Unfortunately, genomic science is not at all equipped to address this question – it simply does not have the ability to establish (or rule out, for that matter) the historicity of any particular individual in the ancient past.[169]

In other words, even the most predominant theistic evolutionary supporters agree that the text and social sciences seem to point toward a historical Adam and Eve, and genomic science is not equipped to dismiss YEC.

Similarly, Hugh Ross and his OEC ministry Reason to Believe seem confused on the topic:

> The Genesis 1 narrative begins with the creation of the universe and culminates with God's special creation of Adam and Eve. Historic Christianity holds that Adam and Eve were the first two humans, uniquely made in God's image, and that all humanity has descended from them. The biblical

---

[168] Josh McDowell and Sean McDowell, *Evidence That Demands a Verdict: Life-Changing Truth for a Skeptical World* (Nashville, TN: Thomas Nelson, 2017, p.428-30)
[169] BioLogos, "Adam, Eve, and Human Population Genetics - Articles," BioLogos (BioLogos, November 12, 2014, https://biologos.org/articles/series/genetics-and-the-historical-adam-responses-to-popular-arguments/adam-eve-and-human-population-genetics)

genealogies (both Old and New Testament), Jesus' teachings, and Paul's epistles all refer to Adam as a real individual.

<u>Genetic, linguistic and pathogen studies support a historical Adam and Eve.</u> [emphasis added] This research indicates that humanity arose 1) recently (within the last hundred thousand years or so), 2) at a single location (close to where Bible scholars place the Garden of Eden), and 3) from a small population, arguably as small as a single pair. Much scientific work remains to be done toward refining details, but ample evidence supports the historic Christian idea that all humanity descended from two historical persons, Adam and Eve.[170]

Hugh Ross and Fazale Rana find too many theological and social science-based reasons to not accept an historical Adam and Eve. This goes against their concordist nature, even as they try to defend a historical Adam and Eve while keeping their OEC suppositions. While evolutionary biologists argue for the idea that there were many first humans, not just two, Fazale Rana describes why he is reluctant to accept their theory:

The idea that humanity arose as a population is a theory-laden concept that is a necessary entailment of the evolutionary paradigm. Because of the central importance of Adam and Eve's historicity to the Christian faith, I am reluctant to embrace the idea that humanity began as a population, not a pair. But, I'm as equally reluctant to accept this scientific claim—mainstream or not—knowing that the population size measurements are based on simplified, idealized methods that struggle to take into account population dynamics that can influence population size estimates and haven't been validated. Questions about the validity of the mathematical relationships that form the basis of these methods compound these problems. To put it another way: Even if I accepted the notion of common descent, I still wouldn't be convinced that humans arose as a population because of the scientific questions that surround the population size estimates. In RTB's view, science has yet to

---

[170] "Historical Adam," Reasons to Believe (Reasons to Believe), (https://www.reasons.org/explore/publications/rtb-101/historical-adam)

falsify the notion that humanity descended from a primordial pair.[171]

It seems that the OEC position, which wishes to maintain an OEC base/ontology but keep a historical Adam and Eve would not pass Occam's Razor as the simplest explanation of the data (if God exists). With the fall of naturalism, like logical positivism a century ago, it is ironic that Christians, of all people, need to maintain a naturalistic perspective on life and biblical exegesis. I have communicated these concerns to Hugh Ross, whom I greatly respect, but he maintains his original concordist views on scripture, which usually puts the natural sciences one step ahead of scripture and the social sciences so that both must conform to the natural sciences (except when you want to keep something like the Virgin Birth or Resurrection). This mode of eisegesis may be commendable in the mid-20th century, but is it in the 21st century?

Changing Tradition?

Reasons to Believe and Hugh Ross have shown great tact in defending a historical Adam and Eve, but they seem to remain inconsistent as is outlined in their answer to theistic-evolutionist and New Testament professor JR Kirk, who writes:

> Where, then, are we left, if the pressures of scientific inquiry lead us to take down the spire of a literal, historical Adam? For many, the cognitive dissonance between the sciences and a historical Adam has already become too great to continue holding both. We therefore have to carefully determine whether the cause of Christ, and of truth, is better served by indicating that choice must be made between the two, or by retelling the narrative about the origins of humanity as we now understand it in light of the death and resurrection of Christ.[172]

RTB responds:

> This is a tricky topic and I appreciate Kirk's thoughtful approach to it. Still, the thought of "retelling" the biblical

---

[171] Fazale Rana, "Adam and Eve: A Primordial Pair or a Population?" The Cell's Design (Reasons to Believe, July 6, 2016, https://www.reasons.org/explore/blogs/the-cells-design/read/the-cells-design/2016/07/06/adam-and-eve-a-primordial-pair-or-a-population)
[172] Maureen (Guest Writer), "Adam, Eve, and Changing Tradition," Take Two (Reasons to Believe, August 16, 2013, https://www.reasons.org/explore/blogs/take-two/read/take-two/2013/08/16/adam-eve-and-changing-tradition)

origins story makes me a little uneasy. Would we be retelling the story in order to accommodate modern views, or because scientific data or theological understanding actually warrant a change? If the first reason, there's a lot of stuff in the Bible that people would like to change to suit modern philosophies and tastes—how much, then, should we alter to accommodate them? If the second reason, what if the scientific foundation for human evolution is not as solid as is generally believed? RTB biochemist Fuz Rana lays out several lines of evidence that buttress the traditional view of Adam and Eve while showing that it's reasonable to question the evolutionary view:

- **Molecular anthropology** – Genetic studies suggest that humanity had a recent origin in East Africa from a small population that expanded rapidly and migrated. These findings integrate well with the origins explanations in Genesis.

- **Differences between humans and hominids** – More and more research, including genetic studies, indicates that hominids are dead ends and side branches, rather than humanity's evolutionary predecessors.

- **Cultural big bang** – Archaeological discoveries reveal tools and pseudo-cultural practices among hominids remained static for tens of thousands of years. But when modern humans appeared, the sophistication of tools and tool manufacturing increased dramatically, and religious and artistic expression appeared for the first time. These findings line up with biblical view of humans uniquely as God's image bearers.

From the theological side of things, rejecting an historical Adam and Eve does raise legitimate concerns. How does the evolutionary view of humanity impact the genre of Genesis? How does it influence our understanding of God's role as Creator and Redeemer? What about the doctrine of original sin? Clearly, the historical Adam and Eve is a tradition that not only warrants careful handling and thoughtful dialogue but also may be worth keeping.[173]

Even RTB understands the ramifications and inconsistencies of their view, or so it seems. Would Occam's razor fall more on the side of adding an arbitrary, additional fourteen billion years to the equation? What about a population of mindless Adam and Eve hominids? A non-literal Fall? It seems that Reasons to Believe, William Lane Craig, and OEC in general, have one foot in a naturalistic world and the other in a non-naturalistic one. If this is the case, YEC theory is obviously the less contrived and more in adherence to Occam's Razor, let alone perspicuity and historical exegesis. Nonetheless, let us analyze all components of Genesis 1–11 before making such sweeping generalizations.

Human Origins

Author and Dr. Ann Gauger – 2016 (Seattle, Washington)

I had the privilege of conversing with all three of the authors of the 2012 book *Science and Human Origins* (Ann Gauger, Douglas Axe, and Casey Luskin) over the years. Their work was a major influence on my earlier book, for which Casey Luskin provided the foreword. In their 2012 work, they systematically break down, from a secular understanding, why Adam and Eve make good scientific sense. They, like Ross, fall more into the OEC camp, but none of them have expressed great reasons for it, other than staying more credible with mainline science. Gauger has helped William Lane Craig in his current research on a historical Adam and Eve; I am surprised that Craig says he is leaning towards a non-historical Adam and Eve, since this is not

---

[173] Ibid.

Gauger's viewpoint. Is it good exegete (historically, philosophically, or anthropologically) to posit that we need millions of years in order to maintain a historical Adam and Eve (or to follow a concordist view that there was a herd of mindless primates from which God chose two to be the beginning of humanity)?

This seems more of a knee-jerk reaction to keep our Enlightenment paradigm of millions or billions of years *plus* the Bible in retreat to modern science. Once again, naturalism bred with non-naturalism is self-refuting in the manner of a square circle, so I am at a loss when someone attempts to sway me into adopting it. I have discussed this with both Ross and Gauger and attempted to reconcile these components, but Ross is wed to his concordist views and Gauger to her PDC of millions of years (and Roman Catholicism) and a pseudo-historical Adam and Eve. Without compelling reasons based on scripture or science, I remain unconvinced that I should adopt such a radical view.

> The problem seems to be a matter of time. Dr. Ross [and Gauger] believes...that Adam and Eve were real people, the parents of all humanity, and the agents through whom sin entered human history. However, [they] also buy into secular claims about the age of the Earth.... Dr. Ross realizes that the timing of Adam and Eve's entry onto the stage of history cannot be reconciled with the ancient dates assigned to Neanderthals. He therefore maintains that God created Adam and Eve after the human-like animals we call Neanderthals...and that Neanderthals had no biological relationship to true humans. The same would be true for any other archaic humans deemed to be of great age.[174]

As of January 2020, Gauger has acknowledged what I have said all along: "Ultimately a coalescent event can't tell you what went before. Was there a previous population, or was there no pre-existing population? Bottleneck to two, of de novo creation? These questions will have to be addressed by other methods."[175] These other methods are found largely within the social, not the natural sciences as I pointed out to Gauger in 2016. Again, OEC is largely a shell-game where one discipline, say biology, will claim that it's the historian that has solid proof for OEC, but then the historian punts to the astronomer

---

[174] Elizabeth Mitchell, "Does Hugh Ross Believe in Soulless Ancient Humans?" Answers in Genesis, April 20, 2015, (https://answersingenesis.org/human-evolution/origins/does-hugh-ross-believe-in-soulless-ancient-humans/)

[175] Ann Gauger, "Reflections on Our Ancient Past," Evolution News, January 10, 2020, (https://evolutionnews.org/2020/01/reflections-on-our-ancient-past/)

and the astronomer to the geologist, etc. So the question remains: If you are a Christian what are your grounds for adopting the OEC position? No appeal to authority, hand-waving or more of the shell-game; what are your reasons?

> Even though Dr. Ross denies evolution, he accepts the evolutionary scientists' interpretation of the fossil record insofar as the timing of the Neanderthals' appearance 150,000 to 200,000 years ago, their extinction about 30,000 years ago, and their coexistence with humans in Europe for about 10,000 years.[176] Also, despite the evolutionary assumptions and circular reasoning on which it is based, Ross applies the molecular clock dating of human origins to Adam and Eve, presuming that God made the first "real" humans around $100,000 \pm 20,000$ years ago.[177]

Thus, because Dr. Ross accepts the biblical truth that Adam and Eve were the parents of all modern humans and that they brought sin and death this world, he cannot permit the idea that Neanderthals—who are supposed to have been on the earthly scene thousands of years too soon—were actually humans. By default, then, in Ross's estimation, Neanderthals and their fellow human-like travelers in the ancient world-before-Adam must have just been animals. In *Navigating Genesis*, Ross even suggests that God created these bipedal, thinking, feeling, intelligent, human-looking beings to put the fear of man into animals before Adam's race was born. This of course ignores the clear biblical statement (Genesis 9:2) that God put a fear of man into animals in the wake of Noah's Flood, nearly two thousand years later (tens of thousands in Ross's reckoning). When we decide to pick and choose which parts of Scripture to believe and which parts to twist in order to compromise with secular, worldview-dependent, Bible-denying claims, such discrepancies are bound to happen.[178]

---

[176] Fazale Rana, "Does New Date for Neanderthal Mean the End of Human-Neanderthal Interbreeding?" Reasons to Believe, (June 15, 2011, http://www.reasons.org/articles/does-new-date-for-neanderthal-extinction-mean-the-end-of-human-neanderthal-interbreeding), as quoted in Mitchell, "Soulless Ancient Humans," (https://answersingenesis.org/human-evolution/origins/does-hugh-ross-believe-in-soulless-ancient-humans/)

[177] Fazale Rana, "Were They Real? The Scientific Case for Adam and Eve," Reasons to Believe, (October 1, 2010, http://www.reasons.org/articles/were-they-real-the-scientific-case-for-adam-and-eve), as quoted in Mitchell, "Soulless Ancient Humans," (https://answersingenesis.org/human-evolution/origins/does-hugh-ross-believe-in-soulless-ancient-humans/)

[178] Mitchell, "Soulless Ancient Humans?" (https://answersingenesis.org/human-evolution/origins/does-hugh-ross-believe-in-soulless-ancient-humans/)

Attempting to denote the first humans as mindless hominids seems self-refuting from a Christian ontology and, from a secular perspective, without warrant or proof. Again, it seems the social sciences, as well as Occam's Razor, are firmly in favor of YEC theory for a historical Adam and Eve.

Whether it is the Upanishads, Sumerian, Efik of Nigeria, Norse, Fang tribe of West Africa, Blackfeet of North America, Biami of Papa New Guinea, Bukusu tribes of Kenya, or the Agikuyu tribes, all have narratives of a first set of parents (man and woman) that falls into a recent creation. Similarly, anthropology, sociology, and history all support these narratives in what secularists often refer to as the Neolithic Revolution. Most OEC and secular sides recognize the recent creation of humanity, civilization, writing, language, and the arts; they just add millions of years in front of it. We cannot seem to get away from the fact that the Bible, theology, church history, and the social sciences all fall heavily on the side of a historical Adam and Eve within a YEC framework. As we look into the natural sciences, it is possible that OEC theories will be so strong that they override the biblical and social sciences, but so far, we have not seen strong reasons for accepting OEC, as regards Adam and Eve as historian of science Terry Mortenson articulates:

> It seems that if one is a biblical Christian, the historicity of Adam is abundantly clear from both the Old and New Testaments. Right from the beginning, the text describes real time and names people and places. Genesis 1 speaks of years and seasons and days with evenings and mornings governed by the sun, moon, and stars. Genesis 2 describes the location of the Garden of Eden and names four rivers. Genesis 4 names the city that Cain built. Genesis 6–8 describes certain events on specific days of different months of the 600th and 601st years of Noah's life. The eleven occurrences of the Hebrew word *toledoth* scattered through Genesis (in Genesis 2:4, 5:1, -6:9, 10:1, and so on) and translated as "this the account of" or "these are the generations of" tie the whole book together as one historical record. Few evangelicals doubt the historicity of Genesis 12–50, but there is no break in the literary style between chapters Genesis 11 and Genesis 12. The Abraham and Terah of Genesis 11 are the same men in Genesis 12. The genealogies of Genesis 5 and Genesis 11 connect Adam to Noah to Abraham so that all of the men named were equally historical. The Hebrew verb forms in Genesis 1, which is often claimed to be a unique genre, show conclusively that

the first chapter of the Bible is historical narrative just like
the rest of Genesis.[179]

In any straightforward reading of the Bible, it is clear that Adam was a
historical person. Scripture teaches that all humanity descended from a
historical Adam and Eve.[180] Similarly, the social sciences and histories of
different cultures seem to support a YEC worldview with a historical Adam
and Eve. It seems all but certain, if one is a Christian, that a historical Adam
and Eve birthed the entire human race. In *The Quest for the Historical Adam*,
William VanDoodewaard does a phenomenal job of detailing a real and
historical Adam within the Bible and history.[181] Practically all social sciences
are on the side of a historical and literal Adam and Eve. Perhaps the natural
sciences will prove this fallacious, but if all we had to use were the following:

1. Being a self-proclaimed Christian
2. The Bible
3. The social sciences (all cultures)

...one would conclude that a historical Adam and Eve are grounded in reality
and history, and the social sciences support this conclusion, just as one would
expect if the Genesis account were literal.

A Historical Noah's Flood

I touched upon this from a non-naturalistic vs. naturalistic viewpoint in *The
Philosophy of History,* but we need to review this from an OEC vs. YEC
perspective now. The YEC position is clear: the social science reason there
are so many flood legends (at least 270) is because it is a true and historical
event. Even my secular colleagues recognize that the closest thing to a
universal history resides within the odd narrative surrounding Noah's Flood
as recorded in the Bible. On the flipside, my OEC colleagues either believe
in a local flood or are forced to believe in a universal flood, which would seem
to negate billions of years of history (both of which are problematic for the
OEC position). As a student of ancient history, I have no doubt that people
have historically believed in a real and global flood.

---

[179] Terry Mortenson, "In Defense of the Historical Adam," Answers in Genesis, July 28,
2015, (https://answersingenesis.org/adam-and-eve/defense-of-historical-adam/)

[180] Josh McDowell and Sean McDowell, *Evidence That Demands a Verdict: Life-Changing
Truth for a Skeptical World* (Nashville, TN: Thomas Nelson, 2017, p.441)

[181] William VanDoodewaard, *The Quest for the Historical Adam: Genesis, Hermeneutics,
and Human Origins* (Grand Rapids, MI: Reformation Heritage Books, 2015)

As noted by Peter Enns in his book, *Inspiration and Incarnation*, it seems possible that the cross-cultural flood stories may have a common origin:

> As with the Enuma Elish, one should not conclude that the biblical account is directly dependent on these flood stories. Still, the obvious similarities between them indicate a connection on some level. Perhaps one borrowed from the other; or perhaps all of the stories have older precursors. The second option is quite possible, since, as mentioned above, there exists a Sumerian flood story that is considered older than either the Akkadian or biblical versions.[182]

John Currid proposes that the biblical account of the Flood perhaps originates from the flood of the Ancient Near East. A common origin does not necessarily infer that one source built off another, but that each account delivered a completely different version of a common event.[183, 184]

> If the biblical stories are true, one would be surprised not to find some reference to these truths in extrabiblical literature. And indeed in ancient Near Eastern myth we do see some kernels of historical truth. However, pagan authors vulgarized or bastardized those truths – they distorted fact by dressing it up with polytheism, magic, violence, and paganism. Fact became myth. From this angle the common references would appear to support rather than deny the historicity of the biblical story.[185]

Some, like Currid, take a more polemic approach, to say that the biblical story is designed to mock stories from the ancient Near East while providing the true Flood account. Is this a plausible possibility? It is mostly agreed that the writing in the ancient Near East, when analyzing Genesis 6–9, which encompasses the flood story holistically, is written in the form of historical narrative, and this clearly bears the markings of that genre:

---

[182] Peter Enns, *Inspiration and Incarnation: Evangelicals and the Problem of the Old Testament* (Grand Rapids, MI: Baker Academic, a division of Baker Publishing Group, 2015, p.29); McDowell, *Evidence*, 390

[183] John D. Currid is the Carl McMurray professor of Old Testament at Reformed Theological Seminary in Charlotte, North Carolina, and the author of several books and Old Testament commentaries. A PhD graduate in Syro-Palestinian archaeology (University of Chicago), he has extensive archaeological field experience from projects throughout Israel and Tunisia.

[184] McDowell, *Evidence*, 391.

[185] John D. Currid, *Ancient Egypt and the Old Testament* (Grand Rapids, MI: Baker Books, 1999, p.32)

A most important grammatical marker in biblical Hebrew is a device called a vav-consecutive-plus-imperfect. Often simply translate as "and it was," the device is the way in which a Hebrew writer presents events in a historical sequence. It appears commonly throughout Hebrew narrative but rarely in other genres such as poetry. In Genesis 6:5-22, that device appears at least a dozen times. Also, in Hebrew narrative the writers often employ a word that serves as a sign of the coming direct object – it is the word 'et. It almost never occurs in poetry, but it is clear, distinctive marker of historical prose. The sign of the direct object appears at least fifteen times in Genesis 6:5-22... And the style of writing used in the cosmological texts in the ancient near east is best described as "mythic narrative".[186]

We can conclude that "the Genesis writer is a radical monotheist. His presentation of the Flood account not only relays the event in a historical manner, it also contains harsh and radical rebukes of pagan myths."[187] Evidence from the Old Testament, New Testament, and ancient history seems to indicate that Adam and Eve were viewed as historical persons, and the Flood was viewed as a real and global event. If YEC is viably true, then what we see in ancient history and the social sciences is exactly what we would expect—historic accounts of a first human pair and a great Flood that impacted the world, followed by a great spreading out of civilization all less than 8000 years ago.

[186] John D. Currid, *Against the Gods: the Polemical Theology of the Old Testament* (Wheaton, IL: Crossway, 2013), p.58)
[187] Ibid.

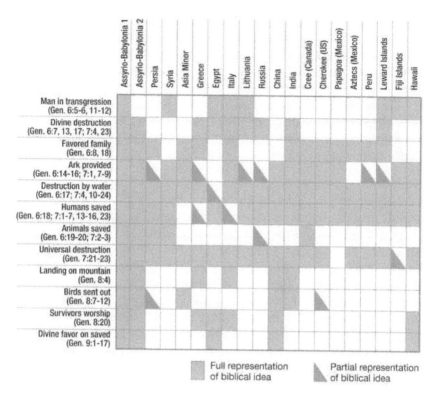

Chart adapted from B.C. Nelson, The Deluge Story in Stone, Appendix 11, Flood Traditions, Figure 38, Augsburg, Minneapolis, 1931.[188]

Though there are 270–400+ flood legends that include a worldwide flood and a boat with an elect group of people and animals all orchestrated by God, only the Bible gives a coherent, step-by-step process that aligns to a sensible ark model and a geologically consistent model. We therefore see in Genesis 6:5–7 that the reason for the Flood is man's wickedness and sin. Old Testament professor Kenneth Mathews notes, "Genesis repeatedly attributes the flood to the wickedness of man and explains that the corruption of the earth has merited the response of a moral God. There is no flood story comparable to the moral stature of Genesis."[189]

---

[188] Monty White, "Flood Legends," Answers in Genesis, March 29, 2007, (https://answersingenesis.org/the-flood/flood-legends/flood-legends/)
[189] K. A. Mathews, *Genesis*, vol. 1 (Nashville, TN: Broadman & Holman Publishers, 1996, p.101)

The ultimate question regarding the Flood at this point, similar to a historical Adam and Eve is, "What best accounts for all of these Flood accounts?" Since we have already shown in my previous work why a naturalistic hypothesis is weak, we should look at it from an OEC vs YEC perspective. In YEC, these legends and myths exist because they are historically true. In OEC, we must either balance old-earth creationism with the stories of a global flood (the minority perspective in OEC) or turn it into a local or non-global flood. Occam's Razor would seem to be on the side of YEC, but perhaps we're missing something.

The various flood stories not only share many common parallels, but they are also mostly agreed to as having a historic base by even the most ardent naturalistic anthropologist or physical historian. The overlapping ancient histories can help us gauge shared commonalities between the Genesis account and other ancient origin histories (the Eridu Genesis, Enki and Ninhursag, Enki and the Ordering of the World, Enki, Ninmakh and the creation of Humankind, Epic of Atrakhasis, Enuma Elish, Baal Cycle, Heliopolis Pyramid Text, Memphis Creation Story, Epic of Gilgamesh, etc.). Are these similarities coincidental or are they telling the same ancient story, changed over time? For example, the Sumerian King List correlates to the persons and dynasties of Adam through Noah from Genesis. By the mid-twentieth century, most archaeologists had confirmed that there was enough evidence for a great flood in the archaeological strata to warrant the belief in a massive flood occurring in Mesopotamia. While some may debate whether this flood was global in scale, the sedimentary rock strata does confirm that the world was at one point underwater (there is much disagreement on when this occurred and if it was all at the same time, as we'll review in the next chapter); the point is that even the most skeptical of persons will admit that flooding on a grand scale did, indeed, occur, and this is why flood legends are shared by most cultures, making this the closest thing the historian has to a "universally recorded history," which leaves it even harder to ignore.

The existence of the flood traditions all over the world seems consistent with the Genesis account, as Nozomi Osanai and others have continued to bring to light. While a naturalist can argue that the flood legends exist simply because flooding has occurred in most parts of the earth at one time or another, the detailed nature of the many common elements are too many to place it in the category of "coincidence." Even people who live far from the sea or in mountainous areas have flood legends that are similar to the Genesis account. For instance, the Pawnee tribe in Nebraska tells of the creator Ti-ra-wa, who destroyed the first people, who were giants, by water due to his indignation about their corruption. Then he created a man and a woman like present people, who became the Pawnees' ancestors. The Miao tribe, who reside in southwest China, had a story similar to the Genesis account even before they met Christian missionaries. According to their tradition, when God destroyed the whole world by the flood because of wickedness of man, Nuah the righteous man and his wife Matriarch, together with their three sons, Lo Han, Lo Shen, and Jah-hu, survived by building a broad ship and embarking on it with pairs of animals.[190] The following a brief summary of over two hundred flood traditions from all over the world and what percentage of commonality each share with one another:

- Is there a favored family? 88%
- Were they forewarned? 66%
- Is the flood due to wickedness of man? 66%
- Is catastrophe only a flood? 95%
- Was the flood global? 95%
- Is the survival due to a boat? 70%
- Were animals also saved? 67%
- Did animals play any part? 73%
- Did survivors land on a mountain? 57%
- Was the geography local? 82%
- Were birds sent out? 35%
- Was the rainbow mentioned? 7%
- Did survivors offer a sacrifice? 13%
- Were specifically eight persons saved? 9%[191]

Ninety-five percent of the above totals have common elements with the Genesis Flood narrative. Although it is impossible to study all of the flood traditions around the world here, it seems to be historically certain that a flood of some type did happen and does offer further credence to the Genesis account, and therefore it seems reasonable to think that the Genesis account is consistent with secular historical and sociological records. Explorer and sociologist Graham Hancock has written extensively on the subject and believes that the case can be made for a global flood being the one area of ancient history that is global in its historicity. Did over two hundred cultures just dream up the same story by coincidence?

> [Flood legends] turn up in Vedic India, in the pre-Columbian Americas, in ancient Egypt.... They were told by the Sumerians, the Babylonians, the Greeks, the Arabs and the Jews. They were repeated in China and south-east Asia, in

---

[190] Nozomi Osanai, "Secular Sources for a Global Flood," Answers in Genesis, (http://www.answersingenesis.org/articles/csgeg/comparison- secular-historical-records)
[191] Ibid.

prehistoric northern Europe and across the Pacific. Almost universally, where truly ancient traditions have been preserved, even amongst mountain peoples and desert nomads, vivid descriptions have been passed down of global floods in which the majority of mankind perished.

To take these myths seriously, and especially to countenance the possibility that they might be telling the truth, would be a risky posture for any modern scholar to adopt, inviting ridicule and rebuke from colleagues. The academic consensus today, and for the century, has been that the myths are either pure fantasy or the fantastic elaboration of local and limited deluges—caused for example by rivers overflowing, or tidal waves....

Not all mainstream academics toe this line. But amongst those who don't it seems to have been generally agreed that almost any explanation, however harebrained, is more acceptable than a simple literal interpretation of the myth of a global flood—i.e. that there actually was a global flood or floods. My guess is that such thinking will not much longer survive the steady accumulation of scientific evidence which suggests that a series of gigantic cataclysms, exactly like those described in the flood myths, changed the face of the earth completely....[192]

Hancock sees himself as a journalist who asks questions based upon observation and as someone who provides a counterbalance to what he perceives as the "unquestioned" acceptance and support given to orthodox views by the education system, the media, and society at large. I agree with this open philosophy and believe Hancock (whether right or wrong) is allowing the evidences to speak, as opposed to mere orthodoxy.

Similar to the plausibility surrounding the various flood legends, the vast majority of linguists confirm that humankind did, indeed, share a common language, as the Bible states, in the ancient past as well as confirming that the first civilizations did spring up in Sumer, the Indus Valley, and then into Egypt (as the Bible describes). The point being is that the Genesis account does record a well-balanced holistic record for a plausible inference to the best explanation; Genesis 1–11 does seem to meet the criteria for a non-

---

[192] Graham Hancock and Santha Faiia, *Underworld: the Mysterious Origins of Civilization* (Toronto: Anchor Canada, 2003, p.34,35)

naturalistic account of the history of origins not only of the universe and mankind, but also on a historical flood.[193]

A Different Approach

Professor of geology at Calvin College, Davis Young does not agree with Hugh Ross concerning the extent of the Flood. Interestingly enough, he does not even agree with his own earlier writings (as Young changes his viewpoint from day-age theory to the even more bankrupt position of theistic evolution). In 1977, he wrote *Creation and the Flood*, in which he promoted the idea of a global yet tranquil flood.[194] He now believes in a local flood but he differs with Ross because he does not believe that it wiped out all of mankind. Young has abandoned one bad idea for another one. This is a common practice among those who insist on allowing man's fallible teachings to be their guide rather than the unchanging Word of God; again, completely understandable from the secular viewpoint but we're talking specifically about Christians here. Here is Young's view in his own words:

> But archeological investigations have established the presence of human beings in the Americas, Australia, and south-eastern Asia long before the advent of the sort of Near Eastern civilization described in the Bible and thus long before the biblical deluge could have taken place. In the light of a wealth of mutually supportive evidence from a variety of disciplines and sources, it is simply no longer tenable to insist that a deluge drowned every human on the face of the globe except Noah's family.[195]

Young does not accept that the Flood wiped out all of humanity because he believes that people have been living in the "Americas, Australia, and southeastern Asia" since well before the timing of the Genesis flood. He believes this "fact" has been well established by several disciplines of science, which he calls "extra-biblical" evidence.

---

[193] Stroud, *Philosophy*, 177

[194] Davis A. Young, *Creation and the Flood* (Grand Rapids, MI: Baker, 1977, p. 172–174, 210–212), as quoted in Lisle and Chaffey, "A Local Flood?" (https://answersingenesis.org/the-flood/global/defense-a-local-flood/)

[195] Davis A. Young, *The Biblical Flood: A Case Study of the Church's Response to Extrabiblical Evidence* (Grand Rapids, MI: William B. Eerdmans Publishing, 1995, p. 242), as quoted in Lisle and Chaffey, "A Local Flood?" (https://answersingenesis.org/the-flood/global/defense-a-local-flood/)

First, notice that Young's rejection of a worldwide flood is based on secular scientific majority opinion rather than the text itself. In fact, Young seems to imply that the New Testament authors believed in a worldwide flood. He wrote, "These New Testament writers clearly assumed the historical existence of Noah and the deluge, and they viewed the deluge as a unique event." The only way this event could have been unique is if it were worldwide, since there have been countless local floods, some of them quite large in geographic extent.

Think about that for a minute. If the New Testament authors accepted a global flood, and wrote about it, then why would Young reject it? Is he actually claiming that the Bible is wrong? Yes, indirectly anyway. First Peter 3:20 clearly states that only eight people survived the Flood. Young does not accept this even though there is strong extra-biblical support for a worldwide flood from non-biblical sources as already discussed.

Literally hundreds of ancient cultures tell of a massive worldwide flood in which only one family survived, with animals, on a large boat as already touched upon. In fact, many of these ancient stories are not limited to the Flood. Some of these cultures tell stories that correspond to the major events of the first 11 chapters of the Bible, such as the creation, the fall of Adam and Eve, the Flood, and the Tower of Babel. (Whether it is Hugh Ross's local-flood or Young's tranquil-flood, the evidence does not seem to be on their side. They could end up being correct, but their faith-based assertions hold less credibility than the concept of a global flood from the lens of the social sciences.)

In 1997, Ethel Nelson, a missionary to China, published *God's Promise to the Chinese*, in which she demonstrated how the ancient Chinese language, through its use of picture-characters instead of letters, revealed their knowledge of creation and the Flood.[196] This fascinating discovery lends tremendous extra-biblical support for the veracity of Genesis.[197]

Questions tackled include:

- Do the ancient Chinese characters have a biblical meaning little understood before?
- What was the meaning of the 4,000-year-old Border Sacrifice that the Chinese emperors observed annually?

---

[196] Ethel R. Nelson, *God's Promise to the Chinese* (Dunlap, TN: Read Books Publishers, 1997), quoted in Lisle and Chaffey, "A Local Flood?" (https://answersingenesis.org/the-flood/global/defense-a-local-flood/)

[197] Jason Lisle and Tim Chaffey, "Defense—A Local Flood?" Answers in Genesis, February 2, 2012, (https://answersingenesis.org/the-flood/global/defense-a-local-flood/)

- Who was Shang Ti, worshiped in the Border Sacrifice? Painstaking analysis of the most ancient forms of Chinese writing reveals the original thoughts and beliefs of their inventor.[198]

boat

vessel   eight   people

The Discovery of Genesis, C.H. Kang and Ethel Nelson, p. 55

The Chinese pictogram for "boat" is composed of three symbols: vessel, eight, people. There are many other relatable characters covered in The Discovery of Genesis.[199]

Much could be said on the Chinese language, but there is some merit in establishing the existence of a historical flood through the development of language and writing; add to this the historical narratives held by other cultures throughout time and we seem overwhelmingly on the side of a global flood, just as the Bible states, at least from a social science perspective. Moreover, local flood theory that attempts to adopt a concordist viewpoint and assumes modern scientific understanding is beyond question is full of

---

[198] "Chinese Characters and Genesis," Creation.com | Creation Ministries International, (https://creation.com/chinese-characters-and-genesis)
[199] C. H. Kang and Ethel R. Nelson, *The Discovery of Genesis: How the Truth of Genesis Were Found Hidden in the Chinese Language* (St. Louis: Concordia Publ. House, 1985) Image courtesy of Creation.com.

119

question-begging and assertions that have little to no evidence. When the evidence is brought to bear, it is overwhelmingly agreed on by secular and non-secular academia that from a social science perspective, the Flood of Noah stands up incredibly well, as it is less contrived than local flood theories. A historic flood is imbedded so deeply in history and the social sciences that it cannot be dismissed. Whether it is Graham Hancock's secular analysis in *Underworld* for over four hundred flood legends having a common source, or Duane Gish's over 270 flood legends, all seem to agree that from a biblical and social science perspective, Noah's Flood is as absolute as anything within ancient history, remaining one of the strongest and most plausibly true.[200,201,202]

A Historical Tower of Babel and Table of Nations:

When I talk to my OEC colleagues they usually scoff at a 10,000-year-old Creation, a historical Adam and Eve, the Flood and the Tower of Babel, but can rarely defend their skepticism. The Tower of Babel has a long, rich history from a variety of cultures, which is strange if it's all myth, and which could point to a possible historical ontology that (again) aligns quite well with YEC biblical narrative.

> Have you ever stopped to marvel at the vast variety of languages on Earth? According to Ethnologue, there are about 7,000 total languages found throughout the world.[203] Where exactly did they all come from? Although there are many hypotheses regarding the origin of language, there is not one general consensus amongst scholars. The oldest belief — that there was a single language that eventually evolved into many—is detailed in many Tower of Babel stories from various cultures. The similarities and differences of these fascinating tales still leave us with unanswered questions....All of these stories, despite coming from different cultures and religions, bear an uncanny resemblance

[200] Hancock and Faiia, *Underworld*.

[201] White, "Flood Legends."

[202] In some ways, Hugh Ross is more consistent than most of my OEC colleagues in that he recognizes that if you support billions of years of history then you must reject a global flood, a traditional Adam and Eve, and a Tower of Babel. OEC theorists who wish to accept billions of years of history but also accept biblical events would do well to realize that they cannot have their cake and eat it, too. I respect that Ross realizes this and is consistent in his beliefs.

[203] "Languages of the World," Ethnologue, (https://www.ethnologue.com/), quoted in "The Tower of Babel Story: A Cross-Cultural Tale," Gaia, September 27, 2017, (https://www.gaia.com/article/tower-babel-story-cross-cultural-tale)

to one another. Can this be brushed aside as a bizarre coincidence, or is there some truth to the story of the Tower of Babel? [204]

Is it a coincidence, like the creation accounts, historical first couple and global flood, that there also seems to be a good explanation for the formation of writing/language/civilization accounted for within the Bible that closely aligns with what we know of history?

As I described in *The Philosophy of History*, naturalistic and OEC theorists attempt to explain most of these events with, "Revolution!" Ironically, when the naturalist is not sure how to explain origins or a related topic, they use words like "bang/explosion/revolution". This is the same tack that OEC theorists take, but they add God or the Bible to the beginning of it, hoping to have one foot squarely in the world of the scientific elite while keeping the other within their own presentism-based, theological framework. Therefore, it should be worthwhile to review the Neolithic Revolution from a YEC vs. OEC perspective. If YEC theory is plausibly accurate, we should see the social sciences align coherently with an assumption of a recent Creation. Moreover, it should appear that the OEC position is inconsistent and ad hoc or contrived.

NEOLITHIC REVOLUTION?

I have gone deeply into this topic in my graduate and post-graduate studies in ancient history, and these points seem well suited to weigh YEC against OEC when testing whether an OEC perspective is needed to properly understand the flow of history. The traditional cradle of civilization is in Mesopotamia, where (according to standard dating), the Neolithic Revolution began around twelve thousand years ago. One feature of this revolution was organized agricultural activity, including farming and animal domestication. While the timing of this revolution is more recent than evidence of modern human behavior as discussed in the typical high school textbook, these discoveries place the development of organized agriculture before the Neolithic Revolution and closer to the earliest evidence for modern human behavior.[205] Even Josh and Sean McDowell were forced to conclude, "Scripture, the book of nature (including genetic, paleontological, and archaeological evidence), and linguistic evidence join together to present a cumulative case for the historicity of Genesis 1-11."[206] As a historian, I know that anything much

[204] "The Tower of Babel Story: A Cross-Cultural Tale," Gaia, September 27, 2017, (https://www.gaia.com/article/tower-babel-story-cross-cultural-tale)
[205] McDowell, *Evidence*, 440.
[206] Ibid, 442.

before Hammurabi (1750 BC) is guess-work and conjecture, so just for fun, let's see how far we can really take the data.

At the point of civilization, we move from *prehistory* into history with the advent of civilization. They typical history book will start with a story of homo sapiens evolving from simple dwellings to civilizations such as Sumer. They will then utilize a naturalistic explanation of language formation as well as writing. But does a naturalistic philosophy of history adequately account for these? They do not and that is why you have most refer to this time of civilization, language and writing as being a surprise because it is almost as if these three phenomena erupted simultaneously (Neolithic Revolution). None of this is a surprise to the YEC position since these would be expected in a post-flood world where technology, language and writing already existed. But to the OEC side it is much more complicated to explain. Areas that I feel should be briefly reviewed (from an OEC vs YEC perspective) include:

1. Language

2. Writing

3. Civilization

4. Religion

The first thing that even the most ardent OEC will acknowledge is that from primitive times into the Neolithic age and from Neolithic to modern civilization; each of these successions literally burst onto the scene without much if any gradualistic signs present if a naturally old succession of events occurred. Language, writing, civilization, and religion all seem to be in an advanced stage of development all the way up until the advent of what we call modern civilization that originated in the areas usually referred to as the Fertile Crescent. We really have no record to follow or way of gauging a naturalistic (or OEC) viewpoint of each of these phenomena slowly progressing over time into their modern forms. Ancient Sumerian language or cuneiform writing is not less sophisticated than today's modern languages. Moreover, languages that still implore a pictogram form such as Chinese or Japanese are no more primitive for doing so than the modern English I am using now. In circa 3500–3000 BC, the earliest civilizations in the river valleys of the Tigris-Euphrates, Nile, and Indus emerged from Neolithic villages, which we know little about. With this, many historians infer a gradual progression of human development, including domestication of plants and animals.

Similarly, we see great organization, which included canals and irrigation systems and more advanced building and governmental systems forming. While what I have just commented on is for the most part universally agreed on by historians, what is not agreed on is that prior to this time we have anything better than an inference or assertion usually based on naturalistic presuppositions. For example, it is not uncommon to see a random date of 100,000 to 50,000 BC used to signify "when" primitive man began using fire.[207] First of all, this is a very large area of error—this should at least signal the reader that what they are reading is very subjective. Moreover, it is an assertion presupposing that a form of naturalism is true, though an OEC would presumably agree that naturalism is false, they normally will accept these types of dates *a priori*. While there is nothing wrong with making an assertion, we should not read this as a credible hypothesis unless the evidence is there to support it. Compare noted expert on early dynastic periods of development, John Anthony West, on the developmental periods of ancient Egypt:

> What is remarkable is that there are no traces of evolution from simple to sophisticated, and the same is true of mathematics, medicine, astronomy and architecture and of Egypt's amazingly rich and convoluted religion mythological system. The majority of Egyptologists will not consider the implications of Egypt's early sophistication. These implications are startling. How does a complex civilization spring full-blown into being? Look at a 1905 automobile and compare it to a modern one. There is no mistaking the process of 'development.' But in Egypt there are no parallels. Everything is right there at the start. The answer to the mystery [of how civilization seems to explode into history] is of course obvious but, because it is repellent to the prevailing cast of modern thinking, it is seldom considered.[208]

Other more mainstream figures have also confessed puzzlement at the suddenness with which Egyptian civilization appeared. Walter Emery of the University of London (professor of Egyptology) commented:

> At a period approximately 3400 years before Christ, a great change took place in Egypt, and the country passed rapidly

---

[207] DM. Bowman, Fire in the Earth System. *Science Magazine*, (Oct. 2012, http://www.sciencemag.org/content/324/5926/481), quoted in Stroud, *Philosophy*, 145-9.
[208] Anthony R. West, *Serpent in the Sky: the High Wisdom of Ancient Egypt* (London: Wilwood House, 1979), quoted in Stroud, *Philosophy*, 145-9.

from a state of Neolithic culture with a complex tribal character to one of well-organized monarchy. At the same time the art of writing appears, monumental architecture and the arts and crafts develop to an astonishing degree, and all the evidence points to the existence of a luxurious civilization. All this was achieved within a comparatively short period of time, for there appears to be little or no background to these fundamental developments in writing and architecture.[209]

When we turn to the historical development and origin of language and writing, it only seems to get worse when one attempts to understand it through a strictly naturalistic process as my secular colleagues and many of my OEC ones do. There is no denying that secular sources universally agree that writing, language and civilization came onto the scene rapidly in the Middle East around 3500–4000 BC, which lines up perfectly with YEC theory. Director and professor at the German Federal Institute of Physics and Technology, Dr. Werner Gitt has commented, "Man's natural language is the most comprehensive as well as the most differentiated means of expression. This special gift has been given to human beings only, allowing us to express all our feelings and our deepest beliefs, as well as to describe the interrelationships prevailing in nature, in life, and in the field of technology. Language is the calculus required for formulating all kinds of thoughts; it is also essential for conveying information."[210]

When we turn from spoken to written languages, we quickly discover that we can only speak of true writing when pictograms/drawings representing the spoken words of a given language through their shapes and sequencing began to be used. The spoken word acquires a temporal dimension through writing; historical traditions usually require permanent records to be kept, and the same holds for science in most communities. Various civilizations seem to have invented their own writing technique—the Sumerians used pictograms about 3500 BC, Egyptian hieroglyphics originated 3000 BC, in the Middle East cuneiform writing was in use around 2500 BC, and Chinese ideograms date from 1500 BC.[211]

---

[209] Graham Hancock and Santha Faiia, *Fingerprints of the Gods* (New York: Crown Trade Paperbacks, 1995, Quoting Dr. Emery), quoted in Stroud, *Philosophy*, 145-9.

[210] Werner W. Gitt, *In the Beginning Was Information: a Scientist Explains the Incredible Design in Nature* (Green Forest, AR: Master Books, 2007), quoted in Stroud, *Philosophy*, 145-9.

[211] Stroud, *Philosophy*, 145-9.

Ironically, history's relatively short life cycle leans heavily towards YEC, since if OEC hypotheses were correct, there would be a much longer record of human history than Sumerian culture, so secularists (and many OEC) stamp "revolution" on it and hope no one asks too many questions.

> The Neolithic [Revolution (aka – explosion)] was the wide-scale transition of many human cultures from a lifestyle of hunting and gathering to one of agriculture and settlement which supported an increasingly large population. Archaeological data indicates that various forms of plants and animal domestication evolved in separate locations worldwide, starting no earlier than 12000 years ago (10000–5000 BC) by even the most secular sources. However, the Neolithic Revolution involved far more than the adoption of a limited set of food-producing techniques. During the next millennia it would transform the small and mobile groups of hunter-gatherers that had hitherto dominated human history into sedentary societies based in built-up villages and towns, which radically modified their natural environment by means of specialized food-crop cultivation that allowed extensive surplus food production. These developments provided the basis for high population density settlements, specialized and complex labor diversification, trading economies, the development of non-portable art, architecture, and culture, centralized administrations and political structures, hierarchical ideologies, and depersonalized systems of knowledge (e.g., property regimes and writing). The first full-blown manifestation of the entire Neolithic complex is seen in the Middle Eastern Sumerian cities (ca. 3500 BC), whose emergence also inaugurates the end of the prehistoric Neolithic period.[212]

Again, we hear the word "revolution" to describe anything that shows no signs of naturalistic evolution (or seems to recent); when the scientist or, in this case, the historian does not understand something they simply put "bang/explosion/revolution" after it and hope no one will ask too many questions. Is this good logic? I remember when I simply asked a professor of history this very question, and they could not answer any of my questions concerning what evidences they were using to extrapolate these explosions; what was directing them, and why did they happen all at once instead of

---

[212] Appel-Bocquet, Jean-Pierre. *When the World's Population Took Off:* The Springboard of the Neolithic Dem. (Sce CE, Oct. 2012), quoted in Stroud, *Philosophy*, 145-9.

gradually? I was met with silence and an angry reply that it is an established fact, so there is no point in questioning it. Sound familiar? It's the same thing I usually hear from OEC. As a then historian in training, I simply found this methodology not only illogical but also woefully naive and self-refuting. The one thing I do agree with and have found well established historically in the above quote is the last sentence concerning "the first full-blown" civilization of Sumerian cities approximately 3500 BC. Susan Wise Bauer is honest enough to admit that any dating before Hammurabi is problematic and anything before about 1750 BC is complete guesswork by the historian, and these stories of Neolithic explosions may or may not be accurate as they must assume an enormous amount of contrived assertions that goes well beyond the evidence. Dr. Bauer recognizes this in her own writings and studies in which the historian is limited to the hierarchal structure that supposes science as occupying the top chair:

> Trained in a university system where science was revered as practically infallible, historians too often tried to position themselves as scientists: searching for cold hard facts and dismissing any historical material which seemed to depart from the realities of Newton's universe. To concentrate on physical evidence to the exclusion of myth and story is to put all of our faith in the explanations for human behavior in that which can be touched, smelled, seen, and weighed [positivism]: it shows a mechanical view of human nature, and a blind faith in the methods of science to explain the mysteries of human behavior....[213]

When the historian looks at the early yet advanced Sumerian civilization, for example, and they see some patterns of tradable goods and similar patterns found in ancient Egypt a century or two later, they may rightly infer that trade routes were established from the Fertile Crescent to Egypt and that Egyptian culture was in part influenced by ancient Sumerian cultures. There are no naturalistic presuppositions built into this; there is simply a logical deduction of the evidences we have to draw forth a conclusion. Whether it is a pre-Enlightenment mindset that I have seen in some biblical believers that the Sumerian civilization must not have existed at 3500 BC because they believe this contradicts their interpretation of when the flood occurred or when the naturalist asserts explosions/bangs/revolutions to force history to meet a presuppositional philosophy they hold, history has been lost. So, I am

---

[213] Susan Bauer. *The History of the Ancient World.* 2007, xxv. Quoted by James Stroud, *Philosophy*, 145-9.

dumbfounded that many of my peers and colleagues feel that I must infer a naturalistic mind-set though there is no evidence to do so.

If YEC were in fact true, then it would make good historical sense why civilization, writing, and language all seemed to explode onto the scene at once and without naturalistic explanation.[214] While jumping into a complete exegetical critique of our records and understanding of ancient civilization would take us quite far off course and be well beyond the scope of this book, we can conclude that the *explosions* concerning the development and origin of language/writing and civilization itself are very unlikely to be attributed to naturalistic causation and thus do not require great ages. This again at least makes YEC theory palatable and seemingly less contrived than OEC for the informed Christian.

For example, we now know that Sumerian writing was well developed and adapted by Akkadian and Elamite civilizations. Also figures such as the famous myth of Gilgamesh was discovered to be more than just a myth but is now recognized as an actual king of the city of Uruk as early as 2900 BC. Though the epic of Gilgamesh has many fantastical stories about very supernatural events, we would be at a great loss if we threw the entire historicity of this king out as fiction because we feel it does not fit our current mode of historic thought it would seem, and more and more historians are slowly beginning to see this. Does Gilgamesh read as a primitive story? Absolutely not—almost anyone taking world literature will find this a required read. Also, a complex and well-established religious system seems to have been well in place at the time of Gilgamesh, which dates centuries before the two oldest religions of Hinduism and Judaism it would appear, so what is the best explanation for this based on naturalism (or OEC)? Again, if the historian is confined to force a naturalistic philosophy into ancient history, history will continue to become more and more jumbled and contrived with more *explosions* having to be included to attempt to describe the inexplicable.

Gilgamesh for example is recorded on the Sumerian King List as the fifth king of Uruk; this list has been found in at least seven different sources and is now considered at least minimally accurate even by the most ardent skeptic.

---

[214] Scientism and logical positivism are dead, so the last thing I need as a historian and philosopher is some biologist telling me about my own trade.

Biblical	Sumerian King List
Adam	Alulim (NIN.KI)
Seth	Alagar (NIN.KI)
Enos	Enmenluanna (BAD.TIBIRA)
Cainan	Enmengalanna (BAD.TIBIRA)
Mahalaleel	Dumuzi the Spepherd (BAD.TIBIRA)
Jared	Ensipazianna (ERIDU)
Enoch	Enmeduranki (SIPPAR)
Methuselah	? Divine Ruler (LARSA)
Lamech	Ubartutu (SHURUPPAK)
Noah	Ziusudra (SHURUPPAK)

Coincidence or not, the King List has rulers who lived before the Great Flood and each of them lived incredibly long lives, like that of the Biblical patriarchs prior to the Flood of Noah.[215]

The Sumerian King List is an ancient list originally recorded in the Sumerian language, listing kings of Sumer from Sumerian and neighboring dynasties, as well as their supposed length of kingship and locations thereof. If we pair this with the Genesis account we find in the Septuagint, Noah's Flood would have taken place around 3300 BC, which if true, would explain why Gilgamesh referred to a "Great Flood" a few generations before him, in which only a few people survived. Similarly, if we review the Sumerian King List's long lifespans, we find parallels to the long lives of the Bible's Adam–Noah preflood world. The list is broken into antediluvian kings and postdiluvian kings before and after a great flood. It lists eight kings before this "great flood" who reigned for fantastically long lengths of time (several thousand years) and then after the flood the lifespan/reigns diminished greatly (to around a hundred years).

While the list was dismissed early on, it has since been authenticated in part with many kings post the flood being substantiated as historic figures, as early as Gilgamesh to much later ones such as Sargon of Akkad. Many have speculated different interpretations to these great dates as well as different meanings, which I believe is a great sign of healthiness since any origin science/history is based on unrepeatable events and cannot simply be ruled out simply based on modern modes of understanding. Bill Arnold, professor of Semitic languages and dean at Columbia University, noted that the

[215] Hank Kraychir, "Ancient Sumerian Writings Reveal Eight Immortal Kings Ruled for 241,200 Years," gnosismasonry.wordpress.com, January 1, 2018, (https://gnosismasonry.wordpress.com/2017/03/01/ancient-sumerian-writings-reveal-eight-immortal-kings-ruled-for-241200-years/), (picture).

Sumerian King Lists, Weidner Chronicle, Babylonian Chronicles all shed light on events discussed in the Old Testament historical books.

> Beyond obvious synchronisms with biblical historical books, these materials also illustrate the contrast between historiography in the ancient Near East and ancient Israel. The lists included here are the raw materials for history writing. The Israelites also had such raw materials, but they moved beyond them to produce genuine historiography, with characterization, interpretive presentation of past events, multiple causal factors, etc.[216]

What can be agreed on by practically all historians as well as other social scientists is that language and writing is amazingly complex and it along with early civilization seems to have erupted onto the scene in a *bang*, just like the origin of the universe and the origin of life. Ancient Mesopotamia still has many secrets that may never be discovered, but what is no secret is that its civilization burst onto the scene along with a sophisticated language, literature, mathematics, philosophy, and art; and naturalism simply does not supply the explanatory scope or plausibility needed. And for the OEC to simply add "God" to the beginning does not add credibility nor answer the challenges I have made in the previous chapter or this one that seems to lie heavily in favor of YEC. Moreover, many historians and anthropologists alike are rethinking the way they have originally viewed religions' origins. There a growing number of evidences that monotheism may have preceded animism and polytheism.[217]

Time constraints will not allow me to go into this in detail here, unfortunately. Nonetheless, all these factors give credibility (indirectly) to the YEC account from practically all social science methodology and understanding. The fascinating piece to me as a historian is that all of these ancient tablets and stories are telling a very similar story that would be expected if there are some truths in them. Though there are many ancient writings that we still do not know how to translate, of the ones we do we see great consistency in reoccurring themes concerning the following:

- Creation by God(s)
- Separation from God(s)

---

[216] Bill T. Arnold and Bryan Beyer, *Readings from the Ancient Near East: Primary Sources for Old Testament Study* (Grand Rapids, MI: Baker Academic, 2004), quoted in Stroud, *Philosophy*, 155.
[217] Stroud, *Philosophy*, 155-6.

- Antediluvian series of kings or persons who lived or ruled for long periods of time
- A great flood that separated pre/post flood world
- A scattering of people groups and languages
- History beginning in the Mesopotamian regions of the Middle East...

When moving into the tenth chapter of the book of Genesis, we find an area that seems to be quite accessible to the historian concerning the genealogy of humankind. Even higher critics have often admitted that the tenth chapter of Genesis oftentimes referred to as the "table of nations" is a remarkably accurate historical document, which accounts for the genealogy of all nations from a post-flood narrative. There is no comparable catalog of ancient nations available from any other source. It is unparalleled in its antiquity and comprehensiveness. Dr. William F. Albright, who was known as the world's leading authority on the archaeology of the Near East (and himself did not believe in the infallibility of the Bible), said concerning the table of nations in Genesis 10: "It stands absolutely alone in ancient literature, without a remote parallel, even among the Greeks, where we find the closest approach to a distribution of peoples in genealogical framework...The Table of Nations remains an astonishingly accurate document."[218]

Here we find the one link between the historic nations of antiquity and the prehistoric times pre-Noah and the antediluvians recorded in Genesis. While many other than Dr. Albright have studied the table of nations, I stumbled across a research document by Bill Cooper of the United Kingdom called *After the Flood* where Cooper painstakingly provides genealogical sketches, documented manuscripts, and much more to trace the sons of Noah to the Chinese, the Aryan race of India, the European cultures, etc., from this table of nations:

> The test I devised was a simple one. If the names of the individuals, families, peoples, and tribes listed in the Table of Nations were genuine, then those names should appear also in the records of other nations in the Middle East. While I would have been quite content if I could have vindicated 40% of these; today I can say that the names so far vindicated in the Table of Nations make up over 99% of the list, and I shall make no further comment on that other than to say that no other ancient historical document of purely human

---

[218] Bill Cooper, *After the Flood: the Early Post-Flood History of Europe* (Chichester: New Wine Press, 1995), quoted in Stroud, *Philosophy*, 178.

authorship could be expected to yield such a level of corroboration as that![219]

While a historian could still say these are not 100 percent certain, they would likewise have to admit that as of today they remain highly credible for their historical and genealogical accuracies, which I find quite astonishing. When we read Genesis 11:1–9…we see an explanation (thus providing explanatory scope) for why these nations were scattered into different groups after this great flood and eventually how languages changed in the event known as the Tower of Babel. There is considerable evidence now that the world did, indeed, have a single language at one time. Linguists find this theory helpful in categorizing languages. Sanskrit was the classical language of India, and today is considered the primary bridge between Hebrew and other Semitic languages, and the Greek/Phoenician and Latin of Western civilization. Gothic, Celtic, and Persian/Farsi languages are now known as the Indo-European family of languages. But the similarities are not confined to this family. Wayne Jackson stated that the ancient languages of Assyria and Egypt had much in common with those of the Mayan and Incan peoples of the Americas. Language scholars were rapidly concluding that all languages had a common root in the 1970s. Even secular scholars now largely acknowledge that all languages did come from one common root just as the Bible describes.

So where does this leave us when reviewing YEC and OEC using McCullagh's five criteria for establishing historicity? It seems from a social science analysis, only #4 would possibly fall more on the OEC side, but this is only if we presuppose an OEC position to begin with, it seems.

1) Be as plausible as possible. (the data must imply something like the hypothesis)
2) Have great explanatory scope. (the hypothesis must explain greater quantity and variety of the data)
3) Have great explanatory power. (the hypothesis must explain the data with a strong degree of probability)
4) Not be disconfirmed by other reasonable belief. (no data that implies the hypothesis is improbable)
5) Not include additional ad hoc components. (the data must not be twisted to fit the theory)[220]

Be as plausible as possible? It seems without question that a high percentage of social scientists, independent of demographics, have posited a relatively

---

[219] Ibid.
[220] McCullagh, *Justifying*, 51-2.

recent creation. Moreover, if naturalism is false, then YEC seems just as coherent as OEC, given the falsity of the premises underlying naturalism.

Have great explanatory scope and power? If God exists and if the Bible is mostly true, then YEC does have greater explanatory scope and power from a social science standpoint. OEC requires much more exegetical gymnastics, so it seems YEC theory holds up well. The quantity and variety of data for a relatively recent creation across cultures and demographics seems to be confirmed through a variety of social science measures coupled with a historiographical approach to how the Bible has been read and understood.

Not to be disconfirmed by other reasonable belief? If one presupposes naturalism, one would definitely support OEC. The problem is that almost no Christian would believe in naturalism since naturalism is the antithesis of non-naturalism and supernaturalism. Even secularists are abandoning naturalism, as I wrote about in detail in *The Philosophy of History*. With this said, I am not aware of data that would necessitate YEC as an improbable hypothesis.

Not include ad hoc components? This is probably the weakest point of OEC. William Lane Craig, for example, must posit billions of years because modern cosmology necessitates it, but he then has to lean towards non-literal biblical events, all the while insisting we maintain a Virgin Birth because that is what Scripture requires. It shows the lengths of inconsistency to which the OEC must go—e.g., inventing framework views, day-age views, gap views, and analogical views—to get around a plain reading of the Scriptures. It is an example of twisting the data to fit one's theory (concordist and non-concordist alike). To assert that all these cultures must have been mistaken or simple minded is disingenuous and we have no strong reasons outside of naturalism to presuppose this to be the case. Occam's Razor is not on the side of OEC when taking all the above points into consideration.

> Millions of Christians today around the world hold a YEC view, as it seems Jesus, the apostles and virtually all orthodox Christians prior to 1800. The idea of millions of years of death, disease, violence, and extinction was seen as utterly incompatible with the Bible's teaching as well as orthodox Christian teaching for two thousand years. Finally, even if the genealogies contain gaps or cannot provide us with an exact date of creation +/- 1000 years still will not get you the millions of years the OEC hopes for and the naturalist must have.[221]

---

[221] Moreland and Reynolds, *Three Views on Creation*, 67-9.

I think we can all agree on the following social-scientific conclusions that support the viability of YEC:

1. **Human population growth:** Less than 0.5% p.a. growth from six people 4,500 years ago would produce today's population. Where are all the people if we have been here much longer?
2. **Stone age human skeletons and artefacts:** There are not enough for 100,000 years of a human population of just one million, let alone more people (10 million?).
3. **Length of recorded history:** Origin of various civilizations, writing, etc., all about the same time several thousand years ago.
4. **Languages:** Similarities in languages claimed to be separated by many tens of thousands of years speaks against the supposed ages (e.g. compare some aboriginal languages in Australia with languages in south-eastern India and Sri Lanka).
5. **Common cultural myths:** speak of recent separation of peoples around the world. An example of this is the frequency of stories of an earth-destroying flood.
6. **Origin of agriculture:** Secular dating puts it somewhere between 7,000–10,000 years ago and yet that same chronology says that modern man has supposedly been around for at least 200,000 years. Surely someone would have worked out much sooner how to sow seeds of plants to produce food.[222]

The above points were strong enough for staunch and credible OEC theorists that I have worked with over the years to endorse many elements of YEC. Highly recognized ID scholar Stephen Meyer commented to me and a small group at a private luncheon in Dallas that: "Though I believe in an old universe I do now believe in a relatively recent creation in regard to life, genetics and history."[223] Based largely on the reasons I have touched upon in the last two chapters. YEC theory is strongly supported by the social science data on practically every front. An entire chapter could be written on human history itself, as there should be a plethora of primitive human history if the OEC position is correct; instead, the fact that written history, language, writing, and civilization appeared less than 10,000 years ago is a strong indicator of YEC. We can no longer assume that the natural sciences are superior to the social sciences, as scientism is in its death throes. It seems to me that without some type of defeater, YEC theory is as plausible and less

---

[222] Don Batten, "Age of the Earth: 101 Evidences for a Young Age of the Earth and the Universe," Creation.com | Creation Ministries International, June 4, 2009, (https://creation.com/age-of-the-earth).
[223] Private luncheon in Dallas Texas, January 2020 at the *Science and Faith Conference.*

contrived than OEC theory.[224] I am aghast when someone as intelligent as William Craig makes ignorant commentary without having done much research. Craig may be an astute religious philosopher, but when it comes to ancient history, he is no better than a layman.

One last hope for OEC – Perhaps the natural sciences will be so one-sided that it will override all the data thus far?

[224] Michael Sudduth, "Defeaters in Epistemology," Internet Encyclopedia of Philosophy, (https://www.iep.utm.edu/ep-defea/).

PART THREE

A New YEC voice?

To our brethren who are committed to the "old earth" perspective, we wish to re-affirm that we consider you our brothers and sisters in Christ, we respect your differing perspective, and we understand the complexity of the scientific issues being debated.

- Logos Research Associates (Mission Statement)

I was asked to serve as emcee in April 2019 for Logos Research Associates' first major meeting with over fifty natural and social scientists from a wide array of fields and disciplines in St. George Utah.[225] It was a great experience challenging major figures within the YEC movement. From the ninety-year-old Dr. Bernard Brandstater to a large group of undergraduates and graduates, each were immersed in their specific field. As always, I pushed back on their geology, history, earth science, physics, anthropology, biology, genetics, and astronomy claims.

One of the scientists I had a chance to visit with and introduce was molecular geneticist and microbiologist Andrew Fabich. Since I had worked for almost four years in a microbiology lab, we had a good starting point for dialogue. It

---

[225] www.logosresearchassociates.org

was, however, an article he wrote titled, "Quit Calling this Ham's Interpretation," that caught my attention.[226] In this article, Dr. Fabich writes:

> If Ken Ham is alone in saying the earth is young, then why am I writing this blog? Because he isn't alone! You know what? Others throughout history have said the earth is young. Even prominent scientists alive today agree with this position and not just here in America. There are young earth creationists in other industrialized nations all around the world. I'm offended by how journalists misrepresent my personal beliefs. My faith isn't based on "thus saith Ken Ham." What's more is that evolutionists would be equally as appalled if we called it "Nye's evolution!" From preschool through PhD in secular education, I've never been taught "Nye's evolution." Calling it "Ham's interpretation" is a straw man argument used in ignorance for emotional reasons.[227]

This ties in beautifully to the two main points I'd like to cover in this chapter:

1. Groups like Answers in Genesis (AIG) do not speak for or represent YEC holistically.
2. Are there good reasons to believe YEC is viable based on the natural sciences?

I will spend the bulk of my time on Point 2, but it is necessary to cover the first point briefly. As Dr. Fabich properly explains, neither Ken Ham nor AIG holds authority in the YEC debate. I have met with Ham and others at AIG, and I am thankful for their passion and efforts to get YEC theories in front of larger audiences. However, groups like AIG are overtly dogmatic and have in some ways kept YEC from being a more robust field of inquiry. YEC has a lot of room to grow and AIG ought not do any further alienating than they already have.

> After much prayer and deliberation over the weekend, the Great Homeschool Convention's Advisory Board has unanimously decided to disinvite Ken and AIG from all future conventions, including the Cincinnati convention next week. The Board believes this to be the Lord's will for our convention and searched the Scriptures for the mind of the Lord and the leadership of the Holy Spirit before arriving at

---

[226] Dr. Andrew Fabich, Dr. Andrew Fabich #fundie, (https://fstdt.com/3DS5)
[227] Ibid.

this decision. The Board believes that Ken's public criticism of the convention itself and other speakers at our convention require him to surrender the spiritual privilege of addressing our homeschool audience. Please know that our Board is 100% young earth and we largely share AIG's perspective from a scientific standpoint. That is why Ken was originally invited and treated so graciously and extremely generously in Memphis and Greenville (far beyond what we do for other speakers or their ministries). Our expression of sacrifice and extraordinary kindness towards Ken and AIG has been returned to us and our attendees with Ken publicly attacking our conventions and other speakers. Our Board believes Ken's comments to be unnecessary, ungodly, and mean-spirited statements that are divisive at best and defamatory at worst.[228]

I have lost track of the times I have been met with a scowl when I mention YEC, usually due to AIG or ICR (Institute for Creation Research) calling YEC theorists "compromising Christians" or some other derogatory term. We must correct this attitude and work together, as even the director of the documentary *Is Genesis History* said, "The world of YEC is a bit parochial with different groups doing their own thing: AIG, ICR, Creation Ministries, Origins, etc. I don't think any of them will play with the others, although individual scientists will. I don't see an immediate solution at this point. In some instances, scientists and/or leaders literally *detest* people in the other groups. It will have to be the younger generation that pulls together."[229] I am neither young nor old, but this internal bickering is ungodly and counterproductive. While I endorse the viability of YEC, I do not endorse AIG as being the best YEC representative.[230]

AIG must not be afraid to be open-minded on the dating of creation. In the words of Ken Ham, "Were you there?" There is nothing compromising in allowing for improvised dating and nothing wrong with saying there was a Creation in six literal days less than 10,000 years ago while not capitulating to 4004 BC because "thus saith Ussher".[231] Logos Research Associates, Walt

---

[228] "Kicked Out of Two Homeschool Conferences," Answers in Genesis, (March 22, 2011, https://answersingenesis.org/ministry-news/core-ministry/kicked-out-of-two-homeschool-conferences/)

[229] Email correspondence.

[230] "Creation Controversy," Kevin Lea's Report on the Austin/Brown Mediation on Grand Lake | Creation Controversy, September 4, 2018, https://creation-controversy.com/)

[231] Smith, "Septuagint's Chronology," (https://biblearchaeology.org/images/Genesis-5-and-11/Smith-Henry-The-Case-for-the-Septuagints-Chronology-in-Gen-5-and-11-ICC.pdf)

Brown, and others have no problem with this. Dr. Brown said 5500 BC is likely the most accurate date of creation, based on the evidence, as more scholars in the field of ancient history and biblical exegesis are starting to agree.[232] When Ken Ham was asked to read and critique Walt Brown's book *In the Beginning*, he refused.[233] My point is simply that groups like AIG need not fear retracting what they have written and repenting their dogmatism when it's almost impossible to get to 4004 BC, a date that they hold dear.[234]

AIG also spends too much energy attacking the Discovery Institute and the theory of intelligent design (ID).[235] I have worked with the Discovery Institute and they have been of immense help to me academically. They also mentored me and provided the foreword to my published master's thesis, and they largely turned the debate around on naturalistic evolution. We have seen many of the world's great minds join the forces of ID and pay for it.[236]

The Discovery Institute invited me to spend two weeks with them in the summer of 2016 for their yearly scientific seminar, where I was able to meet students from around the world. Discovery invited them and paid all expenses for them to learn about ID and why it matters to the future. Most of those affiliated with Discovery are Christians and some are even YEC-oriented, but they also have a group of agnostic and Jewish scientists and fellows. On a shoe-string budget of $4M annually, the Discovery Institute has literally turned the playing field on its head and helped clear the way for God to be looked at afresh in a post-Christian culture. You would think this is a great endeavor, unless you're a dogmatic YEC group like AIG, who has spent time, money, and energy to attack the ID movement:

> One reason *Answers* is not very excited about the Intelligent Design movement is that ID's main argument—that the world is, well, "intelligently designed"—fails to reference the God of the Bible and the Curse's impact on a once-perfect

---

[232] Walter T. Brown, *In the Beginning: Compelling Evidence for Creation and the Flood* (Phoenix, Az Center for Scientific Creation, 2008), p.485-6.

[233] Ibid. pgs. 564-7.

[234] Hardy and Carter, "Biblical Minimum and Maximum," (https://creation.com/biblical-age-of-the-earth)

[235] "Discovering Intelligent Design," Center for Science and Culture, (https://www.discovery.org/id/)

[236] See *Expelled: No Intelligence Allowed* (Vivindi Entertainment, Rocky Mountain Pictures, 2009) and (https://dissentfromdarwin.org/)

world. So, despite the positive aspects of IDM, there are clearly many difficulties with it as well.[237]

AIG has spent much effort in combatting this organization, which is mostly an ally. The attacks from AIG have been aggressive, as described in an article titled "Whatever happened to ID theorist Bill Dembski?" Young-earth creationists knocked one of the most effective advocates for intelligent design out of action.[238]

> Hard-core YE creationists such as Ken Ham were incensed that Dembski would question the reality of a global Flood. They denounced him coast to coast and orchestrated letter-writing campaigns to his employer, demanding his ouster. Dembski was hauled before an inquisition at Southwestern Baptist Theological Seminary. It was made clear that if he did not satisfy them on the global extent of Noah's Flood, he would be immediately fired as a heretic. This put Dembski in an agonizing personal dilemma. If he had been financially solvent, he would have simply resigned right away. However, he had a severely autistic son plus two other children to support and had no other way to pay the medical bills.[239]

Until we can look at AIG (and similar groups) as merely a hybrid of YEC theory and not an overall representative of it, the YEC position will continue to suffer. Many YEC theorists I have worked with agree, so all I can ask of the public is not to judge YEC theory by AIG, just as we should not judge Christ in light of his Christian followers. Let me give a few examples:

Answers in Genesis often hinders YEC science –

Many YEC groups are beginning to accept that 4004 BC cannot be holistically defended biblically, scientifically, or historically, yet AIG insists their view is the "right one" and anything less is compromising. I even took an online course with AIG just to test the waters, and the facilitators became hostile when I challenged their preconceptions with concrete data. Even when we point out that, at best, (as Logos Research biologist Dr. Rob Carter has said)

---

[237] "ID'ed for an Imperfect Argument," Answers in Genesis, October 1, 2010, (https://answersingenesis.org/intelligent-design/ided-for-a-imperfect-argument/)
[238] Buchanan, "Whatever Happened,"
(https://letterstocreationists.wordpress.com/2017/03/19/whatever-happened-to-intelligent-design-theorist-william-dembski/)
[239] Ibid.

we have a number of factors that limit dating precision, AIG will not budge.[240, 241] These factors include:

- Implied precision
- Calendar systems
- Age slippage (birthday conventions and count-ing ages)
- Rounding imprecision accumulation
- Rounding of ages

What this shows is:

> From creation to the Babylonian Captivity, we calculated a per-link imprecision of 219 years (including the 50-yr ambiguity concerning how long Abram remained in Haran), plus an overall systemic imprecision of 89 years. It is not possible to date creation with any more accuracy using just the genealogical data. We should allow for the possibility of ±10 years of imprecision from calendar system changes, and the possibility of up to 3% less solar years before the Exodus if the ancients used 12-lunar-month years or longer blocks of lunar months which would later be converted to 12-lunar-month years. We must also consider the possibility of 1326 additional years if the LXX chrono-genealogies represent the original wording, 301 additional years if the Samaritan Pentateuch is correct, 215 less years for the 'Short Sojourn' view, and 46 fewer or 8 more years due to the ambiguities in the king lists of Judah and Israel. This yields an outside range of 3236 to 5078 years from Creation to the Babylonian Captivity. If the traditional historic date of 587 BC or 586 BC for the Captivity is correct, the earth cannot be more than 7,680 years old (table 4), having been created between 5665 BC and 3822 BC. Note that the only way to get a 'traditional' date of creation of approximately 4000 BC is to use the Short Sojourn calculation and minimal to simple-additive adjustment parameters. This makes it likely that the

---

[240] Hardy and Carter, "Biblical Minimum and Maximum," (https://creation.com/biblical-age-of-the-earth)

[241] *Origins: What's the Biblical Age of the Earth?* (YouTube, 2016, https://www.youtube.com/watch?v=zgR0ukEEZqA)

earth is several hundred years older than most biblical creationists expect.[242]

The above is agreed on by almost all YEC groups, except of course, Ken Ham and AIG. "Those who hold to the inerrancy of the Scriptures should reject all attempts to make the earth older than the Hebrew text [Ussher] warrants, which is about 4000 B.C."[243] AIG does not provide any consistent reasons (biblical, historic, or scientific) for rejecting what other YEC groups agree is true. They simply assert that anyone who disagrees with them are "compromisers."[244]

I got to experience this personally when I encouraged YEC Dr. Rob Carter to make more modest claims. Claims that he could better defend, and we had a friendly discussion on his genetics page with me granting credit to the LXX (Septuagint) dating derived from a pre-Masoretic text, and arguing that history and population growth models are greatly on this side of the slightly older dating of creation around 5500 BC. I only intended to show that a Flood of 3200-3300 BC fits better with history and genetic compilations, but Carter said, "Then all ancient history is corrupted and should be thrown out."[245] I was aghast. The YEC scholar Johnathan Sarfati chimed in and labeled me a "compromiser" in the camp of Hugh Ross.[246] I walked them both through population calculations and asked how much time they estimated came between the end of Noah's Flood and the Tower of Babel and how many people they came up with, using their own math, that this would leave to build the Tower of Babel and scatter across the earth. They would not respond. I was willing to acknowledge 6-day creation less than 10,000 years ago but that is not enough for some of these YEC groups. Do you see why I believe we must break away from these groups for the good of Scripture and to allow the YEC theory room to breathe? Can you imagine the response I would have received if, when I was completing my masters in ancient history, I had told my board that we needed to "throw out all of ancient history"? How can we reach a skeptical generation when we start with a position that we cannot defend, as Carter and Sarfati did in this exchange?

---

[242] Hardy and Carter, "Biblical Minimum and Maximum," (https://creation.com/biblical-age-of-the-earth)

[243] Larry Pierce and Ken Ham, "Are There Gaps in the Genesis Genealogies?" Answers in Genesis, April 8, 2010, (https://answersingenesis.org/bible-timeline/genealogy/gaps-in-the-genesis-genealogies/)

[244] Ken Ham, "Never-Ending List of Christians Who Compromise," Answers in Genesis, September 20, 2013, (https://answersingenesis.org/blogs/ken-ham/2013/09/20/never-ending-list-of-christians-who-compromise/)

[245] Personal correspondence available upon request (also on Rob Carter's Genetics page).

[246] Ibid.

Similarly, Walt Brown, the Associates for Biblical Research, and others agree with me and the late Henry Morris, author of *The Genesis Flood,* that we should allow for flexible dating while maintaining a literal six-day creation.[247,248,249,250] Most flood legends align closer to a date around 3,300 BC, as do the stories of Gilgamesh, the Mayans and various other cultures. The Samaritan Pentateuch and Jewish historian Josephus use the same older dating as the Septuagint and this pre-Masoretic text, which get us to approximately 5,500 BC for the creation date. Likewise, genetics and repopulation logarithms fall much more in line with a Tower of Babel somewhere around 2,850 BC, which would allow time for the world to be repopulated by Noah's sons.[251] But again, AIG dogma cannot allow any of this, no matter what history or the Bible say, and thus they continue to hinder the YEC cause in subtle ways.[252] They are the heaviest funded group, so many YEC supporters feel they must pay homage to AIG. Those who do not are often ostracized.[253] Walt Brown, who acquired his PhD from MIT, dared to deviate from AIG's 4004 BC dating, so AIG was quick to dismiss Brown. "We found a date that agrees with the Ussher date precisely…. This illustrates the futility of Brown's approach."[254] And again we're only scratching the surface.[255]

This is one of the reasons I encourage caution when equating YEC with any one group. Though I may use material from AIG on occasion, I am arguing for the viability of YEC theory independent of AIG. Ken Ham and I are cordial, and I am very grateful for the contributions made by AIG and their affiliates, but AIG does not speak for all YEC theorists. Simply asking, "Were

[247] Walt Brown. *In the Beginning*, 484-6.
[248] Smith, "Septuagint's Chronology," (https://biblearchaeology.org/images/Genesis-5-and-11/Smith-Henry-The-Case-for-the-Septuagints-Chronology-in-Gen-5-and-11-ICC.pdf)
[249] *Were the Pyramids Built Before the Flood? (Masoretic Text vs. Original Hebrew)* (YouTube, 2017, https://www.youtube.com/watch?v=VI1yRTC6kGE)
[250] John C. Whitcomb and Henry Madison Morris, *The Genesis Flood: the Biblical Record and Its Scientific Implications* (Phillipsburg, NJ: P & R Publishing, 1961)
[251] Steve Rudd, April 2019, (http://www.bible.ca/maps/Bible-chronology-age-of-earth-date-Genesis-5-11-Septuagint-text-LXX-original-autograph-primeval-5554BC.jpg)
[252] David McGee, "Creation Date of Adam from Young-Earth Creationism's Perspective," Answers in Genesis, November 28, 2012, (https://answersingenesis.org/bible-characters/adam-and-eve/creation-date-of-adam-from-young-earth-creationism-perspective/)
[253] Carl Wieland, Jonathan Sarfati, and Ken Ham, "Maintaining Creationist Integrity," Creation.com | Creation Ministries International, October 11, 2002, (https://creation.com/maintaining-creationist-integrity-response-to-kent-hovind)
[254] Danny R. Faulkner, "Can One Astronomically Date the Flood within the Hydroplate Model," Answers in Genesis, April 1, 2015, (https://answersingenesis.org/the-flood/can-one-astronomically-date-the-flood-within-the-hydroplate-model/)
[255] I must reiterate that I support and love AIG and Ken Ham holistically but I hold them to a very high standard so they must do better here.

you there?" will not satisfactorily meet the future needs of people's inquiries. Ignoring facts recognized by other YEC groups and showing little humility will only push AIG further from a biblical and scientific framework. This critique of them is done in love and because I know they can do much better in the future.

The YEC I never knew

YEC theory has been around almost as long as history, so it is not a "new" way to describe or understand the world. Moreover, YEC makes good sense of the Bible and theology as well as history and the social sciences. Let's look at YEC theory from the fields of natural sciences. The point is not to "prove" YEC theory, since I don't think that can be done. Instead, ask yourself the same sort of question William Lane Craig asked when he debated Francisco Ayala in 2009 on the topic of intelligent design. Ask, "Has God covered his tracks so well that *YEC* theory is not even viable?"

In this chapter, I will look at a series of events taken as true by most YEC theorists, but considered false or questionable by OEC supporters, and decide if the YEC supposition is viable within a natural science framework. We will again use Douglas Axe's intuition principle, as well as common science, common sense, or plausible science. It will also need to adhere to McCullagh's criteria, providing good explanatory power and being less contrived than competing OEC hypotheses. Even if YEC ends up being false, all we are testing is viability from a natural science perspective. If it is viable, then we have a strong reason to continue to develop and refine YEC theory, perhaps even adopting it in place of OEC theory. If it proves strong from a natural science perspective, and if we have established its superiority in theology and the social sciences, we have a case for elevating YEC theory to the preferred theory for the thinking-Christian it would seem. Biblical and natural events will again be analyzed accordingly:

1. Douglas Axe's concept of common science.[256]
2. McCullagh's steps for historicity[257]
3. Occam's Razor[258]

---

[256] David Klinghoffer, "More Scientists Praise Douglas Axe's *Undeniable*," Evolution News, July 18, 2016, (https://evolutionnews.org/2016/07/more_scientists_1/)

[257] McCullagh, *Justifying*.

[258] "Occam's Razor," Merriam-Webster (Merriam-Webster, https://www.merriam-webster.com/dictionary/Occam's razor)

I bounced this off a number of atheists, skeptics, and OEC/YEC colleagues, and all agreed that if something could pass the smell check of these three points it should be sufficient proof of a reasonable explanation for the natural sciences. If we're talking about Christ's Resurrection using natural vs. non-natural criteria and Theory "A" wins on all three of the above-mentioned points, we should be able to deduce that Theory "A" is *probably* the accurate theory to adopt.

Not your Grandpa's YEC?

In *Three Views on Creation and Evolution,* YEC theory is taken up by Mark Reynolds and Paul Nelson (Logos Research Associates, Discovery Institute, and *Is Genesis History?*). In 1999, this combo argued that YEC theory had made headway in several scientific fields since 1979. They argued (then) that YEC had grown intellectually since the 1961 publication of *The Genesis Flood* with the addition of many great, new minds, like Kurt Wise, John Baumgardner, Steve Austin, and others, coupled with the emergence of intelligent design, which was in its infancy. As Dr. Nelson argues, "If YEC was *pseudoscience* it is the only one that has grown in the manner that it did since usually pseudoscience begins with some semi-credible figure and then tries explaining this *new science* in retrospect of the world around us. Second YEC has been the overwhelming view of the traditional church as well as the sciences [as we have already seen]."[259] They then say, "YEC is intellectually exciting and yet underdeveloped in this book against competing views from OEC and TE."[260]

Fast-forward to 2020, and most YEC views described in that book have now been confirmed. Naturalism is now largely seen as pseudoscience, as I wrote in *The Philosophy of History,* and as the great Alvin Plantinga described as deserving to be jettisoned once and for all, like logical positivism a century ago. YEC theory is still underdeveloped in the natural sciences, though it has gained a lot of ground in the last decade and is still historiographically the position of most of human history. None of this makes YEC true, of course, but it does show that it is going in the right direction and has not experienced any setbacks to warrant its demise.

---

[259] Moreland and Reynolds, *Three Views on Creation and Evolution.*
[260] Ibid.

Watch for logical fallacies!

Watch for logical fallacies from OEC groups when they critique what I have written. OEC theorists are often guilty of the following fallacies when critiquing YEC:

- **Equivocation**: "Science is a very powerful and reliable tool.... So why would [YEC] deny the science of [OEC]?" (This argument equivocates the on the word *science* which can be [operational or origin based]. Operational science is the reliable...tool [ex: a testing of a theory by the scientific method]. Origins science is an attempt to understand past events in light of present evidence [philosophy of science] and is not directly testable or repeatable. The two types of science should not be conflated within an argument.
- **Reification:** "OEC is a fact and the evidence speaks for itself." (Evidence does not actually speak, only people on the topic do.)
- **Hasty Generalization**: "Ken Ham is a YEC theorist, and his research is very sloppy. Therefore, all YEC are bad researchers." (The fact that one YEC theorist is a poor researcher does not mean that all are).
- **Begging the question**: "How do I know OEC is true? Because it's a fact." A person arguing this way has merely assumed what he is trying to prove.... This is one of the most common fallacies committed by old-earth creationists. [Another example]: "Young-earth creationists are wrong because radiometric dating shows that rocks are billions of years old." The problem with this argument is that young-earth creationists do not accept the assumptions in radiometric dating. So by presupposing that radiometric dating is reliable, the arguer has already assumed that young-earth creationists are wrong.
- **Special Pleading**: "You can only use papers submitted in [peer-reviewed,] secular journals; creationist journals do not count." This is an arbitrary double standard. We could equally well argue that only creation-based journals count.
- **False Analogy**: "[YEC] is akin to asking us to believe [in a flat earth]!" Here the critic compares beliefs of a flat earth...to creation. But the notions of a flat earth...can be falsified by operational science.... But [YEC] is about the past.... So the analogy fails.
- **Slippery Slope**: "If we allow for [a YEC interpretation of history], science would come to a halt.... Children...will not search for real explanations!" But there is no rational reason to connect the teaching of [YEC] with the chain of events that are alleged to follow. [If we look at the history of science, we see researchers pursuing knowledge with great gusto, in the hopes of drawing closer to God.]

- **Genetic Fallacy**: "YEC theorists are just a throwback to people before modern science and pre-Enlightenment, so why even listen to them?" Whether or not the statement is true, it is irrelevant.
- **Faulty Appeal to Authority**: "The vast majority of scientists say YEC is wrong, therefore it is wrong!" Scientists have a long history of being wrong, so this statement does nothing to refute YEC or support OEC.[261]

I encourage you to look for these fallacies in discussions with OEC theorists. Many make them without knowing it, but those trained in philosophy know better. I begged atheists to tear apart *The Philosophy of History*, and I encourage OEC to do the same with this work, but if you are going to critique, watch for fallacies, so we can have a good and robust dialog.

Dating Methods – What I won't be discussing in depth

I have worked with RTB and talked to Hugh Ross, though I don't think I have ever spoken to YEC astronomer Jason Lisle, but I found their debates interesting and felt they were on an even playing field, both having PhDs from secular universities—Ross in astronomy and Lisle in astrophysics. Jason Lisle commented in his debates with Ross:

- The tools of science allow us to measure in the present: length, volume, mass, force, density, barometric pressure, velocity, acceleration, energy but not age. We cannot observe or experiment on the past.
- It is impossible to prove the age of something scientifically because we can only observe and experiment on the present. To know the age of something we must have information about two points in time, but scientifically, we can only know one (at most).
- Two things to remember about historical science: Any estimates about the past cannot be scientifically tested or proved. Our ages estimate will be only as reliable as the assumptions that go into it.
- We cannot scientifically know the initial conditions, but in some cases they cannot go beyond a particular value. (this makes it possible to estimate an *upper limit* on the age, but not the true age).

Lisle uses the example of "salt in the ocean," and then breaks down why, using uniformitarianism as a base, we estimate the age of the oceans as less than sixty-two million years, which is far less than the three billion needed by OEC theorists, but gives us the potential of a six thousand-year-old ocean in the YEC model. The only rational way to resolve a debate is with an internal

---

[261] Jason Lisle, *The Ultimate Proof of Creation: Resolving the Origins Debate* (Green Forest, AR: Master Books, 2017), p.123-6.

critique: Assume the presuppositions of the opponent and show that they lead to contradiction. The recession of the moon would limit the age of the earth to 1.4 billion years old (not 4.6B). Similarly, spiral galaxies cannot be more than two billion years old, as the earth's magnetic field decay rate would have been too strong for life to exist as little as ten thousand years ago. Comets last about one hundred thousand years, blue stars last about ten million years, etc. It is mostly uncontroversial that only 10% of dating methods get us to a 4.6B earth and 13.7B year old universe which means 90% of secular dating methods tell us the earth and universe are much younger though only 10,000 years seem equally extreme.[262]

Lisle admits that YEC theory (presupposing uniformitarianism and naturalism) does not align well with secular sources, but neither does OEC. Of course, OEC can factor in "fudge factors," such as us living in a time of unusually high tidal action or that spiral density wave theory accounts for the age of spiral galaxies and the Ort Cloud. But these are all conjectures without scientific basis; OEC theorists must go against their own beliefs in uniformitarianism to allow these fudge factors to fit in and maintain a 13.7 billion-year-old universe and a 4.6 billion-year-old earth. OEC theorists cherry-pick data to fit their vantage, just as the naturalistic side does in many instances. We have all heard about the various dating blunders, in which recent lava flows yielded faulty ages, or surprises within radiocarbon:[263]

> The bottom line is that virtually all biological specimens, no matter how 'old' they are supposed to be, show measurable C14 levels. This effectively limits the age of all buried biota to less than (at most) 250,000 years. (When one takes into account the probability that before the Flood the ratio of radioactive to 'normal' carbon was much lower, the calculated age comes right down into the biblical 'ballpark'.) Interestingly, specimens which appear to definitely be pre-Flood seem to have C14 present, too, and importantly, these cluster around a lower relative amount of C14. This suggests that some C14 was primordial (existing from the very beginning), and not produced by cosmic rays—thus limiting the age of the entire earth to only a few thousand years. This appears to have been somewhat spectacularly supported when Dr Baumgardner sent five diamonds to be analyzed for C14. It was the first time this had been attempted, and the

---

[262] https://www.calvarychapelboston.com/Answers%20chapter4.pdf
[263] Andrew Snelling, "Radioactive 'dating' failure," Creation.com | Creation Ministries International, December 1999, (https://creation.com/radioactive-dating-failure)

answer came back positive—C14 was present. The diamonds, formed deep inside the earth, are assumed by evolutionists to be over a billion years old. Nevertheless, they contained radio-active carbon, even though, if the billion-year age were correct, they 'shouldn't have'.[264]

Even the Museum of Natural History in New York City finally put up a sign admitting that the dating method is more art than science. Dating methods do not really help either side when it comes to ages greater than a few thousand years, it would seem, but I encourage all sides to research the matter on their own. As geologist Tas Walker commented:

- It is impossible to determine the age of something in the past by making measurements of properties in the present.
- Thus, all dates are based on assumptions about the past.
- The only way a scientist can consider his assumptions are valid is if it gives a date that is acceptable.
- If it is not acceptable, then in every case he will change his assumptions after he gets his 'date' in order to give a plausible explanation for his result. This is called interpreting the result.[265]

Some creationists attempt to "throw the baby out with the bathwater" by jettisoning dating measures altogether, but carbon dating works fairly well on things up to three thousand years old. Ironically, the upper limit of carbon dating would be approximately 250,000 years, yet samples dated to millions and even billions of years come back with carbon still in it. The answer from OEC theorists is that "the samples were corrupted." I am not going to go into the dating paradox, as it has been beaten to death; instead I will simply encourage you to research this on your own as it is not overtly helpful or conclusive within my specific research. I hope both sides can agree that we get as many contradictions as answers when we date anything past more than a few thousand years. None of us have a starting point, since our age estimates are only as good as the assumptions we put into them, but for the sake of argument, I am content with giving this one to the OEC side.

---

[264] Carl Wieland, "Radiometric Dating Breakthroughs," Creation.com | Creation Ministries International, March 2004, (https://creation.com/radiometric-dating-breakthroughs)
[265] Dr. Tas Walker and David M., "Do Creationists Cherry-Pick Discordant Dates?" Creation.com | Creation Ministries International, October 28, 2017, (https://creation.com/do-creationists-cherry-pick-discordant-dates)

YEC theorists do not make scientific predictions!

I hear this a lot, though it's demonstrably false, as I point out in *The Philosophy of History*. It is naturalism that makes no predictions, but for this book, let's just keep it between OEC and YEC. While there is no way to do these topics justice, let's break down four big ones:

1. **Time-light cosmological problems** – Incredibly strong cosmological models have been put together in the last two decades that have given YEC theory good speculative models and solve the starlight problem that OEC theorists have long used against YEC. I found this topic interesting, considering its relevance to my astronomy studies.
2. **Catastrophism** (regarding plate tectonics and Noah's flood): There are over twenty predictions from John Baumgardner and others in catastrophic plate tectonics (CPT). In the same vein, I find the discovery of great amounts of water under the Earth's crust supportive of Walt Brown's hydroplate theory (HPT), which builds a strong geologic case for Noah's Flood and its after-effects.
3. **A historical Adam and Eve and created kinds:** Based on population genetics, a historical Adam and Eve is back in business, just as YEC theorists always professed, and the likelihood of their existence has become stronger even within secular circles. Similarly, YEC have long argued against the secular (and often OEC) claim that the Neanderthal shared no commonality with modern humans long before the mapping of the Neanderthal genome. YEC also largely disbelieved the case of *Junk DNA* even though this was the mainline position of the late 20th century.
4. **Created Kinds** – Baraminology has grown and been better refined, though more work is needed to discuss biblically-created *kinds*, in reference to the animals on Noah's Ark and accounting for the life we see in the world today.

Again, the point here is to break these topics down to see if YEC theory is viable, plausible, and testable. If YEC theory is just a "God of the gaps," it explains why OEC theorists frequently accept the latest naturalistic theory and add God to it. A second purpose is to see if YEC has progressed enough as a scientific theory to be taken seriously. We have already established, mostly without controversy I hope, that YEC theory is stronger than competing OEC models in the areas of biblical exegesis, theological-historiography, and the social sciences. Obviously, there are a ton of other topics I could have chosen for analysis, but these four are the ones I normally hear, and they are intertwined with Genesis 1–11, so instead of shying away from the hard questions, let's dive right into them, shall we?

Prediction 1 – Cosmology and Astronomy:

Does YEC theory have a prayer?

"I do believe in the six-day Creation of the world and that there is abundant geological evidence there was a worldwide flood."[266]

– Ben Carson

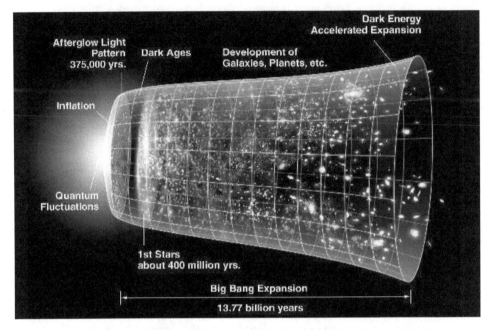

Timeline of the metric expansion of space, where space, including hypothetical, non-observable portions of the universe, is represented at each time by the circular sections. Above: the dramatic expansion occurs in the inflationary epoch, and at the center, the expansion accelerates.[267]

---

[266] Dr. Carson has suffered the way George Washington Carver did almost a century ago for expressing similar views concerning YEC. Despite Dr. Carson's many achievements, Richard Dawkins called Carson, "A deeply depressing disgrace!" In 2004, Carson served on the President's Council on Bioethics, and in 2008, he was awarded the Presidential Medal of Freedom. In 2010, Dr. Carson was elected to the National Academy of Sciences Institute of Medicine, one of the most prestigious honors in medicine. Today he is the Secretary of Housing and Urban Development.

[267] wikipedia.org/wiki/Big_Bang#/media/File:CMB_Timeline300_no_WMAP.jpg

I won't lie – outside of the notion of a "mature creation," largely supported by the late Henry Morris, cosmology has largely been on the side of Hugh Ross and old earth creation when it comes to reconciling distant starlight with YEC. At the same time, Wikipedia ironically quotes me as an advocate of the Big Bang theory.[268] What I concluded from my previous writings and research was that Big Bang models prove a finite past (the universe began to exist and is not eternal or uncaused). I have never endorsed strictly naturalistic understandings built within Big Bang cosmology, since the Big Bang is a materialistic theory, meaning that the only aspects to be considered are naturalistic principles that we can see in operation. I am not a concordist like my friend Hugh Ross. Concordism seems self-refuting since it forces one to adjust one's biblical interpretations (eisegesis) with every new scientific discovery. For example, Hugh Ross says the Bible teaches the Big Bang, but what if the Big Bang model is later shown to be wrong? Ross will have to abandon the Bible or adjust his interpretation to fit the latest discovery and thus all his prior writings endorsing Big Bang cosmology will have to be jettisoned. It is important to spend a little time discussing this topic in greater depth.

Questions like: "Did Adam have a belly button?" and "Was Adam created as a baby?" are legitimate questions for Christians. I see no reason to ridicule the idea of a "mature" creation that would not be based on naturalistic causation. I find it dumbfounding, as do my Eastern Orthodox friends, that so many OEC groups feel we must view astronomy and cosmology through a naturalistic lens, but not the Virgin Birth or Christ's Resurrection. Must God be something we can comprehend, or must we merely need to apprehend? In other words, this is not a "god of the gaps," any more than OEC theorists claim it to be a "time of the gaps." Both YEC and OEC theorists assert that God must have done it *this* way and could not have done it *that* way. This goes back to "God is infinite and humans are finite; therefore, humans cannot fully comprehend God or his ways." I think a little humility from both sides is needed.

I find mature creation and the miraculous actions of God well within reason if the biblical narrative is true, in much the same way that the late A.E. Wilder-Smith maintained when he schooled a young Richard Dawkins in debate.[269] Whether we call this "appearance of age" or "god created with functional

---

[268] "Christian Apologetics," Wikipedia (Wikimedia Foundation), (https://en.wikipedia.org/wiki/Christian_apologetics)
[269] A.E. Wilder-Smith, "Creation and the Appearance of Age," Creation.com | Creation Ministries International, December 1986, (https://creation.com/creation-and-appearance-of-age)

maturity" is an argument in semantics, which is often used by less informed, more dogmatic YEC groups.[270] Outside of mature creation or miraculous creation there are about twenty strong points that YEC theorists use to argue against OEC; e.g., volcanic activity on Earth's moon, recession of the moon from Earth, the presence of a notable magnetic field around the planets, Saturn's rings, the life expectancy of asteroids and comets, the apparent short lives of stars, etc.) All of these point to a much more recent creation than is popularly explained by secularists, but at the same time, most of these do not get you back to ten thousand years. So, are both positions wrong? Let's peel back the layers a bit. While the evidence does not directly support YEC, it does seem to indirectly disprove many elements of OEC.[271]

NGC 4414, a typical spiral galaxy in the constellation Coma Berenices, is about 55,000 light-years in diameter and approximately 60 million light-years from Earth.[272]

---

[270] Jonathan Sarfati, "God Created with Functional Maturity, Not 'Appearance of Age,'" Creation.com | Creation Ministries International, March 10, 2015, (https://creation.com/is-apparent-age-biblical)

[271] The May 2020 issue of *Sky & Telescope* ran an article "Revising the story of planet formation (again)" which echoes this point beautifully. Almost nothing is definite when we're talking about space/time and especially cosmology as has become even more clear in my post-graduate studies in space studies.

[272] "Galaxy," Wikipedia (Wikimedia Foundation, February 24, 2020, https://en.wikipedia.org/wiki/Galaxy)

Surely distant starlight must prove an old universe, right? No one disputes that the stars and galaxies are millions, even billions, of light-years away. Of course, a light year is a distance measurement that indicates how far light, traveling at its presently measured speed of 186,000 miles a second, travels in one year. So, doesn't this prove the light needed millions and billions of years to get here?

This problem assumes that the speed of light has always been the same, and that clocks have always measured time passing at the same rate in all times and places in the history of the universe. It may seem like an open and shut case, but explaining distant starlight is a task for all cosmologies, including the conventional Big Bang model. I have worked with several who have put forth scientifically sound alternative cosmological models that indicate, or at least accommodate, a young universe on the order of 6,000–10,000 years old. These models question the underlying assumptions of conventional models, such as Big Bang theories.

The Big Bang theory has a light time travel problem:

First of all, it should be shown at the outset that even the conventional models have to solve a distant starlight problem. The problem is called the "horizon" problem. In the big bang model, the universe began with a small point called a singularity, which then expands rapidly. Before expansion, this model requires that different regions of the universe started with very different temperatures, yet today we can detect electromagnetic radiation coming from great distances all over the known universe, and this radiation shows that the temperature is very uniform in all places. But how did this happen between regions that are now billions of light years apart? This could happen only by these regions exchanging electromagnetic heat and light energy until the temperature is uniform. This is what happens when an ice-cold glass of water comes to room temperature if we wait long enough. Electromagnetic energy traveling at the current speed of light would not have had time to even out the temperature for points billions of light years apart, since they would have to have exchanged light and heat energy many times. This is why inflation theory was brought in to save the big bang model from this horizon problem. Inflation theory, which actually has no convincing supporting evidence, has the universe expanding slower at first, which supposedly allowed the temperature differences to smooth out before a rapid, explosive inflation after that. As of 2020, there is no known cause for inflation, nor a mechanism to stop it. Therefore, the Big Bang's starlight travel time problem remains, so one cannot dismiss a YEC biblical chronology *a priori*.[273]

Natural or Supernatural?

There are underlying assumptions in conventional models that the processes and rates observed today were always in operation in the past based on uniformitarianism. There is also an upfront exclusion of the possibility of a supernatural creation event, where different processes and rates were brought into play. If we assume instead that a creation event really happened, then there would have been processes that don't happen today, operating at much faster rates than we see today. We can't argue that a supernatural explanation is wrong because something can't be explained by natural means. This is faulty reasoning and exclusion of the supernatural on philosophical grounds, as I meticulously break down in *The Philosophy of History*, so I find it question-begging when OEC theorists criticize YEC cosmologies for not being scientific enough. If one is a Christian, then they would agree with a supernatural beginning; the OEC must be careful to not just be an OE (old earth "non" creationist) or they will simply be a naturalist. See my point? Let's look at alternative cosmological models that have been proposed to deal with the distant starlight problem.[274]

SPEED OF LIGHT

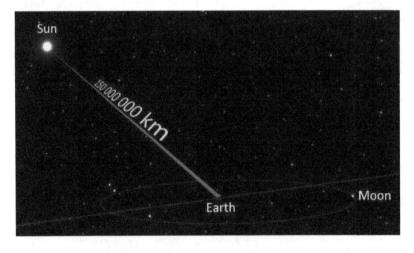

---

[273] Vince Latorre, "Does Distant Starlight Prove a Billions-of-Years-Old Universe? Part 6 of Series," The Bible Can Be Proven, (http://thebiblecanbeproven.com/does-distant-starlight-prove-a-billions-of-years-old-universe-part-6-of-series/)
[274] Ibid.

The past cannot be fully known, nor can we verify the speed of light being constant between points A and B and back from B to A; this is an assumption that we must presuppose, and one on which the theory of relativity hinges. The idea of the speed of light being faster in the past, as proposed by Barry Setterfield, is a possibility and has drawn interest from non-biblical scientists as well. However, this theory, often called C-decay, has largely been fought against by OEC and YEC theorists alike.[275] With that said, there is no reason to believe it is not consistent from A→B and B→A either? Secular sources raise some good questions on the speed of light, but this is not a compelling case from a YEC standpoint by my estimation:

> Modern physics rests on the foundational notion that the speed of light is a constant, which in a vacuum is 186,000 miles per second (299,792 km/s). Einstein established this within his theory of general relativity, first developed in 1906 when he was just 26 years-old. But what if it doesn't? A few albeit controversial incidents in recent years challenge the idea that light always travels at a constant speed. And in fact, we've known for a long time that there are several phenomena that travel faster than light, without violating the theory of relativity. For instance, whereas traveling faster than sound creates a sonic boom, traveling faster than light creates a "luminal boom." Russian scientist Pavel Alekseyevich Cherenkov discovered this in 1934, which won him the Nobel Prize in Physics in 1958. Cherenkov radiation can be observed in the core of a nuclear reactor. When the core is submerged in water to cool it, electrons move through the water faster than the speed of light, causing a luminal boom.
>
> On another front, while no particle with mass can travel faster than light, the fabric of space can and does. According to Inflation Theory, immediately after the Big Bang, the universe doubled in size and then doubled again, in less than a trillionth of a trillionth of a second, much faster than the speed of light. More recently, astronomers have discovered that some galaxies, the distant ones anyway, move away from

---

[275] Stuart Clark, "Cosmic Uncertainty: Is the Speed of Light Really Constant?" New Scientist, March 1, 2017, (https://www.newscientist.com/article/mg23331150-200-cosmic-uncertainty-is-the-speed-of-light-really-constant/)

us faster than light speed, supposedly, pushed along by dark energy. The best estimate for the rate of acceleration for the universe is 68 kilometers per second per megaparsec. By now, instrumentation had improved to the point where the CMB can be successfully probed. As such, in 2016 João Magueijo and Niayesh Afshordi published another paper, this time in the journal Physical Review D. They are currently measuring different areas of the CMB, and studying the distribution of galaxies, seeking clues to support their claim that light in the universe's earliest moments broke free of its presumed speed limit. Again, this is a fringe theory. And yet, the implications are astounding. "The whole of physics is predicated on the constancy of the speed of light," Magueijo told Vice's *Motherboard*. "So we had to find ways to change the speed of light without wrecking the whole thing." Their calculations should be complete by 2021.[276]

New Scientist ran an article in 2017 titled, "Is the Speed of Light really constant?"[277] They discussed in great detail why there was reason to believe the speed of light may have been faster in the past. Some of the research is interesting, but I have not seen anything convincing yet for the YEC position. Perhaps when they finish their calculations next year we will know more, but it seems that trying to build a case based on the change of light speed is a like building a foundation upon sand; therefore, I am compelled to believe that the speed of light is constant until it is shown to be otherwise. Let's look at YEC models that have taken this problem more seriously to see if they are viable.[278]

Dr. Jason Lisle – The Anisotropic Synchrony Convention Model:

Astrophysicist Dr. Jason Lisle (whom we referenced earlier) has refined, or redefined another way to potentially explain the distant starlight problem. He acknowledges the value of the previous models, but also suggests that the time for starlight to get to Earth depends on the convention one uses to measure time. His model is called the Anisotropic Synchrony Convention (ASC) over that of the Einstein Synchrony Convention (ESC) which is the standard use in most physics' textbooks today. In a nutshell, the standards ESC defines the

---

[276] Philip Perry, "Is the Speed of Light Slowing down?" Big Think (Big Think, October 1, 2019, https://bigthink.com/philip-perry/is-the-speed-of-light-slowing-down)

[277] Clark, "Cosmic Uncertainty," (https://www.newscientist.com/article/mg23331150-200-cosmic-uncertainty-is-the-speed-of-light-really-constant/)

[278] Latorre, "Does Distant Starlight," (http://thebiblecanbeproven.com/does-distant-starlight-prove-a-billions-of-years-old-universe-part-6-of-series/)

occurrence of an event at a past moment in time allowing for the finite speed of light; ASC in contrast is saying the ESC is an unprovable assumption so the ASC instead defines the occurrence of an event at the moment it is observed. To keep it simple, a Synchrony convention is a procedure used for synchronizing clocks that are separated by a distance. This theory is based on the fact that the speed of light in one direction, that is the one-way speed of light, actually cannot be objectively measured. What is measured in experiments is the round-trip speed of light, using mirrors to reflect the light back. So, it is possible that the one-way speed of light could actually be instantaneous, even though the round-trip two-way speed of light is constant.

Lisle explains why we can't measure one-way speed of light in: "In order to avoid assuming the time for one-way speed of light, we need to be able to measure the one-way trip. But it is impossible because moving a clock to the mirror may change the time on the clock."[279] Let's look at a quick diagram from the same article that may help clarify.

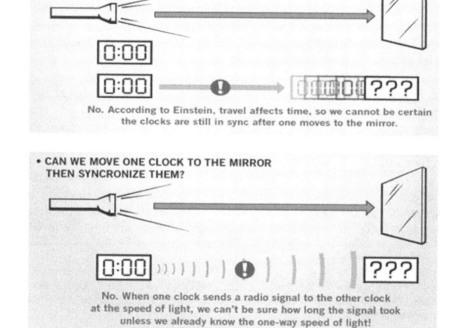

• CAN WE SYNCHRONIZE TWO CLOCKS THEN MOVE ONE TO THE MIRROR?

0:00

0:00 ???

No. According to Einstein, travel affects time, so we cannot be certain the clocks are still in sync after one moves to the mirror.

• CAN WE MOVE ONE CLOCK TO THE MIRROR THEN SYNCRONIZE THEM?

0:00 ???

No. When one clock sends a radio signal to the other clock at the speed of light, we can't be sure how long the signal took unless we already know the one-way speed of light!

---

[279] Dr. Jason Lisle, "Distant Starlight—The Anisotropic Synchrony Convention," *Answers Magazine*, January 2011, pp. 68-71.

In other words, we are free to choose what the speed of light will be in one direction, though the "round-trip" time averaged speed is always constant. The reason that the one-way speed of light cannot be objectively measured is that you need a way to synchronize two clocks separated by a distance. But in order to synchronize two clocks separated by some distance, you have to already know the one-way speed of light. So, it cannot be done without circular reasoning.

We need to have a way of synchronizing clocks to know the one-way speed of light. But we need to know the one-way speed of light in order to synchronize clocks. Einstein was well aware of this dilemma. He said, "It would thus appear as though we were moving here in a logical circle."[280] Einstein's resolution to this dilemma was to suggest that the one-way speed of light is not actually a property of nature but is instead a convention— something that we may choose."[281]

So, we can actually choose a convention, similar to choosing *Local Time* over *Universal Time* on Earth. Anisotropic refers to light having different speeds in different directions, as opposed to the convention Einstein used, isotropic- the same speed of light in all directions. Genesis may imply the Anisotropic Synchrony Convention (ASC), since starlight was made available immediately. So, in this convention the one-way speed of light from the distant galaxies to Earth was instantaneous.

It may seem unlikely that light would not have the same speed in all directions. But even though we may assume for everyday use that light speed is constant in all directions as measured by our clocks, in a relativistic universe, as we approach the speed of light, time and space no longer have absolute values independent of the observer. In his more technical article, Lisle shows that using the Einsteinian convention, with light speed in all directions the same, leads to some interesting results when we have one observer in motion relative to the other.[282] In fact, they will get different answers as to whether some events happened at the same time, or in what

[280] Albert W Einstein, *Relativity: the Special & the General Theory: a Popular Exposition*, trans. R W Lawson (New York: Crown Publishers, 1961), quoted in Latorre, "Does Distant Starlight," (http://thebiblecanbeproven.com/does-distant-starlight-prove-a-billions-of-years-old-universe-part-6-of-series/)
[281] Ibid.
[282] Jason Lisle. "Anisotropic Synchrony Convention——A Solution to the Distant Starlight Problem." *Answers Research Journal*, (3, 2010), quoted in Latorre, "Does Distant Starlight," (http://thebiblecanbeproven.com/does-distant-starlight-prove-a-billions-of-years-old-universe-part-6-of-series/)

order they happened. With ASC we find that two observers see the same events as simultaneous, regardless of their velocity.

He makes the case also that since we can choose a convention, it makes sense to see which one fits the Bible (if we are Christians especially). As we said above, light traveling very fast from the stars to Earth would fit the ASC. Also, people in most of history would not know anything about the speed of light, or lookback time and with ASC, it is not required to know the distance to an object, so ASC best preserves the clarity of Scripture. Things in space would be seen as they happen.

> Think about it – astronomers seem to use ASC when they name a supernova after the year they saw it, rather than the year they believe the light left the source. ASC is just one more possible model that depends on one's starting assumptions rather than the observations.[283]

Lisle dedicates a large portion of his 2018 book *The Physics of Einstein* to answering the various objections to his ASC model, which shows he is not ignoring the critics, but meeting them head on, which is exactly what healthy science should necessitate.[284]

While the above YEC models are consistent with what we know of light-time and fit with an omnipotent God as described in Genesis, I prefer one that utilizes the secular presupposition that the speed of light is constant and still returns a solid model of the universe as well as being acceptable by either ASC or ESC. Time-dilation modeling is one of my favorites and what a part of my MS focus has been directed towards. It could be wrong, but the math and physics behind it are strong, and the theories show how far YEC has come since the 1980s, even if some YEC groups (and most OEC ones) don't like it. Within this vein, I found nuclear physicist Russell Humphreys' model the most intriguing. Though his theory has had some modifications since his original book *Starlight and Time* in 1994, he was the first to take both the Bible and physics seriously while thinking outside the box. He teamed up with Australian physicist John Hartnett, and they helped mold a model of

---

[283] Latorre, "Does Distant Starlight," (http://thebiblecanbeproven.com/does-distant-starlight-prove-a-billions-of-years-old-universe-part-6-of-series/)
[284] Jason Lisle's *The Physics of Einstein: Black Holes, Time Travel, Distant Starlight* is a wonderful book for believer and skeptic alike, providing a good introduction to cosmology and physics.

cosmology from a YEC perspective that continues to grow and be refined today.[285]

Humphreys has made scientific predictions (against NASA scientists) based on his recent creation model, and his predictions were verified when Voyager II measured Uranus and Neptune's magnetic field in 1990. In 2008, and 2011, when probes measured Mercury's magnetic field, they were able to confirm Humphreys' YEC modeling. The predictions dealt with (1) the magnitude and dynamics of planetary magnetic fields, (2) the existence of a cosmic rotation axis, and (3) diffusion of helium through zircons. These predictions are in accord with a young earth interpretation of Genesis 1. In each case, subsequent studies showed the predictions were correct.[286]

I admit that OEC views seem stronger from a naturalistic understanding of starlight and time, but since a growing number of secularists reject naturalism, I believe Christians are free to use the Bible as a litmus test before swallowing everything a concordist view offers. Either way, YEC theory is growing quickly in scope and plausibility. AIG's Danny Faulkner was made to look outdated by Hugh Ross and other cosmologists in their debate several years ago, yet AIG still criticizes time-dilation models for not being orthodox enough.[287,288]

---

[285] I am set to host Dr. Humphrey at several universities in the Summer of 2020, so I look forward to future revisions and working hand-in-hand with great YEC minds.

[286] "Science and Evidence," *Science and Evidence* (blog), November 24, 2015, (https://scienceandevidence.wordpress.com/2015/11/24/magnetic/)

[287] Sarfati, "Intellectually Dishonest," (https://creation.com/william-lane-craig-vs-creation)

[288] Anderson, "Time Dilation," (https://answersingenesis.org/astronomy/starlight/time-dilation-cosmological-models-exegetical-and-theological-considerations/)

Russell Humphreys' Cosmological Model

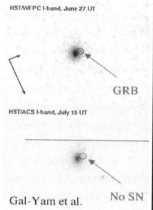

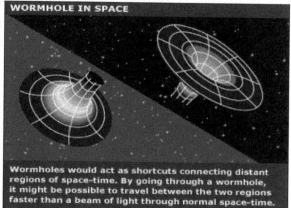

Wormholes would act as shortcuts connecting distant regions of space-time. By going through a wormhole, it might be possible to travel between the two regions faster than a beam of light through normal space-time.

In late May 2011, Physorg reported on a paper by Alon Retter and Shlomo Heller, suggesting that a known gamma-ray burst GRB 060614 might have been a white hole (which are the theoretical opposite of black holes).... Nature publication even commented, "This is brand new territory; we have no theories to guide us." ...If indeed the gamma-ray burst GRB 060614 can be shown to be associated with a white hole, the universe has just become became a more interesting place. A whitehole/blackhole relationship could act as a type of wormhole or be one-directional.[289]

I reviewed various theories over the years, including fellow Logos Research Associate Russell Humphreys' *White Hole Cosmology,* and though I feel YEC theory is moving in the right direction, with some great research paralleled off Genesis, there is still more work needed. My own interest in astronomy, coupled with the gamma-ray burst 060614 (GRB) of 2006, led to my increased interest in white hole cosmological models, including parallels with the concepts of cosmological relativity of the late Moshe Carmeli.[290] A recent physics lecture by Sam Gralla at the University of Arizona substantiated much of Humphreys' cosmology and admitted that current Big Bang cosmology cannot show where the heavy elements came from, what powers gamma-ray bursts, how matter at nuclear density behaves, or how fast black holes can spin, all of which OEC theorists and secularists often falsely claimed are solved. I look forward to hosting Dr. Humphreys' speaking

---

[289] Deborah Byrd, "Have We Seen a White Hole?" EarthSky, May 27, 2009, (https://earthsky.org/space/have-we-seen-a-white-hole)
[290] N. Gehrels et al., "A New γ-Ray Burst Classification Scheme from GRB 060614," Nature News (Nature Publishing Group, December 21, 2006, https://www.nature.com/articles/nature05376)

engagements at several universities in the Summer of 2020, where we will invite physics and astronomy departments to critique our work.[291]

> Since 1979, Humphreys worked for Sandia National Laboratories…in nuclear physics, geophysics, pulsed-power research, and theoretical atomic and nuclear physics. Since 1985, he has been working with Sandia's Particle Beam Fusion Project, and was co-inventor of special laser-triggered "Rimfire" high-voltage switches, now coming into wider use. [The last decade at Sandia saw] greater emphasis on theoretical nuclear physics and radiation hydrodynamics in an effort to help produce the world's first lab-scale thermonuclear fusion. Besides gaining [two other U.S. patents, Dr Humphreys] has been given two awards from Sandia, including an Award for Excellence for contributions to light ion fusion target theory.[292]

In 1994, Russell Humphreys applied the principle of time-dilation to propose a creationist cosmology that would replace the Big Bang. Humphreys derived his new cosmology from the equations of general relativity, replacing the secular assumptions of Big Bang theory with more biblically based ones. A finite universe without boundaries can be represented in two dimensions by the surface of a balloon. An insect crawling on its surface would never encounter a center or an edge, even though the surface is not infinitely large. The quantization of red shifts suggests that distance galaxies are arranged in concentric shells around the Milky Way. In reality, the situation is more complex than this because several different distance intervals exist between the galaxies. Humphreys' theory not only provides the first outline of a creationist cosmology, but also, in principle at least, a solution to the long-standing puzzle of how light from distant stars and galaxies reached the Earth within the biblical time frame.

---

[291] Paul A. Garner, *The New Creationism: Building Scientific Theories on a Biblical Foundation* (Welwyn Garden City, England: EP Books, 2015), p.26-31.
[292] Humphreys, *Starlight and Time*, 4.

Adding acceleration gets gravity

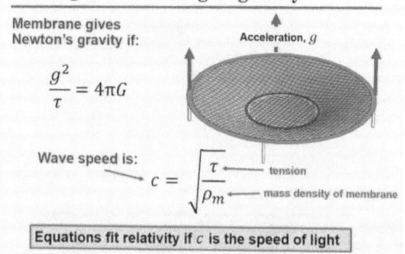

Membrane gives
Newton's gravity if:

$$\frac{g^2}{\tau} = 4\pi G$$

Acceleration, g

Wave speed is:

$$c = \sqrt{\frac{\tau}{\rho_m}}$$

τ ← tension

ρ_m ← mass density of membrane

Equations fit relativity if c is the speed of light

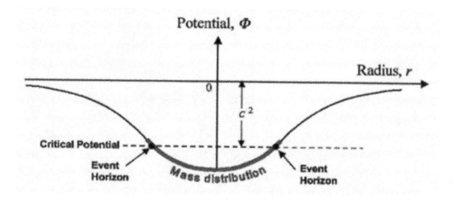

Potential, Φ

Radius, r

0

c^2

Critical Potential

Event Horizon

Mass distribution

Event Horizon

Consider the beginning of the universe (space/time/matter). At the center point, time could theoretically travel much slower, almost at a standstill. If our galaxy was near this center point, it would be plausible for the distant universe to be billions of years old while the equivalent of just days passed on the earth. Time has never been a constant or an absolute, as Einstein discovered a century ago. Time would in essence stand-still below the event horizon as the universe/space/time came into being.[293]

[293] D Russell Humphreys, "Dr Humphreys Responds to Criticism of His Book Starlight and Time," Creation.com | Creation Ministries International, (https://creation.com/dr-humphreys-responds-to-criticism-of-his-book-starlight-and-time)

Humphreys' white-hole cosmology shows that gravitational effects in the early universe could have allowed starlight to travel the required distances while only a short time passed as measured by Earth-based clocks. As with any new theory, Humphreys' cosmology has come in for criticism and modification, and it is unclear whether his version of the theory will survive the challenge of scientific and biblical analysis. Other creationists have been developing their own time-dilation theories to deal with some of the perceived weaknesses in Humphreys' initial work, while at the same time Hugh Ross declined to debate Humphreys.[294] This area of origins research is where creationist contributions are being formulated and debated. Such research shows that it is possible to develop new theories of the universe that incorporate information from both Scripture and our scientific observations. They demonstrate that the Bible can guide our scientific thinking and suggest innovative avenues of enquiry.[295]

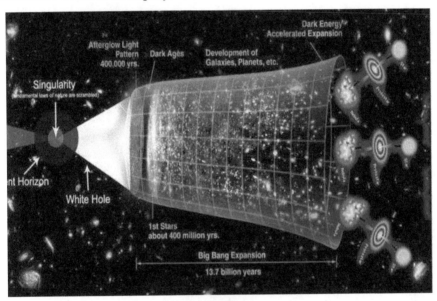

Compare the above model with that of the one at the start of this chapter. Whether the beginning of our universe was a white-hole or <u>simply acted like a white-hole</u> (mathematically), this would show the time dilation models that Humphreys has spent the last 30 years on are going in the right direction. Moreover, they are mathematically sound and completely YEC based.[296]

[294] D Russell Humphreys, "Hugh Ross Avoids Debating Russ Humphreys ... Again," The Institute for Creation Research, March 20, 2003, (https://www.icr.org/article/hugh-ross-avoids-debating-russ-humphreys-again/)
[295] Ibid.
[296] http://bigbangbitbang.blogspot.com/2016/11/the-big-bangbit-bang.html

White hole cosmology is more than a solution to the problem of distant star light; it can serve as a respectable creation cosmology. In this cosmology, the universe would only be thousands of years old, according to a clock on Earth, but according to a clock at the edge of the universe, it would be billions of years old.[297] The key to this model is the idea that time ran slower on Earth than in distant parts of the universe on Day 4 of Creation. Likewise, it relies on presuppositions from the Big Bang, which are based in current scientific trends, but most importantly, are purely biblical in nature, which is vital to provide for a model based on recent creationism. Essentially, God used relativity to let us see a young universe. This solution to the distant starlight problem is both scientifically and biblically sound. The main problem is that it is difficult to test, as are all cosmological models.[298]

Standard big bang cosmology assumes that the universe has no center and no edge, with matter filling all of space, and since there would be no boundary and empty space around the matter, there would be no unique center or center of mass, and no net gravitational force since all galaxies would be surrounded by an even distribution of other galaxies. What many people don't realize is that this is a purely arbitrary assumption, not required by the scientific evidence, but based on the idea that Earth has no special place in the cosmos such as in or near the center (Copernican Principle). What's ironic is that the standard model is always shown to be both bounded and with a center and edge (as the above diagrams show); but this is denied by both big bang theorist as well as OEC (or they simply do not understand this point). Ironic that Humphreys' model more accurately describes what we see anytime we look at these various big bang models in diagram form.

Hawking and Ellis comment on the reason for it: "...we are not able to make cosmological models without some admixture of ideology. In the earliest cosmologies, man placed himself at the center of the universe. Since the time of Copernicus, we have been demoted to a medium sized planet going around a medium sized star on the outer edge of a fairly average galaxy.... We would not claim our position in space is specially distinguished in any way."[299]

[297]Danny R. Faulkner, *Universe by Design: an Explanation of Cosmology and Creation* (Green Forest, AR: Master Books, 2004), pp.101-103.

[298] D Russell Humphreys, "Russell Humphreys Answers Various Critics," The True.Origin Archive: Exposing the Myth of Evolution, 2020, (https://www.trueorigin.org/ca_rh_03.php)

[299] S. W. Hawking and G. F. R. Ellis, *The Large Scale Structure of Space-Time* (London: Cambridge University Press, 1973), quoted in John G. Hartnett, "A New Cosmology: Solution to the Starlight Travel Time Problem," Creation.com | Creation Ministries International, August 2003, https://creation.com/a-new-cosmology-solution-to-the-starlight-travel-time-problem)

Notice that they call this principle an "admixture of ideology". That is, they start up front with the idea that the creation account is false, and that man has no special place in the cosmos. This does not come from observable evidence but from a philosophical conclusion that we are the result of random processes and not from a Creator with a special purpose and place for us. The only physical evidence secularists point out is that the universe is isotropic, that is, it looks about the same in every direction. On the other hand, the creation account in Genesis implies that the universe does have a center (Gen 1:2) from which God causes the expansion of the universe outward from the center of a large mass. And there is good scientific data that indicates the universe may have a center of mass after all.

We also get from relativity theory that gravity affects clocks. A clock at high altitude runs faster than a clock at a lower elevation. This has been verified experimentally many times. This is because the clock at the lower altitude is deeper into the "gravitational well" of the Earth. The deeper into a gravitational well, the more the clocks slow down. So, when someone asks, how long did it take starlight to get here, we need to ask, "whose clocks?" Although this time dilation effect, as it is called, is not much today even for clocks far out into space, there is evidence that the universe has expanded greatly, and when it was much smaller time would have run much faster at the edge of the universe than in the center, which would be deep into the universe's "gravitational well." All these effects fall out using the same equations for General Relativity as the standard model. In this model light from distant stars would have plenty of time to reach earth where clocks would have been running slower. So, what effect makes this possible?

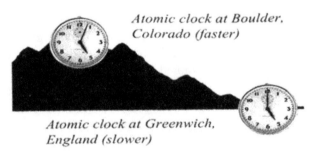

Atomic clock at Boulder, Colorado (faster)

Atomic clock at Greenwich, England (slower)

Gravitational Time Dilation: *The rate at which an atomic clock records time is diminished as gravity increases.*

Here we see an atomic clock placed at a high vs low altitude suffers enough time dilation to change time itself by about 5 microseconds. Time dilation occurs in space based on the mass of an object and its relation to space.

166

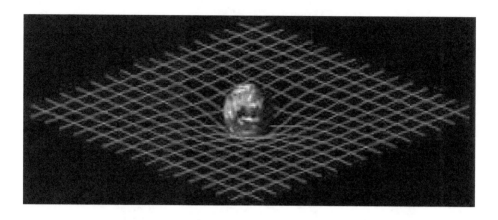

If the universe has a center, then there is a gravitational center of mass. If the universe has expanded, then at one time in the past there was the same amount of matter as today but packed into a smaller space. If the universe was smaller by a factor of fifty, as referenced by Humphreys...relativity allows it to either be inside a black hole or a white hole. All the matter would be contained inside what is called the event horizon of a black hole, the event horizon being where time is greatly slowed or stopped. But black holes do not expand. However, General Relativity allows for a white hole, which reverses the events, and unlike a black hole which holds everything in, the white hole requires that light and matter inside the event horizon expand out, and as they do, the event horizon shrinks in diameter. So, if you have a bounded universe, that has expanded, General Relativity indicates you have a white hole.

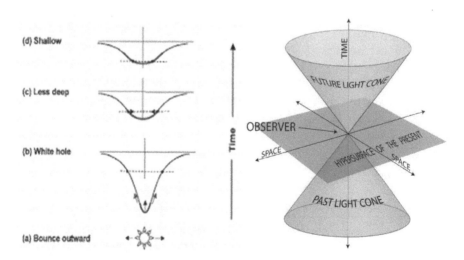

Above Figures: Since time would stand still below the event horizon, as the event horizon got smaller, it would eventually reach earth at the center, on day 4 if we go by the creation account, and while clocks were running fast in the distant universe, they would be stopped or running very slowly on Earth. So, you would see distant objects in the universe age billions of years, and light would have plenty of time to reach Earth. This may sound far-fetched, but it is theoretically sound.[300]

In 2007 Humphreys made some further modifications and came up with a modified version of the original model. He explains in this excerpt from his article referenced below:

> In November of 1915 Albert Einstein published the crowning conclusion of his General Theory of Relativity: a set of sixteen differential equations describing the gravitational field. Solutions to these equations are called *metrics*, because they show how distance-measuring and time-measuring devices (such as rulers and clocks) behave. The equations are so difficult to solve that new metrics, giving solutions under specific conditions, now appear only once every decade or so. Metrics are foundational; they open up new ways to understand space and time. For example, the first metric after Einstein's work, found by Karl Schwarzschild in 1916, not only explained the detailed orbits of planets, but also pointed to the possibility that black holes might exist. In the fall of 2007, I published a new metric as part of an explanation of the 'Pioneer anomaly', a decades-old mystery about the slowing-down of distant spacecraft. Compared to many modern metrics, the new one is rather simple. It describes space and time inside an expanding spherical shell of mass. I was interested in that problem because of the 'waters that are above the heavens' that Psalm 148:4 mentions as still existing today above the highest stars. The waters would be

---

[300] For a layman's summary in *Starlight and Time,* see pages 9-29; for a more technical explanation, see pages 83-128, quoted in John G. Hartnett, "A New Cosmology: Solution to the Starlight Travel Time Problem," Creation.com | Creation Ministries International, August 2003, https://creation.com/a-new-cosmology-solution-to-the-starlight-travel-time-problem)

moving outward along with the expansion of space mentioned in 17 Scripture passages.[301]

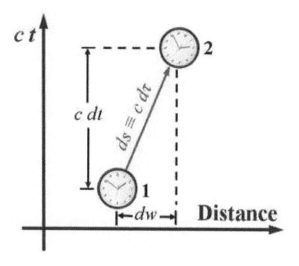

Above Figure: A moving clock measures the spacetime interval *ds* between two events.

According to data in my previous paper, the total mass of the shell of waters is greater than 8.8×10^{52} kg, more than 20 times the total mass of all the stars in all the galaxies the Hubble Space Telescope can observe. However, because the area of the shell is so great, more than 2×10^{53} m², the average areal density of the shell is less than 0.5 kg/m². By now the shell must have thinned out to a tenuous veil of ice particles, or perhaps broken up into planet-sized spheres of water with thick outer shells of ice. It is only the waters' great total mass that has an effect on us, small but now measurable.[302]

[301] D Russell Humphreys, "New Time Dilation Helps Creation Cosmology," *Journal of Creation*, quoted in John G. Hartnett, "A New Cosmology: Solution to the Starlight Travel Time Problem," Creation.com | Creation Ministries International, August 2003, (https://creation.com/a-new-cosmology-solution-to-the-starlight-travel-time-problem)
[302] Ibid.

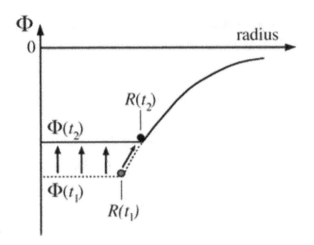

Above Figure: Gravitational potential F inside a spherical shell of mass increases as radius R of the shell increases between two events.

Because of the great mass of the 'waters above', I could neglect the smaller mass of all the galaxies in deriving the metric. Although other distributions of mass could also solve the Pioneer mystery, this one seems more applicable to biblical cosmology. Being relatively simple, the new metric clarifies a new type of time dilation that was implicit in previous metrics but obscured by the effects of motion. This new type, which I call *achronicity*, or 'timelessness', affects not only the narrow volume of space at or just around an 'event horizon' (the critical radius around a black hole at which time stops), but all the volume within the horizon. Within an achronous region, we will see, time is completely stopped. I pointed out a related effect, 'signature change,' in an earlier paper, but all I had to go on then was an older metric, the Klein metric, which was quite complicated. The complexity obscured what that metric suggested could happen to time. The cosmology this paper outlines is a new one that does not stem from the Klein metric."[303]

The new metric Humphreys derived in 2007 has yielded interesting results. One is a straightforward explanation of the Pioneer anomaly.[304] In this paper,

[303] Ibid.
[304] D Russell Humphreys, "Flaw in Creationist Solution to the Pioneer Anomaly?" Creation.com | Creation Ministries International, May 11, 2013,

it has revealed a new type of time dilation, achronicity. The fundamental cause of achronicity appears to be that gravitational potential becomes so negative that the total energy density of the fabric of space becomes negative. That stops the propagation of light, all physical processes, and all physical clocks, thus stopping time itself.

Humphreys has examined the effect only for essentially motionless bodies (having velocities very much less than that of light). He hopes to explore some of the interesting and possibly useful effects of achronicity for non-negligible particle velocities in the near future. The speculative scenario in the previous two sections shows how useful achronicity could be in creation cosmology. Other scenarios are easily possible, and Humphreys hopes that other creationists making alternative cosmologies will find timelessness a good tool."

This new model builds on Humphrey's previous models. As he shows above, it is based on a new solution (metric) of Einstein's General Relativity equations and allows for a new type of time dilation that is an even more powerful solution to the light time travel problem. He uses the illustration of space being stretched out like a trampoline, noting that there are many Bible verses that seem to speak of space as a kind of "material" that can be stretched, rolled, etc. And modern science has a concept of "material" for space as well. As mass of stars are added, it caused the fabric of space to drop below a critical timeless zone, and then as space is then stretched, the created stars and galaxies come out of the timeless zone, and their light follows that zone all the way back to Earth, which is the last to emerge from this timeless zone. What these models show is that there are several possibilities are viable within General Relativity, depending on your beginning assumptions, and that there are several which accommodate a young universe.

This model makes use of well-tested physics (GR) using alternate boundary conditions. Has the effect been significant enough to get starlight here in less than 10,000 years as YEC maintain? That of course is still to be seen. Even if Humphreys is wrong in his scientific interpretations, he has contributed significantly to cosmological studies and encouraged many others, notably Dr. John Hartnett, to further develop time-dilation models.[305] We know that presuppositions are important for the Big Bang theory, but Humphreys has

(https://creation.com/pioneer-anomaly-heat), quoted in Latorre, "Does Distant Starlight," (http://thebiblecanbeproven.com/does-distant-starlight-prove-a-billions-of-years-old-universe-part-6-of-series/)

[305] John W. Hartnett, *Starlight, Time and the New Physics: How We Can See Starlight in Our Young Universe* (Atlanta, GA: Creation Book Publishers, 2010)

worked this through in some detail. Furthermore, he has proven that with different presuppositions, different conclusions are possible. A door has opened. Christian students of cosmology will find this research a great stimulus to their own thinking and for this, Dr. Humphreys, Hartnett, and Lisle are to be commended.[306]

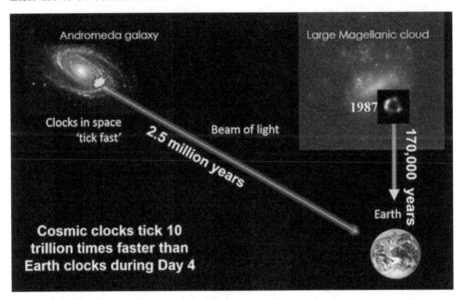

While Cosmological relativity is not yet generally accepted, it is a viable theory of physics that has already been shown to naturally explain several problems in cosmology, including some it was not developed to explain. It also results in a viable young Earth cosmology when applied to a bounded universe.... Harnett has also shown that observations are consistent with a bounded universe inside a white hole with our galaxy at or near the center. This is not to be confused with Dr Humphreys' White hole cosmology since in Hartnett's model the universe is still inside the white hole's event horizon. However, there are obvious similarities in the two cosmologies.[307]

Let's do a few simple calculations based on Dr. Hartnett's own dilation based on Humphreys' original model. Let us suppose that the relative rate of clocks on Earth compared to astronomical clocks during Creation Week was:

[306] Humphreys, "Hugh Ross Avoids," (https://www.icr.org/article/hugh-ross-avoids-debating-russ-humphreys-again/)

[307] "Cosmological Relativity," Cosmological relativity - CreationWiki, the encyclopedia of creation science, (http://creationwiki.org/Cosmological_relativity)

$$\frac{\partial t_0}{\partial t} = 10^{-13}$$

(1)

where t_0 represents time on Earth and t represents time in the cosmos (same for all clocks everywhere except on Earth). By integrating over the 24 hours of Day 4 (assuming = 0.003 years approximately), we can calculate the time available in the cosmos for a photon to travel to Earth. It follows from (1),

$$\int_0^t dt = \int_0^{0.003} \left(\frac{\partial t}{\partial t_0}\right) dt_0 = 10^{13}(0.003) = 30 \text{ billion years}$$

(2)

There is more than enough time during Creation Week. And since light now arriving on Earth left the stars some time during Creation Week, it had plenty of astronomical years to nearly get to Earth. The rest of the journey has been made in the 6,000-7500 years since creation. No accelerated speeds have been assumed, just the constant speed of light that has been repeatably measured for the past 300 years. It is not necessary to suppose that light from all stars in the universe arrived by the close of Creation Week, but at a minimum from our own Milky Way galaxy and maybe farther out to the Virgo Cluster of the order of 70 million light years. The specific dilation rate in (1) is an adjustable parameter of the model, which would determine the extent to how far starlight travelled during Day 4.[308]

The analysis here is mostly undisputable, though the conclusions may not be to the likings of OEC or some YEC theorists. Hartnett, motivated by Humphreys' work, utilized a cosmological relativity to use five dimensions instead of the traditional four dimensions (the fifth being the quantification of the velocity of the expansion of space itself). Hartnett's assumption means that the fabric of space is expanding, and the galaxies are going along for the ride. Good physics and good cosmology (Carmelian) make the YEC perspective plausible and viable.[309]

From the outside, much of what we see from a bounded vs. unbounded universe or time dilation can seem wild, but when compared to the multiverse or string theory, we have much more evidence for time dilation models than

---

[308] Hartnett, "A New Cosmology," (https://creation.com/a-new-cosmology-solution-to-the-starlight-travel-time-problem)

[309] Moshe Carmeli, "Aspects of Cosmological Relativity – PDF" (Beer Sheva, July 25, 1999, https://arxiv.org/pdf/gr-qc/9907080.pdf)

we do for the multiverse. This comes down to a worldview more than anything, as cosmologist George Ellis acknowledges:

> People need to be aware that there is a range of models that could explain the observations. For instance, I can construct you a spherically symmetrical universe with Earth at its center, and you cannot disprove it based on observations. You can only exclude it on philosophical grounds. In my view there is absolutely nothing wrong in that. What I want to bring into the open is the fact that we are using philosophical criteria in choosing our models. A lot of cosmology tries to hide that.[310]

The point of reviewing cosmogonies is to glimpse some of the great work done over the last twenty-five years in YEC cosmology, which is usually recognized as the biggest weakness in the YEC position. None of the OEC groups that I have talked to have a clue about the work Humphreys and others have done. While I find Humphreys' concept a little too *Star Trek like* in some ways, I find it more plausible than any of the multiverse hypotheses that so many of my skeptical (sometimes OEC) colleagues embrace.[311] What is good for the goose is good for the gander, as my grandfather use to say.

---

[310] W Wayt Gibbs, "Thinking Globally, Acting Universally," *Scientific American*, (1995, pp. 28-29)

[311] See *Star Trek: Voyager*/ "Blink of an Eye," (January 19, 2000) for an inverse example of Humphreys' cosmology.

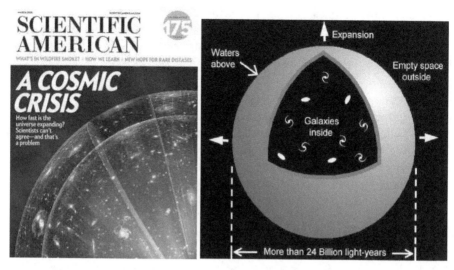

Compare the illustration of our universe from the March 2020 issue of Scientific American to a similar model from Russell Humphreys almost 15 years earlier. Both portray the universe as bounded and finite and ironically in this issue of Scientific American, they admit our current physics is insufficient to support a naturalistic model of the universe.[312]

Ironically, the March 2020 issue of Scientific American ran a cover story on "a cosmic crisis" where Richard Panek describes the same points that Harnett has been discussing for well over a decade. Like Hartnett, Scientific American acknowledges that not only is dark energy and dark matter complete conjecture that makes up about 95% of what we know about the universe, but that we are highly in need of some type of "new physics" (or metaphysics) for us to better understand cosmology today:

> If the source of the Hubble tension is not in the observation of either the late universe or the early universe, then cosmologists have little choice but to pursue option three: "new physics." For nearly a century now scientists have been talking about new physics – forces or phenomena that would fall outside our current knowledge of the universe.[313]

---

[312] https://www.scientificamerican.com/magazine/sa/2020/03-01/
[313] *Scientific American*, "A Cosmic Crisis". March 2020 by Richard Panek.

Could this "new physics" fall in line with Humphreys or Hartnett's work? Time will tell. Likewise, I recently reviewed an article by noted physicist Sean Carroll on space-time in the September 2019 edition of *New Scientist*, in which Carroll rightly acknowledges:

> Space-time is simply the physical universe inside which we and everything else exists. And yet, even after millennia living in it, we still don't know what space-time actually is... We have ideas, each with its own selling points and shortcomings. How in the world can space-time exist in a superposition of different possibilities? That would make it impossible to say for sure that a certain event happened at a definite location in space and time.[314]

If anything, Humphreys' model is meeting the same time dilation problem Carroll discusses head-on, in a way that many OEC groups never have. OEC groups usually cling to the proverbial coat tails of naturalistic scientists and use those same theories but posit God at the beginning, letting their theology and the social sciences fall by the wayside. While OEC cosmology could be true, it seems lazy not to develop one's own cosmological theory. Perhaps OEC theorists are right, but YEC groups are doing good work and analyses. Hugh Ross has said that we know the universe is 13.7B years and that this date will never be adjusted by much, but as of the Fall of 2019, it appears that the universe may be closer to 11.4B years. It will be interesting to see if Ross and others adjust their findings and concordist views or not.

As long as OEC theorists debate YEC scientists that use 20th century, outdated arguments, they will come out looking like the stronger position. The five-hour debate between Ross and Faulkner, followed by a critical analysis and dialogue by a handful of OEC astronomers and cosmologists, showed why the AIG viewpoint of YEC cosmology is somewhat weaker than it should be.[315] It was no coincidence that Dr. Ross chose not to debate Dr. Humphreys and instead chose the easier target of AIG.[316,317] Dr. Humphreys has defended

---

[314] Sean Carroll, "What Is Space-Time? The True Origins of the Fabric of Reality, *New Scientist*, September 11, 2019, (https://www.newscientist.com/article/mg24332470-500-what-is-space-time-the-true-origins-of-the-fabric-of-reality/)

[315] *Hugh Ross vs. Danny Faulkner - How Old Is the Universe?* YouTube (Sentinel Apologetics, 2018), (https://www.youtube.com/watch?v=4vPMcOEnlMY)

[316] Humphreys, "Hugh Ross Avoids," (https://www.icr.org/article/hugh-ross-avoids-debating-russ-humphreys-again/)

[317] I respect Dr. Faulkner, AIG, and ICR, but we must push these groups beyond their own preconceived understandings of 20th century YEC.

his views against several OEC groups and where needed has modified his theory. I see Humphreys' white hole cosmology as a monumental first step towards the correct understanding of the universe, but as Humphreys has acknowledged, his work was just the beginning. He hoped to encourage others to look into this new direction of creation cosmology and that, too, is my hope. Humphreys is going in the right direction if YEC groups like AIG and OEC groups have ears to hear and an open, biblical mind.

Prediction 2 – Is the YEC theory of Noah's flood viable?

I begin this section by reflecting on *Bretz's Flood: The Remarkable Story of a Rebel Geologist and the World's Greatest Flood.*[318] In this remarkable story (and the documentary), Bretz, though atheistic, is attacked for suggesting certain elements of the biblical account are true. This is a recurring theme throughout the historiography of science; doubly ironic is the OEC endorsement of many such attacks. Even *Discover Magazine* said, "Geologists long rejected the notion that cataclysmic flood had ever occurred—until one of them found proof of a Noah-like catastrophe in the wildly eroded river valleys of Washington State."[319]

Dry Falls picture (left) and the Grand Canyon of Arkansas (right). Ironically, when I ask colleagues if there really was a global flood, would what we see in geology and geography be what you would expect? They always say yes, though they remain skeptical, as do OEC theorists.[320]

American geologist J. Harlen Bretz (1882–1981), who mapped the scablands, proposed in various papers published between the years 1919 to 1925, a controversial hypothesis to explain the genesis of this unique landscape: "A flood of unprecedented dimensions eroded the scablands into the solid bedrock."[321]

---

[318] Soennichsen, *Bretz's Flood.*

[319] David R Montgomery, "Biblical-Type Floods Are Real, and They're Absolutely Enormous," Discover, April 29, 2012, (http://discovermagazine.com/2012/jul-aug/06-biblical-type-floods-real-absolutely-enormous)

[320] "Evidence of the Huge Lake and Catastrophic Floods Is Scattered Over Four Western States," HugeFloods.com, (http://hugefloods.angelfire.com/Ice-Age-Floods-5.html), (photo Tom Foster)

[321] David Bressan, "A Concise History of Geological Maps: Mapping Noah's Flood," *Scientific American* (blog), April 10, 2014, (https://blogs.scientificamerican.com/history-of-geology/a-concise-history-of-geological-maps-mapping-noahe28099s-flood/)

No one with an eye for land forms can cross eastern Washington in daylight without encountering and being impressed by the "scabland." Like great scars marring the otherwise fair face to the plateau are these elongated tracts of bare, black rock carved into mazes of buttes and canyons. Everybody on the plateau knows scabland...The popular name is a metaphor. The scablands are wounds only partially healed – great wounds in the epidermis of soil with which Nature protects the underlying rock...The region is unique: let the observer take wings of the morning to the uttermost parts of the earth: he will nowhere find its likeness.[322]

The Geological Society of Washington, D.C., invited Bretz to present his previously published research at a January 12, 1927, meeting, in which several geologists presented competing theories. Bretz considered it an ambush and referred to the group as six "challenging elders." They intended to defeat him in a public debate and end the challenge his theories posed to their conservative interpretation of uniformitarianism. Another geologist at the meeting, J.T. Pardee, had worked with Bretz and had evidence of an ancient glacial lake that lent credence to Bretz's theories. Pardee, however, lacked the academic freedom of Bretz and did not enter the fray. Bretz defended his theories, kicking off an acrimonious forty-year debate over the origin of the Scablands. As he wrote in 1928, "Ideas without precedent are generally looked upon with disfavor and men are shocked if their conceptions of an orderly world are challenged."[323]

Bretz...proposed that huge geologic features in America's Pacific Northwest were formed by catastrophic water flow. He named the Channeled Scablands, with its catastrophically water-carved coulees, dry waterfalls, potholes and huge erratic boulders. At that time, most scientists believed these geologic features were formed by gradual erosion and deposition following the notion of uniformitarianism, which ruled out sudden changes in the landscape by catastrophic events. For most of 40 years, two things prevented the scientific community from accepting Bretz's theory. First, his peers did not come to the Northwest to personally check Bretz's findings. Second, a source for the required humongous water flow had not been identified.... The strong attitude of his superiors not to rock the boat and his job

---

[322] Soennichsen, *Bretz's Flood.*
[323] Quote engraved on monument outside the Dry Falls Museum in Coulee City, WA

security may have prevented him from making it known for almost 40 years.[324]

Today, Bretz's theory is recognized as true; a flood of unprecedented proportions known as the Missoula Flood did indeed occur.

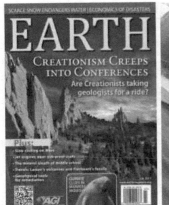

Dr. John Baumgardner, the author, and others touring the unique geologic features of southern Utah (April 2019).

Now take what we read about Bretz and apply it to today. This is why it is important to look at facts instead of popular opinion or the establishment. John Baumgardner is recognized as one of the top geophysicists of the world and has done much to advance a flood model based on a YEC foundation. It was refreshing to read the cover on a 2011 issue of *Earth* magazine: "Creationism Creeps into Conferences."[325]

> In almost every way, the "Garden of the Gods at Colorado Springs" excursion at the annual meeting of the Geological Society of America (GSA) last year was normal – even enjoyable – field trip. But in reality, the trip was <u>anything</u> but a normal geology field trip. Instead, it was an example of a new strategy from creationists to interject their ideas into mainstream geology: They lead field trips and present posters and talks at scientific meetings. They also avoid overtly

[324] Dennis B. Bokovoy, "The Mystery of the Megaflood," Creation.com | Creation Ministries International, September 28, 2005, (https://creation.com/the-mystery-of-the-megaflood)
[325] Steven Newton, "Creationism Creeps into Mainstream Geology," EARTH Magazine, March 28, 2014, (https://www.earthmagazine.org/article/creationism-creeps-mainstream-geology)

stating anything truly contrary to mainstream science. Many attendees seemed unaware of the backgrounds of the five trip co-leaders: Steven Austin, Marcus Ross, Tim Clarey, John Whitmore and Bill Hoesch. The University of Rhode Island even granted [Ross] a doctorate in geology in 2006 even though he professed that Earth was at most 10,000 years old![326]

It is almost comical the way they admit there is nothing wrong with their science except their own prejudices, not based on evidence but on their worldview (many of which are OEC and not atheistic). The article's writers commit a genetic fallacy at least once on every page of this peer-reviewed article. On a good note, however, they conclude by saying, "Geology will not suffer if creationists participate in our meetings, but public relations damage from the misperception that we are systematically hostile [to them] is real."[327] This is a half-truth, as YEC theorists are often discriminated against; in 2017, YEC geologist Andrew Snelling was denied permission to continue research and sample gathering in the Grand Canyon. The courts determined it was due to discrimination against his YEC beliefs.[328]

When I look through 1980's articles by the National Academy of Science or the National Center for Science Education, I see "Six Flood Arguments Creationists Can't Answer," and I find that these arguments have all been answered and overturned.[329] Since 1960s, we have seen a decade-by-decade refining of YEC theorists' arguments for a recent and global biblical flood that has done nothing but grow in plausibility and explanatory scope.

I am not going to provide a detailed breakdown for creationist geology, nor am I going to choose one model that fits the data best. Instead I will show three theories from a YEC perspective to show how the field has grown and matured over the last fifty years. There are other good, speculative, geologic theories, such as expanding earth theory and shock dynamics geology theory,

---

[326] Ibid., 32-7.
[327] Ibid.
[328] Amanda Reilly, "Update: Creationist Geologist Wins Permit to Collect Rocks in Grand Canyon after Lawsuit," Science, December 8, 2017, (https://www.sciencemag.org/news/2017/06/update-creationist-geologist-wins-permit-collect-rocks-grand-canyon-after-lawsuit)
[329] Robert J Shadewald, ed., "Six 'Flood' Arguments Creationists Can't Answer" National Center for Science Education | National Center for Science Education, November 24, 2008, (https://ncse.ngo/cej/3/3/six-flood-arguments-creationists-cant-answer)

and I encourage readers to investigate those as well, though my focus will remain on the following three models:

1. Catastrophic plate tectonics (CPT)

2. Hydroplate theory (HPT)

3. Canopy theory (CT)

I am grateful to be able to work with John Baumgardner, founder of CPT, Walt Brown, founder of HPT and various others on differing canopy theories. I was also able to explore these theories in my post-graduate studies from a secular lens. CPT and HPT have grown in intellectual integrity, even with their YEC underpinnings. Special thanks to Logos Research Associates and the many people in Utah and Arizona that helped me do fieldwork on these topics, as well as those that helped me better analyze Iceland's 1996 flood.

The author with Steve Austin (geologist) in Utah, surveying Snow Canyon Overlook. "Cementing in mounds and cross-bedded sandstone is remarkably uniform and hard, showing that the cement was uniformly dissolved throughout water that saturated the sand."[330] Is PT, CPT, or HPT a better explanation for such features?

Before we jump into a YEC understanding of the Flood and whether the models are plausible and provide a greater explanatory scope than do the various naturalistic OEC viewpoints, let's review the concept of a local flood. Many OEC theorists think the Flood was a local flood, confined to the area around Mesopotamia. This idea comes not from Scripture or the social

---

[330] "Liquefaction During the Compression Event," In the Beginning: Compelling Evidence for Creation and the Flood, (Center for Scientific Creation, February 27, 2020), (https://www.creationscience.com/onlinebook/Liquefaction7.html)

sciences, but from an inference of "billions of years" within Earth history. This is why if Hugh Ross rejects a recent creation cosmology then he must also deny (or redefine) a global flood, Tower of Babel, and a literal Adam and Eve if he wishes to be consistent with his OEC. If you want to prove a 4.6 billion-year-old earth, then you cannot support a global flood, as Ross and I have discussed.[331] Let's analyze the concept of the local flood hypothesis and some of the problems it creates:

- If the Flood was local, why did Noah have to build an Ark? He could have walked to the other side of the mountains and missed it.
- If the Flood was local, why did God send the animals to the Ark so they would escape death? There would have been other animals to reproduce that kind if these particular ones had died.
- If the Flood was local, why was the Ark big enough to hold all kinds of land vertebrate animals that have ever existed? If only Mesopotamian animals were aboard, the Ark could have been much smaller.
- If the Flood was local, why would birds have been sent on board? These could simply have winged across to a nearby mountain range.
- If the Flood was local, how could the waters rise to 15 cubits (8 meters) above the mountains (Genesis 7:20)? Water seeks its own level. It couldn't rise to cover the local mountains while leaving the rest of the world untouched.
- If the Flood was local, people who did not happen to be living in the vicinity would not be affected by it. They would have escaped God's judgment on sin. If this happened, what did Christ mean when He likened the coming judgment of all men to the judgment of 'all' men (Matthew 24:37–39) in the days of Noah?
- If the Flood was local, God would have repeatedly broken His promise never to send such a flood again.[332]

These are questions that should pop into our heads when we hear an argument for a local flood. There are some good, secular reasons for avoiding a global flood, but perhaps the elites of academia are just afraid a global flood sounds too biblical. Their answer during Bretz's time was, "No! It's because he is wrong!" But later it was acknowledged that it was because it sounded too biblical. It could be the same today.

---

[331] I have suggested to Ross that he can keep his 13.7 billion-year creation, but why reinvent everything else? As a concordist, he argues it's all or nothing. If you want 13.7 billion years, you need to jettison it all to be consistent.

[332] "Noah's Flood Covered the Whole Earth," Creation.com | Creation Ministries International, June 1999, (https://creation.com/noahs-flood-covered-the-whole-earth)

Traditionally, for scientists operating from a naturalistic premise, the geological sciences have provided the chronological framework to allow other scientific disciplines to place their data in an historical context. The main principle of uniformitarianism has motivated research into present geological processes so that rocks these scientists regard as ancient can be interpreted in terms of such processes. In the last thirty years there has been a major shift in thinking amongst evolutionary geologists with the development of plate tectonics—all modern geological processes are now seen as part of a global interaction of plate tectonics, which itself has been adopted as the interpretative geological paradigm.

> By contrast, scientists working from a YEC perspective view all significant geological events within a Biblical chronological framework. Nevertheless, there is still a need for scientific models of these events because the Biblical record is not exhaustive, nor is it intended as a scientific treatise. In particular, creation scientists need to understand the Biblical Flood by addressing the hydrology and sedimentation that occurred during the cataclysm and in the subsequent years as the Earth settled down. Modern geological processes, while instructive, do not have the same standing as for long-age uniformitarian scientists. This is because geological processes during Creation and the Flood were different from what we observe today. So creationists have a greater need to develop an integrated approach from many scientific disciplines. As well as the geological sciences, inputs from many other disciplines are needed, such as fluid flow, heat transfer, plate tectonics, volcanology, planetary astronomy, and mathematics.[333]

On a good note, the scientific study of the seaworthiness of the Ark has all but been settled. I give AIG credit for building a scale model of Noah's Ark so one can get an idea of the meticulous dimensions listed in Genesis. Once we bounce this against what we know of sea vessel design, it is mind-boggling how accurate the Book of Genesis is:

> Noah's Ark was the focus of a major 1993 scientific study headed by Dr. Seon Hong at the world-class ship research center KRISO, based in Daejeon, South Korea. Dr. Hong's

---

[333] Andy McIntosh, Steve Taylor, and Tom Edmondson, "Flood Models: The Need for an Integrated Approach," Answers in Genesis, April 1, 2000, (https://answersingenesis.org/the-flood/flood-models-the-need-for-an-integrated-approach/)

team compared twelve hulls of different proportions to discover which design was most practical. No hull shape was found to significantly outperform the 4,300-year-old biblical design. In fact, the Ark's careful balance is easily lost if the proportions are modified, rendering the vessel either unstable, prone to fracture, or dangerously uncomfortable. The study also confirmed that the Ark could handle waves as high as 100ft.[334]

The Bible got it right, it seems, so now the question is more about the Flood and the models describing it. Let's review the top three models popularly held by YEC theorists for plausibility and explanatory scope. I encourage careful scrutiny of all the interpretations so that we can make informed decisions.

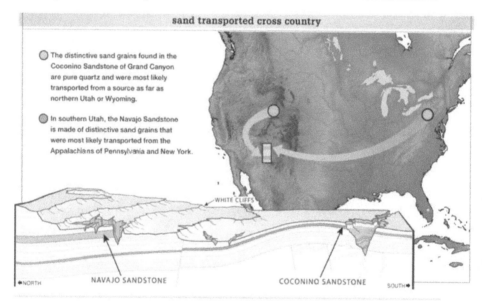

It is mostly agreed today that wind deposition (cross-beds) would have an angle of around 32 degrees but if underwater closer to 20 degrees. The Coconino appears closer to 20; similarly, the Navajo sandstone wide array of depositions across the country would seem to lean towards a global flood (not just wind) as a better explanation to what we see. So which theory best takes this into consideration?[335]

[334] Tim Lovett, "Thinking Outside the Box: Size and Shape of the Ark," Answers in Genesis, March 19, 2007, (https://answersingenesis.org/noahs-ark/thinking-outside-the-box/)
[335] https://answersingenesis.org/geology/rock-layers/sedimentary-layers-show-millions-of-years-of-geological-activity/ (special thanks personal Ray Strom and John Whitmore)

Both hydroplate theory (HPT) and catastrophic plate tectonics (CPT) have continued to grow in explanatory scope and plausibility while canopy theory (CT) has fallen out of favor. John Morris (son of Henry Morris and president of ICR) has said even though "all evidence is against CT he still holds to it in some ways."[336] While there is nothing wrong with this, it shows how bias can hurt scientific inquiry. Though Morris recognizes the weakness of CT, he maintains it because his father and ICR have long maintained it. I continue to encourage Christians not to look exclusively to AIG or ICR as the voice of YEC theorists. If these groups were holistically biblical, they wouldn't hold to any man-made theory so tightly, but as the Bible warns, man's egotism and hubris often forms more of a hinderance than a support to the Christian cause.[337] Let's review these competing, but not mutually exclusive, flood-theories.[338]

---

[336] *RSR's Global Flood and Hydroplate Theory* (YouTube, 2018),
(https://www.youtube.com/watch?v=tpQSPaJ-X_U&feature=youtu.be&t=6680)
[337] "Creation Controversy," Kevin Lea's Report, (https://creation-controversy.com/)
[338] Special thanks to: Jonathan Sarfati, "Flood Models and Biblical Realism," Creation.com | Creation Ministries International, December 2010, (https://creation.com/flood-models-biblical-realism)

Canopy Theory (CT)

The canopy theory, as a model for the beginning of the Flood, aligns strongly with the 20th century concept of an "antediluvian paradise" where the world was literally perfect before the Fall of Adam and Eve. This asserts that the "waters above" most likely referred to a canopy of water vapor, which condensed and collapsed to provide most of the rain for the Genesis Flood. A few decades ago, this was very popular since it seemed to explain many things about rain, rainbows and longevity. Now it is rejected by most informed creationists but often times referenced by OEC, which only show they are working with outdated materials.[339]

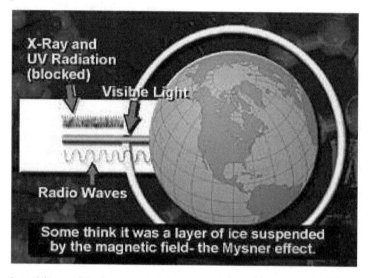

The real problem with the canopy theory was that some creationists gave the impression that it was a direct teaching of Scripture; Creation Ministries International (CMI) cautioned against such dogmatism back in 1989 when the model was still very popular among many creationist writers. After all, for most of church history, no one had seen a canopy in the actual text of Scripture... Furthermore, it seems to contradict Scripture, since Psalm 148:4 says: "Praise him, you highest heavens, and you waters above the heavens!" Clearly these waters could not have been a canopy that collapsed during the Flood since they were still present during the time of the Psalmist over a thousand years later.

---

[339] Johnathon Sarfati, "Noah: The Man, The Ark, The Flood," *Digging Deeper Links For,* (https://www.stmatthewmilan.org/web_documents/noah_digdeep.pdf)

Many of the arguments for the canopy were also faulty on scientific grounds. For example, one argument is that the canopy would protect us from damaging radiation and explain the extremely long lifespans recorded in Genesis. But water vapor is obviously not a great shield from UV. When it comes to cosmic radiation, there is no evidence that this is involved in longevity, and as stated above, the cause of decreasing lifespans was genetic rather than environmental.

What water absorbs very well is infrared, as any vibrational spectroscopist knows. It is actually a far more important greenhouse gas than CO_2, accounting for about 66% of the atmospheric greenhouse effect on Earth, or maybe even as much as 95%. This leads to the major scientific problem with the canopy theory—a water vapor canopy thick enough to provide more than about a meter's worth of floodwater would cook the earth.[340]

The Canopy Theory in a Nutshell

The canopy theory is an honorable attempt to interpret Scripture correctly, and to account for the waters of the Flood. The theory starts with Day Two of the creation week:

> Then God said, "Let there be a firmament in the midst of the waters, and let it divide the waters from the waters." Thus God made the firmament, and divided the waters, which *were* under the firmament from the waters, which *were* above the firmament; and it was so. And God called the firmament Heaven. So the evening and the morning were the second day. (Genesis 1:6-8)

This passage is clearly talking about the creation of a firmament and the division of waters into waters above and below the firmament. The basis of the Canopy Theory is that the firmament represents the Earth's atmosphere and the waters above are in the form of a canopy, which surrounded the Earth before the Flood. It is thought that this canopy could have been the source, or at least a source, for the waters of the Flood. The Flood would have been initiated, therefore, by the collapse of this canopy. It is thought that the pre-Flood canopy would have caused conditions of environment and weather before the Flood to be very different from those of today. The actual nature of the canopy differs in competing interpretations, with some assuming it to

---

[340] Ibid.

be a canopy of water vapor, and others suggesting a crystalline canopy. It must be emphasized that many creationists have held to and taught the Canopy Theory in the past. In quoting a number of great creationist writers, who supported the Canopy Theory, it must not be thought that I am intending to be disrespectful of their position. My rejection of their support for the Canopy Theory is merely an indication that our understanding moves on and should not be taken to imply anything other than the immense respect that I have for such thinkers.

Primary among these has to be the late Dr. Henry Morris, the father of modern creationism. In his wonderful book, *The Genesis Record*, he writes:

> The "waters above the firmament" thus probably constituted a vast blanket of water vapor above the troposphere and possibly above the stratosphere as well, in the high-temperature region now known as the ionosphere and extending far into space.

Dr. Morris went on to list some of the ways in which a vapor canopy might have made pre-Flood conditions different from today. These include:

- Uniform world temperatures
- Uniform warmth
- Shielding cosmic radiation, leading to longer pre-Flood lifespans
- Uniform worldwide moisture, with no deserts or ice caps

In 1976, Morris was satisfied that such a vapor canopy would provide the water required for the Flood.

> A worldwide rain lasting forty days would be quite impossible under present atmospheric conditions; so this phenomenon required an utterly different source of atmospheric waters than now obtains. This we have already seen to be the "waters above the firmament", the vast thermal blanket of invisible water vapor that maintained the greenhouse effect in the antediluvian world. These waters somehow were to condense and fall on the earth.[341]

---

[341] Henry M. Morris, *The Genesis Record: a Scientific and Devotional Commentary on the Book of Beginnings* (Grand Rapids, MI: Baker Book House, 2009), quoted in "Explaining the Flood without the Canopy," Creation Today, (https://creationtoday.org/explaining-the-flood-without-the-canopy/)

Problems with the Canopy Theory

A number of significant scientific problems have come to light, which cast doubt on the canopy theory. Canopy theorists have used the canopy concept to explain a number of pre-Flood effects. For example, they have suggested that the canopy would have increased atmospheric pressure at the Earth's surface. They claim that this would affect pre-Flood life. Genesis 6 refers to "giants," and it is suggested that humans would not have been able to grow to giant height without increased pressure. However, giant height of seven or eight feet is completely feasible with normal atmospheric pressure. Canopy theorists have also claimed that the giant insects seen in the fossil record would not have been able to breathe without increased oxygen partial pressure. Again, this can be shown not to be the case. Indeed, increased oxygen partial pressure can actually be shown to have a deleterious effect on longevity of humans.

> On the subject of longevity, it has been suggested that the longevity of humans before the Flood was due to greater atmospheric pressure. However, a better explanation of this longevity is the comparative absence of mutations among the human gene pool. The level of mutations would have greatly increased after the Flood, so this could explain the rapid decrease in longevity. Scientist Dr. Larry Vardiman has taken a close interest in the canopy theory, having calculated many different models for how it could have worked. To the best of my knowledge, he still holds to a version of the canopy theory. Nevertheless, his research has pointed out a number of problems with the theory.
>
> It must be remembered that water vapor is probably the most significant of the so-called "greenhouse gases." So any vapor canopy would trap more heat from the sun, leading to increased temperatures at the Earth's surface. Vardiman's computer models showed that "any canopy containing more than about 20 inches (51 cm) of water produced such a strong greenhouse effect that surface temperatures became unsuitable for life." Vardiman proposed that cirrus clouds near the top of the canopy could have helped against this effect, but other researchers, such as Andrew Snelling, have

suggested that these would mitigate insufficiently the problems caused by the canopy.[342]

Similarly, Dr. Walt Brown showed canopy theory to be bad science in the 1980s. Henry Morris (ICR) broke ties with Dr. Brown because he was more committed to a humanistic theory more than biblical and scientific correction.[343]

Clearly, 20 inches of water is insufficient to explain the water of the Flood. However, even if further factors are introduced to allow the canopy to increase in size, it is still only possible to produce a canopy that would deposit one meter of water on the Earth. Some creationists have suggested that the canopy would not therefore be the only source of water. This indeed makes sense. A better model for how the Flood began is catastrophic plate tectonics or Hydroplate theory models, which shows that the major source of water would probably have been within the mantle. But, if no canopy can be proposed that would represent a significant percentage of the water required for the Flood, one wonders why one needs a canopy theory at all, especially as we now move on to some Scriptural objections to the canopy theory. These arguments are significant. If a few scientific results looked problematic, but we could show that Scripture clearly taught a canopy, then we would know that the scientific results were currently incomplete, and we would trust Scripture. However, it is obvious that the canopy is not required by Scripture, and is even probably incorrect, according to Scripture….

It has been hard for many modern creationists to let go of the vapor canopy theory. Dr. Carl Wieland expressed this emotional difficulty, in answering a critic on the Creation Ministries International website. While showing why the canopy theory does not make sense, Dr. Wieland admitted: "Having lectured using the 'canopy' idea many years ago, I can certainly understand its appeal. Emotionally, it was hard

---

[342] "Explaining the Flood without the Canopy," Creation Today, (https://creationtoday.org/explaining-the-flood-without-the-canopy/)
[343] "Vapor Canopy and the Hydroplate Theory," Albright's Flood Models Controversy Series | KGOV.com, July 22, 2016, (https://kgov.com/vapor-canopy-theory-jane-albright-series-on-global-flood-models-controversy)

to 'let go.'"[344] I had similar emotions. Nevertheless, we must face the fact that the canopy theory was not Scripture, but rather a scientific model to aid our understanding. Scriptural analysis and modern scientific understandings both show that the canopy model is not necessary. It seems today that the effects, for which the canopy theory was developed to explain, are actually better explained by other means.[345]

Good, self-correcting science will eliminate weaker theories. Walt Brown single-handedly helped put the proverbial nail in the coffin for canopy theory back in the 1980s, which ultimately cost him his job with ICR. Henry Morris was more worried about his own published stance supporting canopy theory over the truth, but the truth is persistent. Today, canopy theory is rejected by almost all creationists. Even the son of the late Henry Morris, John Morris, has acknowledged that the evidence is against them, though he still hopes it is true.[346] This shows how jaded and hypocritical many creationists are, despite the evidence and biblical exegesis. While it is still possible to salvage the canopy theory, neither Kent Hovind nor anyone from ICR has anything to lose abandoning an old theory that no longer can be deemed biblical or scientific. We should thank Walt Brown for his constant push towards biblical and scientific truth, even if it cost him his job and apologetics career.

> Canopy theories have misled many, delaying understanding of the flood, geology, and, therefore, earth's true age. The flood water came from below, not above. Failure to understand this has caused many to doubt the historical accuracy of the flood to explain the fossils buried in the earth's sedimentary layers, the theory of organic evolution fills the vacuum – an explanation that also removes or minimizes need for the Creator.[347]

---

[344] Carl Wieland, "Blame CMI? And What about the 'Canopy' Theory?" Creation.com | Creation Ministries International, April 17, 2010, (http://creation.com/cannot-blame-cmi), quoted in "Explaining the Flood without the Canopy," Creation Today, (https://creationtoday.org/explaining-the-flood-without-the-canopy/)

[345] "Explaining the Flood," (https://creationtoday.org/explaining-the-flood-without-the-canopy/)

[346] "Vapor Canopy," (https://kgov.com/vapor-canopy-theory-jane-albright-series-on-global-flood-models-controversy)

[347] Walt Brown. *In the Beginning.*

While I respect Kent Hovind and ICR, both are likely false in their attempt to resurrect this type canopy theory. Now let us put our focus on the two remaining theories—CPT and HPT.

Catastrophic Plate Tectonics (CPT)

This is probably the most popular model among informed creationists today. This accepts much of the evidence adduced to support uniformitarian plate tectonics but solves a number of problems. The CPT model begins with a pre-Flood super-continent (possibly indicated by Genesis 1:9 and maintained by most secular geologists). While uniformitarian models assume that the ocean plates have always had the temperature profile they display today, the CPT model starts with some additional cold rock in regions just offshore surrounding the supercontinent. Since this rock was colder, it was denser than the mantle below. At the start of the Flood year, this began to sink.

But how can it sink more rapidly than ocean plate subducts today? The answer lies in laboratory experiments that show that the silicate minerals that make up the mantle can weaken dramatically, by factors of a billion or more, at mantle temperatures and stresses. If a cold blob of rock is sufficiently large, it can enter a regime in which the stresses in the envelope surrounding it become large enough to weaken the rock in that envelope, which allows the blob to sink faster, resulting in the stresses becoming a bit larger still, and causing the rock inside the surrounding envelope to weaken even more. Moreover, as the blob sinks ever faster, the volume of the envelope of weakened rock grows ever larger. Rather quickly the sinking velocity of the blob of dense rock can reach values of several km/hour, on the order of a billion times faster than is happening today. This is called *runaway subduction*.[348]

---

[348] Sarfati, "Flood Models," (https://creation.com/flood-models-biblical-realism)

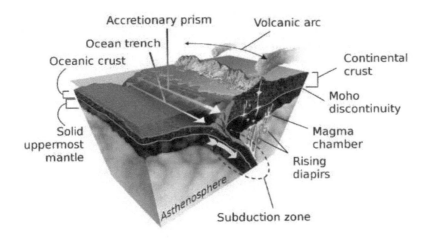

Top – Diagram of the geological process of subduction.[349] **Bottom** – Baumgardner's CPT model showing the computational viability of runaway subduction being a driving mechanism for the Genesis Flood.[350]

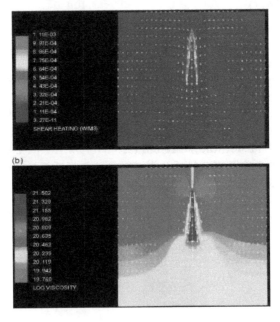

---

[349] K D Schroeder, "Subduction-en.svg," *Wikimedia Commons* (Creative Commons Attribution-ShareAlike 4.0, May 26, 2016),
(https://commons.wikimedia.org/wiki/File:Subduction-en.svg)
[350] "John Baumgardner," LogosResearchers, (https://www.logosresearchassociates.org/john-baumgardner)

The sinking ocean floor would drag the rest of the floor along, in conveyor belt fashion, and displace mantle material, starting large-scale movement throughout the entire mantle. However, as the ocean floor sank and rapidly subducted adjacent to the pre-Flood super-continent's margins, elsewhere the earth's crust would be under such tensional stress that it would be torn apart (rifted), breaking up both the pre-Flood super-continent and the ocean floor.

> Thus, ocean plates separated along some 60,000 km where seafloor spreading was occurring. Within these spreading zones hot mantle material was rising to the surface to fill the gap caused by the rapidly separating plates. Being at the ocean bottom, this hot mantle material vaporized copious amounts of ocean water, producing a linear chain of superheated steam jets along the whole length of the spreading ridge system. This is consistent with the biblical description of the "fountains of the great deep" (Genesis 7:11; 8:2). This steam would disperse, condensing in the atmosphere to fall as intense global rain ("and the flood-gates of heaven were opened", Genesis 7:11). This could account for the rain persisting for 40 days and 40 nights (Genesis 7:12).

> Not only is CPT backed up by supercomputer modelling that even impresses uniformitarians, but it has also provided further fruitful research avenues for creationists, including a mechanism for Earth's rapid magnetic field reversals and hydrothermal solutions to carve huge caves. All the same, weather experts have been modelling the weather for decades, yet there are still many flaws; some argue that we should not place too much faith in modelling for plate tectonics either. Defenders argue that there are fewer unknowns in a confined solid-state modelling of CPT than in the fluid (liquid and gas) dynamics and variable solar activity modelled in weather simulations. [351]

I regularly correspond with Dr. Baumgardner on many of these points, and his research is recognized by many secular publications.

[351] Sarfati, "Flood Models," (https://creation.com/flood-models-biblical-realism)

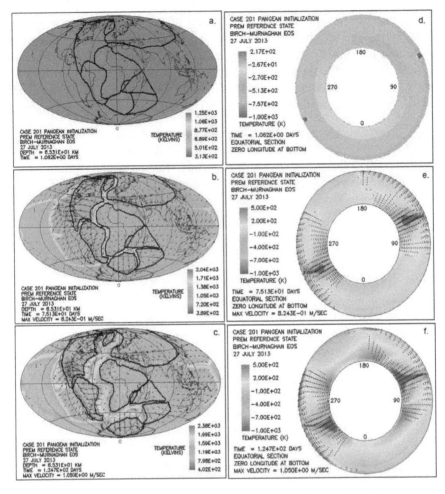

Numerical simulation of the CPT process in 3D spherical shell geometry suggests that subduction of the pre-Flood ocean lithosphere around a pre-Flood supercontinent (Pangea) leads to a distribution of continents similar to today's earth. Baumgardner's design of this computer program used by geophysicists worldwide, has led to a higher degree of credibility for creation scientists.

Dr. Baumgardner has continued to revise his theory through refining and self-criticism as well as working with many other professional geologists, physicists and earth scientists makes CPT one of the most promising theories, explaining the data supporting uniformitarian plate tectonics, and solving a number of its problems. Its strong points include explaining high-pressure minerals and simultaneous uplift of all of today's high mountains.

Furthermore, under Uniformitarian PT, plates are moving too slowly to penetrate past the upper layers of the mantle; rather, they should blend in long before they reach the lower mantle. Yet studies show that the subducted plates have penetrated much further and are still relatively cool. This is consistent with the subduction being fast enough to penetrate the mantle, and recently enough so they haven't had time to heat up.

> But CPT is not a direct teaching of Scripture, so it is legitimate for creationists to question or reject it as a model, and a number of knowledgeable creationist geologists and engineers like Walt Brown do. Opponents argue that it concedes too much to uniformitarianism, and that it doesn't explain the whole of the Flood like a theory such as Hydroplate theory potentially does.[352]

In the plus column, we have confirmed,

> There is a ring of relatively cool material in the lower mantle that corresponds to past and present subduction zones surrounding a hot zone under the Pacific, and hotter material being squeezed up under Africa as predicted by Catastrophic plate tectonics. A more recent discovery of a slab of oceanic crust in the lower mantle was also predicted by Catastrophic plate tectonics. No other theory predicts nor readily explains this evidence as well as CPT. [353]

It has only been within the last sixty years that plate tectonic theory has come into its own. There is more research needed for all earth science theories, but Baumgardner and CPT are going in the right direction, both biblically and scientifically.

Some of the problems with CPT include getting rid of the excess heat generated through rapid turnover of the mantle and replacement of oceanic crust. It is hardly satisfactory to suggest that God miraculously removed the heat. If one is going to resort to "God of the Gaps" reasoning for a tiny part of the model, then why not just be done with a search for a mechanism and say, "God caused the Flood supernaturally"? After all, the Flood was a major disjunction in biblical history, and clearly a time of special intervention by God. Biblical creationists need not be closed to miraculous causes for such

---

[352] Sarfati, "Flood Models," (https://creation.com/flood-models-biblical-realism)
[353] "Catastrophic Plate Tectonics," CreationWiki, the Encyclopedia of Creation Science, (https://www.creationwiki.org/Catastrophic_plate_tectonics)

one-off, special events, rather than worry about scientific rigor or economy of miracles. After all, we don't need to find a quasi-naturalistic explanation for the Resurrection or feeding the 5,000. This is different from ordinary, repeatable, operational science, where "God did it" and is one of the large criticisms (rightly so in my opinion) leveled against CPT by scientist like Walt Brown. Since models like CPT are trying to make an operational-science cause of the Flood, an ad hoc appeal to the miraculous is likewise less than acceptable…[354]

Similarly, Baumgardner must rely heavily on tsunamis to account for the Flood sediment record. While this is certainly possible, it seems too contrived and needs further revision.[355]

CPT Predictions

Like many Flood models, CPT predicts the following:

- A consistent, worldwide, initiation event in the geologic column.

- Most body fossils assigned to Flood deposits were deposited allochthonously (including coal, forests, and reefs).

- Most ichnofossils assigned to Flood deposits are grazing, moving, or escape evidences, not long-term living traces.

- Sediments assigned to the Flood were deposited subaqueously, without long-term unconformities between them.[356]

Dr. Baumgardner has incorporated research from a number of scientists in a variety of fields, but he has also subjected his theory to peer review by both Christian and non-Christian scientists. In 2012, he answered "101 questions" about his model in an extensive review that critiqued the CPT model and a variety of different models from both OEC and YEC.[357]

This review was 1,645 pages, showing how far YEC sciences have come in the last few decades. It is also self-critical and holds up well against

---

[354] Sarfati, "Flood Models," (https://creation.com/flood-models-biblical-realism)

[355] John Baumgardner, "Understanding How the Flood Sediment Record Was Formed: The Role of Large Tsunamis," ed. J H Whitmore (Pittsburgh: Creation Science Fellowship, 2018), (https://digitalcommons.cedarville.edu/cgi/viewcontent.cgi?article=1020&context=icc_proce edings)

[356] https://www.christianforums.com/threads/the-flood-manifesto.4815436/

[357] John Baumgardner, "Home of Global Flood," Global Flood, 2017, (http://www.GlobalFlood.org/)

competing OEC models.[358] OEC theorists roll their eyes at modern-day YEC flood geology, but it is my experience that they have not kept up with the times.

It was a pleasure to talk to Dr. Baumgardner and to walk with him, Steve Austin, John Whitmore, Ray Strom, and many others through the Red Hills Desert Gardens, Snow Canyon Overlook, Diamond Valley Cinder Cone, Shnabkaib, Moenkopi, and the Grand Staircase in April 2019. The most impressive part of the theory of CPT is that it has the largest consensus amongst physicists, geologists, geophysicists, earth scientists, and others— mostly inside the YEC network, but steadily growing into the mainstream.

There are thousands of pages of material on CPT, but I hope to represent each point fairly and coherently, let scientists speak for themselves, and encourage OEC groups to critique and defend their own models. If they are confident in their viewpoints, a rebuttal of YEC theory, replaced with their own, stronger theory in these three areas is an understandable request. Dr. Baumgardner has been an immense help, showing the merits of YEC and how it has self-corrected and grown over the last thirty-five years. Let's look at areas where CPT has grown and corrected itself, as any good scientific theory should.[359]

1986 First International Conference on Creationism Proceedings – This is the initial publication describing the process of runaway subduction as an important aspect of the Genesis Flood

1990 Second International Conference on Creationism Proceedings – This paper describes a more realistic 2D simulation of the runaway process as well a 3D simulation that employs a subducting ocean lithosphere around the perimeter of a Pangean supercontinent.

1994 Third International Conference on Creationism Proceedings – This paper assesses a much more potent weakening mechanism than simple thermal weakening to enable the runaway process, namely, the strongly non-linear, strain-rate dependent deformation mechanism known as power-law creep.

1994 Third International Conference on Creationism Proceedings – This paper describes major advances made in the 3D modeling of Flood tectonics relative to the 1990 paper.

---

[358] If you would like to download "The Flood Science Review," please send an email to info@IJNP.org, and we will send you a link where you can download our eBook.
[359] Baumgardner, "Home of Global Flood," (http://www.GlobalFlood.org/)

1994 Third International Conference on Creationism Proceedings – A joint paper by Austin, Baumgardner, Humphreys, Snelling, Vardiman, and Wise that provides an overview of how the Genesis Flood, with rapid plate tectonics as its primary physical mechanism, resurfaced the entire earth in the time span of only a few months....

1997 U.S. New and World Report (June 16 issue) – This article, written by a secular reporter, nevertheless presents a surprisingly accurate account of Baumgardner's conversion and subsequent Christian journey.

2000 Geophysical Astrophysical Fluid Dynamics – This highly technical paper reports a portion of the research work of Woo-Sun Yang for his Ph.D. at the University of Illinois, in particular, his development of a numerical scheme able to cope with the extreme viscosity changes that arise in the context of runaway subduction.

2002 Journal of Creation –Forum on Catastrophic Plate Tectonics – This paper is the first of six articles in a forum on the topic of catastrophic plate tectonics as a prominent aspect of the mechanics of the Genesis Flood.

2003 Fifth International Conference on Creationism Proceedings – This important paper reports several groundbreaking advances in modeling the runaway subduction phenomenon.

2005 Institute for Creation Research Impact Article – This article addresses an ongoing enigma for the standard geological community of why all the high mountain ranges of the world—including the Himalayas, the Alps, the Andes, and the Rockies—experienced most of the uplift to their present elevations in what amounts to a blink of the eye, relative to the standard geological time scale.

2011 Flood Science Review conducted by In Jesus' Name Productions – This set of 101 questions and answers is an outcome of a major peer review of Flood models that began early in 2009 and continued through the summer of 2011.

2012 Journal of Creation – This article focuses on the question of whether or not the primary plate tectonic processes of seafloor spreading and subduction are occurring in the present day.

2013 *Journal of Creation* – This paper is a response to a claim in an earlier *Journal of Creation* article that the motions documented by NASA's network of over 2,000 GPS stations do not imply that the plates are moving in a coherent manner, converging at subduction zones, and diverging at mid-ocean ridges, primarily because the required plate driving forces do not exist.

2018 Eighth International Conference on Creationism Proceedings – This paper applies numerical modeling to explore the question of whether repetitive giant tsunamis generated by catastrophic plate tectonics during the Genesis Flood can plausibly account for the Flood sediment record.

2019 International Journal of Plasticity – This paper provides more detail on the latest deformation model for silicate rocks which yields catastrophic mantle runaway behavior under the conditions of the Genesis Flood.

The above examples should show how CPT has been self-critical and refined itself over the decades, as any good scientific theory should. The PDF section on critiques against CPT found on Dr. Baumgardner's website (www.GlobalFlood.org) is large and self-critical. From the Wilson Cycle to the quantity and character of the sediments in the deep ocean trenches, these critiques have done helped to evolve and progress the CPT model:

> To make progress in reconstructing truthfully the Earth's past and interpreting correctly the massive quantity of geologic observations now available, specifically in light of what God Himself has revealed on this topic, we simply cannot afford as creationists to be careless in how we approach this task. We cannot indulge in building straw-man illusions. We cannot pick and choose what data we address and what data we ignore. Rather, we must do our best to bring all the data to bear on any candidate model we construct. Without question we must be discerning as we draw upon work done by researches who view the world through evolutionary [and often OEC] glasses. But God gives such discernment. I personally believe the plate tectonics revolution of the 1960s, together with just a bit more physics insight, has now provided Christians the key to re-establish biblical authority by demonstrating the early chapters of the book of Genesis, and especially the account of the Flood, is authentic history. I am persuaded we are now able to do this in a way that has not been possible for almost two centuries. As young-earth creationists, I believe we must begin to pull together, communicating with one another, to bring to fruition a

vibrant and credible defense for the hope that is in us, relevant to the time in which we live.[360]

Baumgardner vigorously defends CPT and breaks down where competing models fail. His critiques of Walt Brown's hydroplate theory (HPT) has forced Brown to update future editions of his book to allow for an increased thickness in the pre-flood granitic crust and modify his lack of mechanism for transforming the distribution of continental crust into the present one. In a similar vein, Baumgardner tears apart critiques of his CPT model by scientists like Michael Oard, and after answering the critiques, bombards Oard with questions that Oard either cannot or chooses not to answer. Moreover, he answered in great detail "101 questions" pertaining to CPT and competing models, showing that he has no problem stepping into the lion's den, and yet he has the humility to adjust his theory as needed.[361]

Hydroplate Theory

I had the privilege of speaking with Dr. Brown repeatedly on the strengths and weaknesses of hydroplate theory (HPT) and hope to visit him later this year at his Center for Scientific Creation in Phoenix, Arizona, which he has been running since his retirement from the military in 1980. I initially assumed his theory was inundated with problems or out of date since most YEC groups sided with CPT theory, but through careful research and discussions with engineers, physicists and geologists, I have realized that hydroplate theory answers some of the questions that PT and CPT does not.[362]

Dr. Brown's story is an interesting one, as is the history of HPT.

> Dr. [Walter T.] Brown received a Ph.D. in mechanical engineering from Massachusetts Institute of Technology (MIT) where he was a National Science Foundation Fellow. He has taught college courses in physics, mathematics, and computer science. Brown is a retired full colonel (Air Force), West Point graduate, and former Army ranger and paratrooper. Assignments during his 21 years in the military included: Director of Benet Research, Development, and

---

[360] John Baumgardner, "Dealing Carefully with the Data," Creation.com | Creation Ministries International, April 2002, (https://creation.com/dealing-carefully-with-the-data-baumgardner)
[361] Baumgardner, "Home of Global Flood," (http://www.GlobalFlood.org/)
[362] You can read the entire book for free online at:
http://www.creationscience.com/onlinebook/

Engineering Laboratories in Albany, New York; tenured associate professor at the U.S. Air Force Academy; and Chief of Science and Technology Studies at the Air War College. Since retiring from the military in 1980, Dr. Brown has been the Director of the Center for Scientific Creation and has worked full time in research, writing, and speaking on origins. For much of his life, Walt Brown was an evolutionist, but after many years of study, he became convinced of the scientific validity of creation and a global flood. Walt Brown's book titled *In the Beginning* is an exhaustive thesis detailing the hydroplate theory, which provides badly needed substantiation and the mechanisms responsible for the global flood.[363]

Dr. Brown dates his first version of hydroplate theory to 1972. He directs the Center for Scientific Creation in Phoenix, AZ, and has expanded his thinking to include the probable mechanism of the Flood, the likely physical events of Creation, and the lingering and *predictable* consequences of the greatest disaster earth has ever known.[364] Dr. Brown worked with the late Dr. Henry Morris, considered the father of the modern Creation movement and founder of Institute for Creation Research (ICR). Dr. Brown insisted on taking the evidence where it led, though it confronted Dr. Morris's canopy theory (CT). This caused a rift between ICR and Dr. Brown, a rift that is sadly still alive and well. When I asked Henry Morris IV about Walt Brown, he emailed back, "ICR does not endorse Walt Brown's HPT; he is too far invested in his own theory to give it up."[365] Over the decades, though, the creation movement followed Walt's lead and abandoned canopy theory and its scientific misdirection. As the messenger, Walt paid the price.[366] Whether Dr. Brown is right or wrong, to his credit, he pushed back on a scientifically untenable and non-biblical model of the Flood in the name of truth over tradition.[367]

In 1993, the television network CBS ran a special on the search for Noah's Ark featuring Dr. Brown and his hydroplate theory, which got it in front of a

---

[363] "Walt Brown," CreationWiki, the Encyclopedia of Creation Science, last mod. December 5, 2013, (http://creationwiki.org/Walt_Brown#cite_note-2)
[364] "Walter T. Brown," Creation Science Hall of Fame (new), February 1, 2012, (https://creationsciencehalloffame.org/piece/walter-t-brown)
[365] Personal correspondence available on request.
[366] "Vapor Canopy," (https://kgov.com/vapor-canopy-theory-jane-albright-series-on-global-flood-models-controversy)
[367] Bodie Hodge, "The Collapse of the Canopy Model," Answers in Genesis, September 25, 2009, https://answersingenesis.org/environmental-science/the-collapse-of-the-canopy-model/)

larger audience and opened it up to healthy scrutiny. Walt's response was that of any good scientist; he jettisoned what he could not properly defend, issued an apology for any mistakes he made, and corrected them in future editions of his work. His book *In the Beginning: Compelling Evidence for Creation and the Flood* is now on its 9th edition. This type of revisionism is healthy. What makes hydroplate theory different?

The hydroplate theory is a relatively new model of Earth history that posits before the Global flood, a massive amount of water was trapped underneath the crust. The pressure on the water caused the plates to break and separate. The escaping water then flooded the whole earth. Because these plates were broken, moved, and affected by water, (Hydro = water) these plates are considered hydroplates.[368]

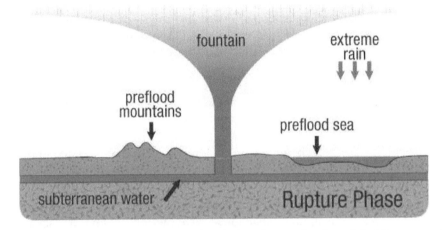

Dr. Brown's only starting assumption is that the preflood earth held a mass of water that surrounded the earth underneath the crust which is in-line with the "fountains of the great deep" described in Genesis.[369] It might have held as much as half of the water in our oceans today. The average thickness of this subterranean waters was at least 1 mile; above the water was a granite crust and beneath the water was Earth's mantle. This water was seemingly held in coterminous chambers forming a thin spherical shell. The shell was possibly 60 miles below the earth's surface. Increasing pressure on the water started stretching the crust. This "stretching" created a microscopic crack which violently grew about 3 miles per second. This crack found the weakest parts

---

[368] "The Hydroplate Theory: An Overview," In the Beginning: Compelling Evidence for Creation and the Flood, last updated February 27, 2020, (https://www.creationscience.com/onlinebook/HydroplateOverview2.html)
[369] https://inhisimage.blog/2018/02/12/fountains-of-the-deep/

of the crust and broke through them. This crack encompassed the globe in about two hours.

As the crack raced around the Earth, the 60-mile-thick crust opened up like a rip in a tightly stretched cloth. Pressure in the subterranean chamber directly beneath the rupture suddenly dropped to nearly atmospheric pressure. This caused *supercritical water* to explode with great violence out of the 6o-mile-deep slit. All along this globe-circling rupture, whose path approximates today's Mid-Oceanic Ridge, a fountain of water jetted hypersonically into and far above the atmosphere. Some of the water fragmented into an ocean of droplets that fell as torrential rain while some of the water shot high above the stratosphere creating ice crystals that fell in certain areas. These extreme hails buried, asphyxiated, and instantly froze many animals. This includes the frozen mammoths found today.

These fountains eroded the rock on both sides of the crack creating massive amounts of sediment all over the world. The sediment buried many animals and plants establishing the fossil record. The width was so colossal that the rock beneath was compelled upward by pressure and became the mid-oceanic ridge. Then the hydroplates slid down and away from the inclining mid-Atlantic ridge. Once the gradually advancing plates reached speeds of about 45 miles per hour they would collide, compress and buckle. The plates that buckled downward became ocean trenches and those that buckled upward became mountains. This explains why large mountain ranges are in correlation to their oceanic ridges.[370]

[370] "Hydroplate Theory," CreationWiki, the Encyclopedia of Creation Science, last mod. November 20, 2018, (http://creationwiki.org/Hydroplate_theory#cite_note-1)

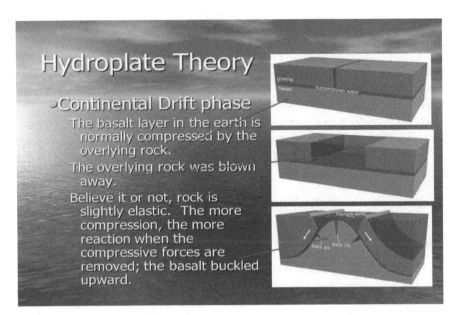

Hydroplate Theory

- Continental Drift phase

  The basalt layer in the earth is normally compressed by the overlying rock.

  The overlying rock was blown away.

  Believe it or not, rock is slightly elastic. The more compression, the more reaction when the compressive forces are removed; the basalt buckled upward.

One of the most important difference between the hydroplate theory and catastrophic plate tectonics lies in what each theory takes for granted, and what each theory explains. Catastrophic plate tectonics takes for granted the hot mantle and core and invokes a *miracle* to explain the event that started the cataclysm. The hydroplate theory says that the mantle-and-core structure of the inner earth *is a consequence* of the Global Flood, as are the high mountains of today. The hydroplate theory makes only *one* assumption, for a subcrustal ocean. And now we find evidence even for that.[371]

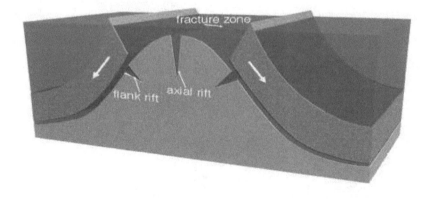

---

[371] Terry A Hurlbut, "Hydroplate Theory v. Catastrophic Plate Tectonics," Conservative News and Views, December 8, 2014, (https://www.conservativenewsandviews.com/2011/12/14/creation/hydroplate-theory-v-catastrophic-plate-tectonics/)

Geophysicists have confirmed since 2007 that there are still "oceans of water" deep within the earth's crust.[372] The deepest hole ever drilled on (Kola Borehole) reached a depth of 7.6 miles in 1992, and "to everyone's surprise was hot, flowing mineralized water (including salt water) encased in…granite," which seems to add credibility to Brown's theory.[373] Similarly, geologists have verified that entire mountains were moved seventy miles in less than an hour by a great catastrophe that has been described in a similar manner to that of HPT.[374] Last, and most recently (2015), geologists discovered a layer between the tectonic plates and the mantle that helps explain how tectonic plates slide on the earth's surface (similar to what Brown long predicted).[375]

> Using ricocheted vibrations from dyna-mite blasts, researchers glimpsed a layer of gooey material sandwiched between the Pacific tectonic plate and the underlying mantle. If present beneath all plates, the layer of partially melted rock could help explain how tectonic plates slide around Earth's surface so easily…. Professor Stern says the thinner layer beneath the plate appears to contain pockets of molten rock that make it easier for the plates to slide. "This means that the plates can be pushed and pulled around without strong resistance at the base. A weak slippery base also explains why tectonic plates can sometimes abruptly change the direction in which they're slipping. It's a bit like a ski sliding on snow."[376]

What science is finding is incredibly consistent with what Walt Brown long predicted:

> The New Zealand team suggests the jelly rock gains its consistency from a higher concentration of water or magma than is present in the lithosphere above it. But it would not have to be too high. While the lithosphere contains 0.1% magma, even a 2% concentration of magma might be enough

[372] Ker Than, "Huge 'Ocean' Discovered Inside Earth," LiveScience (Purch, February 28, 2007), (https://www.livescience.com/1312-huge-ocean-discovered-earth.html)
[373] Martin G. Selbrede, "Dr. Walt Brown's Hydroplate Theory," Chalcedon, September 7, 1998, (https://chalcedon.edu/magazine/dr-walt-browns-hydroplate-theory)
[374] Debbie Cobb, "That Time A Mountain In Wyoming Moved 70 Miles in Under An Hour," Y95 COUNTRY, September 26, 2018, (https://y95country.com/that-time-a-mountain-in-wyoming-moved-70-miles-in-under-an-hour/)
[375] "Geologists Discover Tectonic Plate's Slippery Underbelly," Geology In, (http://www.geologyin.com/2015/02/geologists-discover-tectonic-plates.html)
[376] Ibid.

to explain the consistency of the rock in the channel. The finding of the jelly channel might also help resolve a 50-year debate about whether the plates move as a result of being pushed or pulled. An early idea was that magma being extruded from the mid-oceanic ridges was pushing the plates apart. Another pushing force might come from slowly creeping convection currents beneath the plates that act like rollers beneath a conveyer belt.[377]

Similarly, HPT seems to have a stronger ability to describe the fountains of the great deep being water based (as the Bible states) instead of magma based, as CPT states.[378] This is also the catalyst of all the sedimentation we see around the world, whereas CPT must imagine great tsunamis to acquire an adequate amount of sedimentation across the continents. HPT also seems to have a stronger scientific answer for too much heat being generated: CPT posits a miracle occurred to solve the excessive heat problem, whereas HPT theory applies the buildup of super-critical water[379] jettisoning into the air by directed energy.[380]

---

[377] Cathal O'Connell and Elizabeth Finkle, "Geologists Solve the Mystery of What Tectonic Plates Float On," Cosmos, February 16, 2015, (https://cosmosmagazine.com/geoscience/geologists-solve-mystery-what-tectonic-plates-float)

[378] Dr. Baumgardner rightly says that hydrogen ions exist within the mineral lattices of upper mantle rocks. Water from this source would be minuscule compared with the readily abundant ocean water. Many people seem confused on this point; the presence of great amounts of water presupposed by Dr. Brown is completely without evidence. Brown admits this point as his only presupposition, but it is a presupposition seemingly confirmed by Genesis 7:11 when it references clearly "the fountains of the great deep" connected with the water of the great flood of Noah it would seem?

[379] Physicist have confirmed Brown's math that one might get water to erupt from the earth at 2 miles per second if it were not supercritical; but once you factor in SC water (think of a pressure cooker on a massive scale) it is not difficult to calculate the needed 7 MPS needed to achieve earth's escape velocity.

[380] Baumgardner has been very helpful, even acknowledging, "There is simply no way within the known laws of physics for rock tens of miles thick to cool from near melting point in only a few thousand years." Ironically Dr. Baumgardner was unwilling to dialog with Dr. Brown when I offered to set it up in June 2020.

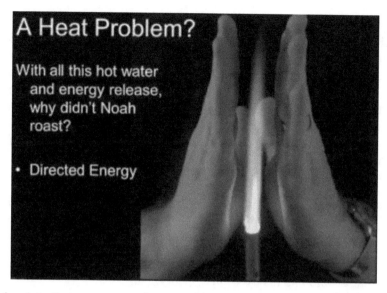

Hydroplate theory seems to have greater explanatory scope and be less ad hoc in its dealings with certain elements of the flood, including the alleged heat problem associated with the eruption of fountains that would deposit great heat on the surface of the earth and the oceans, as well as supercritical water heating the atmosphere.[381]

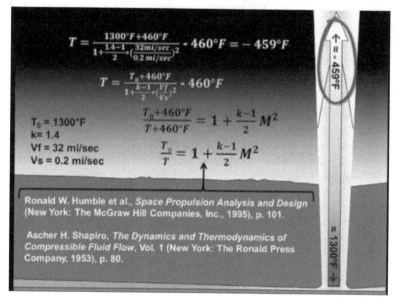

[381] "RSR Answers the Hydroplate Theory Heat Problem," Real Science Radio, March 22, 2019, (https://kgov.com/hydroplate-theory-heat-problem-walt-brown)

Recently, Answers in Genesis published their own animation of how the Global Flood started.[382] Answers in Genesis, like ICR, more or less accepts catastrophic plate tectonics. One would expect any animation for catastrophic plate tectonics to depict a volcanic breach, an upward thrust of magma, one side of the breach diving or subducting below the other, and the steam plume that gave the earth forty days and nights of rain. Instead, it shows a crack developing in an ocean floor (how deep that floor might be, is not clear), and then a wall of water rushing out of it. In other words, AIG's animation, that is supposed to show how catastrophic plate tectonics worked, is more consistent with the hydroplate theory.[383]

Brown has seen different versions of this animation since 2009. He shared with CNAV two misgivings that he had about the animation:

1. Naïve viewers might mistakenly assume that Brown "stole" some ideas from catastrophic plate tectonics in developing his hydroplate theory.

2. In any event, neither the animation, nor its Web page, nor the related display in the Creation Museum directs the viewer to the information behind the hydroplate theory.[384]

While I wish Brown would incorporate more YEC persons in a variety of fields to provide critical analyses against HPT, as Baumgardner has with CPT, I like that hydroplate theory is independent of plate tectonics. In other words, some geologists are still very skeptical of plate tectonics. If plate tectonics were proven false, then so too would CPT. HPT would be unimpacted since it does not rely on plate tectonics in the traditional sense. Also, HPT made radical presuppositions, such as water under the crust serving to help plate shifts, but these predictions have been shown to be growingly accurate. I am less convinced in Brown's theories concerning Ice Ages or the origin of comets, even though some of his initial predictions have been confirmed and remain plausible. However, Brown's theory does make many interconnected

---

[382] This animation shows regularly at the Creation Museum in Petersburg, KY, as well as my own creation history museum in Eureka Springs, AR.

[383] Walt Brown dates the Flood to approximately 3290 BC and the Creation to 5532 BC, +/- 100 years, which aligns with my own dating when considering other flood legends from around the world, coupled with the Septuagint and pre-Masoretic text of the Old Testament. http://creationicc.org/2018_papers/14%20Smith%20Septuagint%20Chronology%20final.pdf for more information.)

[384] Hurlbut, "Hydroplate Theory v. Catastrophic," (https://www.conservativenewsandviews.com/2011/12/14/creation/hydroplate-theory-v-catastrophic-plate-tectonics/)

predictions that have an incredible amount of explanatory scope while at the same time providing logically sound reasons why one would find saltwater in comets as well as elements of organic life.[385]

I find the Flood narrative almost irrefutable from a social science and theological standpoint, but the theories of CPT and HPT are equally strong from a natural science perspective, as well. CPT is basically on the same ground as plate tectonics, but HPT is independent of plate tectonics, and many of the predictions it has made have been shown to be true in the last forty years. Time will tell how well these theories hold up, but no one can deny that they are viable interpretations of the world we see today.[386]

Buckled Mountain. Textbooks and museums frequently refer to some uplifting force that formed mountains. Can you see that an uplifting force, by itself, would not produce this pattern? Horizontal compression was needed to buckle these sedimentary layers near the Sullivan River in southern British Columbia, Canada. Such layers—seen worldwide—must have been soft, like wet sand, at the time of compression.[387]

---

[385] Michael J. Oard, "Analysis of Walt Brown's Flood Model," Creation.com | Creation Ministries International, April 7, 2013, https://creation.com/hydroplate-theory)

[386] A.C. McIntosh, T Edmonson, and S Taylor, "Flood Models: The Need for an Integrated Approach," Creation.com | Creation Ministries International, (https://creation.com/flood-models-the-need-for-an-integrated-approach)

[387] Walt Brown, "In the Beginning: Compelling Evidence for Creation and the Flood," Center for Scientific Creation, (http://www.CreationScience.com/)

Table 3. Evidence vs. Theories: Origin of Ocean Trenches, Earthquakes, and the Ring of Fire

Evidence to be Explained	Hydroplate Theory — Trenches, earthquakes, and the Ring of Fire are a result of shifts inside the Earth during the flood, including the rising of the Atlantic floor and the subsidence of the Pacific floor. Driven by Gravity		Plate Tectonic Theory — Trenches, earthquakes, and the Ring of Fire are produced by subducting plates that have been diving into the mantle for hundreds of millions of years. Driven by Heat	
The Ring of Fire	●	1	◉	2
Gravity Anomalies	●	3	◉	4
Core-Mantle Boundary	●	5	◉	6
Flood Basalts	●	7	◉	8
How Are Plates Made?	●	9	◉	10
Water in the Upper Mantle	○	11	◉	12
Seamounts and Tablemounts	●	13	◉	14
Stretched Oceanic Ridges	●	15	◉	16
Scattered Volcanoes	●	17	◉	18
Continental Material under Ocean Floor	○	19	◉	20
Images of Earth's Interior	●	21	○	22
Fast Seismic Waves	●	23	◉	24
Fossils in Trenches	●	25	◉	26
Deep Earthquakes	●	27	◉	28
Earthquakes Far from Plate Boundaries	●	29	◉	30
Earthquakes Correlate with Low Tides	●	31	○	32
Earthquake Driving Force	●	33	◉	34
Plate Reversals	●	35	◉	36
Earthquakes Drop Local Gravity	●	37	◉	38
Tension Failures	●	39	◉	40
Wide Earthquakes	●	41	◉	42
Reasonable Driving Mechanism	●	43	◉	44
Displaced Material	●	45	◉	46
Frictional Resistance	●	47	◉	48
Arcs and Cusps	●	49	◉	50
Concentrated Trenches	●	51	◉	52
Undistorted Layers in Trenches	●	53	◉	54
Initiation	●	55	◉	56
"Fossil" (Ancient) Trenches	●	57	◉	58
Other	◉	59–61	◉	62–65

Key:
● Explained by theory.
○ Theory has moderate problems with this item.
◉ Theory has serious problems with this item.
Numbers in this table refer to amplifying explanations on pages 166–178.

One concept I really enjoyed in Walt Brown's book (In the Beginning) is that in each section he compares HPT to all mainstream theories to see how they compare scientifically. He then goes into detail on each of these theories, point by point, to show why HPT is the strongest point in his estimation. *It was for these reasons that Drs. Kuebler and Fowler (non-creationists) found HPT superior in many ways to any other YEC flood model in their formidable book (The Evolution Controversy).[388]

[388] Fowler, Thomas. Kuebler, Daniel. *The Evolution Controversy: A Survey of Competing Theories.* Baker Academic. 2007.

Though I mostly disagree with meteorologist Michael Oard's flood-impact model (impact-vertical tectonics), I do agree with some of his criticisms against both HPT and CPT. Moreover, I agree that most likely certain elements of different flood models may be accurate. An integrated approach may in fact be the best of both worlds.

> The hydroplate theory and CPT are usually regarded as mutually exclusive. But this need not be so. There is considerable room for volcanic activity during the continental drift phase of the hydroplate theory. The breaking of the Earth's crust (possibly by an impact) may well have released large volumes of subterranean waters into the atmosphere and led to the rapid movement of the broken continental plates from the impact center. Subsequently, a subduction mechanism may then have taken over from the initial catastrophe, driving continuous upheavals in the Earth's mantle under the seas, and sustaining the disaster for the rest of the Flood year.[389]

I am dumbfounded by how well certain evidences in geology and earth science have come in line, over the last twenty years, with the notion of the great deep bursting open as described in Genesis. *New Scientist* ran an article "Massive Ocean Discovered towards Earth's Core" in 2014, and we have since seen a growing level of substantiating evidences for what a great, prehistoric ocean in the crust of the earth. Some anti-creation sites tie together these underground oceans and ringwoodite, but they show their own ignorance when they do so, especially when one considers not only what ringwoodite is but how it relates to underground oceans of the distant past. As *New Scientist* (and *National Geographic*) state:

> A reservoir of water three times the volume of all the oceans has been discovered deep beneath the Earth's surface. The finding could help explain where Earth's seas came from. The water is hidden inside a blue rock called ringwoodite that lies 700 kilometers underground in the mantle, the layer of hot rock between Earth's surface and its core. Some geologists think water arrived in comets as they struck the planet, but the new discovery supports an alternative idea that the oceans gradually oozed out of the interior of the early Earth. "It's good evidence the Earth's water came from

---

[389] McIntosh, Edmonson, and Taylor, "Integrated Approach," (https://creation.com/flood-models-the-need-for-an-integrated-approach)

within," says Steven Jacobsen of Northwestern University in Evanston, Illinois.[390]

There is an impressive amount of substantiating evidence for a global flood that matches theologically, historically, and scientifically with what is described in the book of Genesis. Yet another coincidence? Surely not.

> We could go on and on discussing the evidence. It's dramatic. It's exciting. It solves many persistent geological problems. But the connection with Noah's Flood can only be appreciated by those who are willing to see. Those who continue to hold onto their blind spots won't be able to make the connection. This bias is a major problem. Evolutionary/OEC geologists think they are dealing with facts and can't see that they are only dealing with interpretations. It gives a false sense of superiority and a strong incentive to shut down debate. We would see great progress if evolutionist geologists could at least see that there is another way of looking at things and stop trying to censor ideas that differ from their own. In other words, it's time evolutionary/OEC geologists, who presently dominate the geological profession, stopped censoring and discriminating against views they do not agree with. It's time they were professional enough to put their assumptions on the table and discuss these issues on their merits, without setting up straw men and without calling people names. I'm confident that if this happened, they would see that Noah's Flood was indeed a real event that explains the evidence and has big ramifications in many areas of public life in the western world.[391]

It is obvious that geology and earth science are advanced in their critique against an OEC interpretation in which Noah's Flood is denied. The social sciences and theology are overwhelmingly in favor of Noah's Flood, and the natural sciences seem to be falling in line. I look forward to further findings from a deeper, more serious, dive into catastrophism and the historicity of a global flood. I find these theories more biblically and scientifically based than

---

[390] Andy Coghlan, "Massive 'Ocean' Discovered towards Earth's Core," New Scientist, June 12, 2014, (https://www.newscientist.com/article/dn25723-massive-ocean-discovered-towards-earths-core/)

[391] Tas Walker, "It's Time for Evolutionist Geologists to Face the Evidence," Creation.com | Creation Ministries International, November 12, 2013, (https://creation.com/evolutionist-geologists-must-face-the-evidence)

the various local flood theories that Hugh Ross, William Lane Craig, and others posit. Moreover, those who take a global flood, old earth/universe stance are doubly inconsistent. YEC theories have done nothing but grow in plausibility and explanatory scope over the decades.

I wish I had the time to dive into the correlation between the Flood and the Ice Ages, but time constraints prevent me from doing so. Meteorologist Michael Oard has done some great work on the Ice Age and seems to be supported from a multitude of disciplines, so I suggest referencing Oard's published works and his articles on CMI.[392] And even if Oard's and Walt Brown's (rock-ice) Ice Age models both turn out to not be fully accurate, they do have great explanatory scope and provide a very plausible cause for the Ice Age being caused by the Global Flood (an area that both OEC local flood theorists and secularist struggle to give account for as they have over 70 theories to date on causes of the Ice Age(s).[393]

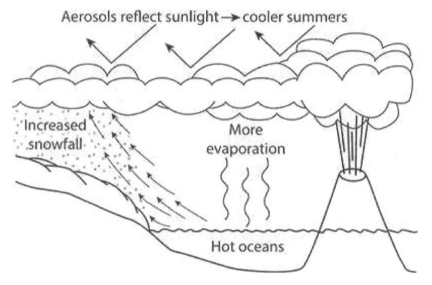

Similar to cosmology, the geological models presented by YEC researchers have many areas to work through, but I am amazed at how far the YEC position has come over the years on virtually no budget. Not only are the scientific models viable, they provide a consistent understanding of the world while taking the Bible seriously.[394]

---

[392] https://creation.com/michael-j-oard
[393] https://www.icr.org/article/the-bible-best-explains-the-ice-age Jake Hebert, Ph.D. 2018. The Bible Best Explains the Ice Age. Acts & Facts. 47 (11) - picture
[394] Michael J. Oard, "What Cause the Ice Age?" Creation.com | Creation Ministries International, July 2014, (https://creation.com/what-caused-ice-age)

Prediction 3 – YEC and a Historical Adam and Eve?

The theory of a historical Adam and Eve and the genetics surrounding a population spike from the time of Noah's Ark seem to be strong indicators in favor of YEC.[395] We have already seen that the social sciences and biblical exegesis are on the YEC side concerning a historical Adam and Eve, but what about the natural sciences? We will look at the two points below:

1. The decay in the human genome due to multiple harmful mutations each generation is consistent with an origin several thousand years ago. This has been confirmed by realistic modelling of population genetics, which shows that genomes are young, in the order of thousands of years.[396]

2. Very limited variation in the DNA sequence on the human X and Y chromosome around the world is consistent with a recent origin of mankind—thousands not millions of years.

On the first point, I hosted geneticist John Sanford in 2016 at two universities while he spoke on genetic entropy and again in 2019, when I went to Utah and served as emcee for Logos Research Associates.[397] This is no mere

---

[395] Robert Carter and Chris Hardy, "Modelling Biblical Human Population Growth," Creation.com | Creation Ministries International, April 2015, (https://creation.com/biblical-human-population-growth-model)

[396] See J. Sanford et al., "Mendel's Accountant: a Biologically Realistic Forward-Time Population Genetics Program," Scalable Computing: Practice and Experience,8(2):147–165, 2007, (https://www.scpe.org/index.php/scpe/article/view/407)

[397] We also hosted Dr. Sanford in a Q&A online forum July 2020.

creationist propaganda, as Sanford and other YEC theorists from Logos Research Associates have published these findings in *Journal of Mathematical Biology*, *Theoretical Biology and Medical Modeling*, and various other academic journals.[398, 399] While there is obviously no way to do justice to Sanford or other creation scientists, I can summarize the main points and direct you to take a deeper look into their research. While many OEC theorists are good at digesting and defending another group's works, they often do so at the cost of sacrificing the heart of the biblical narrative. You can sense this when OEC groups like *Cross Examined*, with Frank Turek, wish to remain OEC but cannot completely reconcile it with the Bible. They accuse YEC groups of conflation and setting up a false dichotomy, and maybe some of them do, but what about the points I raise?

Frank Turek gives lip-service to modern science by endorsing billions of elapsed years since Creation while maintaining a historic Adam and Eve, but instead of explaining why we keep a fairly recent creation for Adam and Eve as well as billions of years of creation, he abruptly ends his discussion: "The existence of a historical Adam and Eve, however, is foundational to a full and proper understanding of the Gospel and Christ's role as the *second Adam*. 'For as in Adam all die, so in Christ, all will be made alive.'" (1 Corinthians 15:22)[400] I have seen these same inconsistencies in my conversations with Hank Hanegraaff, but when I asked him questions I pose in this book, he acknowledged most of them, including death before sin and a historical Adam and Eve but again insisted we follow secular scientists when interpreting Genesis. He avoided Noah's Flood, but did acknowledge that we cannot give these up *a priori*. Perhaps there is no reason to give them up at all?

I first met Dr. John Sanford at the University of Arkansas in 2016. Though I had mostly only hosted OEC groups at that point, I had always respected the YEC position and knew it went far beyond what AIG would have the world think. I was moved by Dr. Sanford's humility and genuine love for the Lord, as well as his wish to help reach the next generation—specifically, millennials. We had dinner on the university campus, set up for his talk, and had a nice crowd of about seventy people—professors, students, Christians,

[398] William F Basener and John C Sanford, "The Fundamental Theorem of Natural Selection with Mutations," Springer Link, November 7, 2017, (https://link.springer.com/article/10.1007/s00285-017-1190-x)

[399] John Sanford et al., "The Waiting Time Problem in a Model Hominin Population," *National Center for Biotechnology Information*, 2015, (https://www.ncbi.nlm.nih.gov/pmc/articles/PMC4573302/pdf/12976_2015_Article_16.pdf)

[400] Jonathan McLatchie, "Did They Really Exist? A Biblical and Scientific Defence of Adam and Eve," Cross Examined, August 22, 2019, (https://crossexamined.org/did-they-really-exist-a-biblical-and-scientific-defence-of-adam-and-eve/)

and skeptics. I was surprised by the genuine interest and questions from the audience. I was equally surprised by Dr. Sanford's acknowledgment of his belief in YEC and awareness that it wasn't the most important topic. He and others at Logos Research Associates had been working with Ratio Christi (an apologetics ministry focused on college campuses) to bring a new level of credibility to YEC theory. Last, I was floored by Dr. Sanford's expertise. He'd worked with OEC theorists William Dembski, Michael Behe, Philip Johnson, Bruce Gordon, Douglas Axe, Johnathan Wells, and a slew of others at Cornell University, where he taught for over thirty years, researching the nature of biological information from a multiplicity of angles documented in *Biological Information: New Perspectives*. It was, however, his work on genetic entropy that most intrigued me and led me to begin working with Logos Research Associates.

> In *Genetic Entropy*, Dr. Sanford presents compelling scientific evidences that the genomes of all living creatures are degenerating due to the accumulation of slightly harmful mutations. Both living populations and numerical simulation experiments (that model digital populations using sophisticated computer modeling) have consistently demonstrated that the clear majority of mutations cannot be effectively eliminated from the genome through natural selection. By escaping purifying selection, these mutations are continuously accumulating in the genomes of all living creatures resulting in the continuous erosion of genetic information over generational time. The end result is the inevitable extinction of all living populations. This phenomenon is known as "Genetic Entropy." Genetic Entropy has been acknowledged by leading population geneticists from the time of the neo-Darwinian Synthesis (1930) to the present day.[401]

So, what is Genetic Entropy? It is the genetic degeneration of living things. Genetic entropy is the systematic breakdown of the internal biological information systems that make life alive. Genetic entropy results from genetic mutations, which are typographical errors in the programming of life (life's instruction manuals). Mutations systematically erode the information that encodes life's many essential functions. Biological information consists of a large set of specifications, and random mutations systematically scramble

---

[401] John C Sanford, "About *Genetic Entropy*," Genetic Entroy.org, 2018, (https://www.geneticentropy.org/order-book)

these specifications – gradually but relentlessly destroying the programming instructions essential to life.

> Genetic entropy is most easily understood on a personal level. In our bodies there are roughly 3 new mutations (word-processing errors), every cell division. Our cells become more mutant, and more divergent from each other every day. By the time we are old, each of our cells has accumulated tens of thousands of mutations. Mutation accumulation is the primary reason we grow old and die. This level of genetic entropy is easy to understand. There is another level of genetic entropy that affects us as a population. Because mutations arise in all of our cells, including our reproductive cells, we pass many of our new mutations to our children. So, mutations continuously accumulate in the population – with each generation being more mutant than the last. So not only do we undergo genetic degeneration personally, we also are undergoing genetic degeneration as a population. This is essentially evolution going the wrong way. Natural selection can slow down, but cannot stop, genetic entropy on the population level.

> Apart from intelligence, information and information systems always degenerate. This is obviously true in the human realm, but is equally true in the biological realm, (contrary to what evolutionists and many OEC claim). The more technical definition of entropy, as used by engineers and physicists, is simply a measure of disorder. Technically, apart from any external intervention, all functional systems degenerate, consistently moving from order to disorder (because entropy always increases in any closed system). For the biologist it is more useful to employ the more general use of the word entropy, which conveys that since physical entropy is ever-increasing (disorder is always increasing), therefore there is universal tendency for all biological information systems to degenerate over time – apart from intelligent intervention.[402]

When considering beneficial mutations that add "new" information to the genome, I had the privilege of asking the author of *Darwin's Black Box,* (and

---

[402] John Sanford, "What's Genetic Entropy?" Genetic Entropy, 2018, (https://www.geneticentropy.org/whats-genetic-entropy)

OEC) Dr. Michael Behe, if there were any beneficial mutations that he knew of while I was in Seattle with the Discovery Institute. He thought for a moment and said, "No overtly beneficial mutations that I am aware of exist." I followed this up in January 2020, in Dallas, asking if he knew of any beneficial mutation that <u>added new information</u>. He didn't know of a single one.

So how does this factor into YEC vs OEC? It corroborates the notion of a recent Adam and Eve and it helps substantiate what the Bible and much of history has long recounted: a pre-Flood group of people living incredibly long lives. After Noah's Flood, lifespans began to decline rapidly. Ironically, this steep decline matches what we know of genetic entropy, and the degeneration can be traced to less than 10,000 years ago, adding credence to YEC theory.[403]

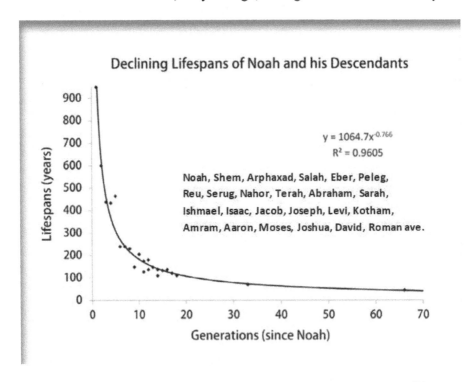

Human lifespans in early history, as recorded in the Bible.[404]

---

[403] A S Kondrashov, "Contamination of the Genome by Very Slightly Deleterious Mutations: Why Have We Not Died 100 Times Over?" Journal of Theoretical Biology (U.S. National Library of Medicine, August 21, 1995), (https://www.ncbi.nlm.nih.gov/pubmed/7475094)
[404] John C. Sanford and John R. Baumgardner, *Genetic Entropy* (Waterloo, NY: FMS Publications, 2014), p.164-8.

When Biblical lifespans (scale above) are plotted across generations after Noah, we see a dramatic decline in life expectancy. The pattern of decline reveals a very clear biological decay curve. Fitting the data to the "line of best fit" reveals an exponential curve following the formula $y = 1064.7x^{0.766}$. The curve fits the data very well, with a coefficient of determination of 0.96 (1.0 would be a perfect fit). It seems highly unlikely this biblical data could have resulted from an ancient fabrication. The curve is very consistent with the concept of genomic degeneration caused by mutation accumulation. The curve is very similar to the theoretical curves shown below.[405]

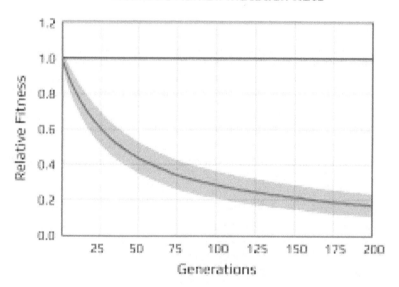

Fitness Decline Simulation Using Realistic Human Mutation Rate

Fitness decline relative to the starting population is shown. On the left axis is shown fitness, while generations are plotted along the bottom axis (200 generations equal 4,000–6,000 years). Reducing the mutation rate by half of increasing population size ten-fold did not fundamentally change the observed downward trajectory. The trajectory shown in this simulation experiment is remarkably similar to biblical lifespans. The shaded area reflects the standard deviation of population fitness.[406]

[405] Ibid. https://kolbecenter.org/god-family-genetics-bible-perspective/
[406] Ibid.

Did Noah Really Live to Be 950 Years Old? [407]

The answer, if you're an OEC theorist, is that they are either false or exaggerations, or you give no response. The fact that humanity is genetically degenerating due to mutation accumulation amounts to "evolution going backwards" and is the antithesis of Darwinian thought while strongly supporting a YEC understanding of reality. Remarkably, such degeneration is very consistent with the Bible. In many places, the Bible indicates that we are dying people in a dying world, and that creation itself is wearing out. (Psa 39:5&11; Psa 102:25-26; Mat 24:35; Ro 8:22; Heb 1:10-12; 1Pe 1:24-25).

The most obvious outward evidences for genetic degeneration are aging, death, and shortened average lifespans. The degeneration of man is explicitly recorded in the words of Jacob, who said to the Pharaoh "I have traveled this earth for 130 hard years. But my life has been short compared to the lives of my ancestors" (Genesis 47:9, NLT). The extreme longevity of the early patriarchs is very well documented in Genesis, Exodus, Numbers, Deuteronomy, and Joshua. The Bible records the age at death of the first 25 Patriarchs in the lineage that goes from Adam to Moses. All of these early Patriarchs lived to be extremely old. This was also true of their Biblical contemporaries, such as Ishmael, who lived at the same time. Likewise, we can infer that Cain was extremely long-lived, since he established a city that was populated by his offspring (Gen 4:17). So extreme longevity was not unique to any single-family lineage but was probably characteristic of all of humanity at that time.

We do not normally think of the Bible as a source of scientific data. However, the recorded ages of the Patriarchs do in fact constitute real data, which can be analyzed scientifically. Numerous scholars have done this. We likewise have done this – going a bit further than previous analyses. The results are fascinating and have incredible implications.

If we plot the first 10 generations from Adam to Noah, we see that most of the Patriarchs lived to be over 900 years old. Longevity was stable in that period, and the trend-line is nearly flat. During this part of history, the only exception was Enoch – who was "taken up to heaven without dying" (Gen 5:24; Heb 11:5), when he was still relatively young (365 years old). In modern times, most people are not able (or willing) to believe that people could have ever lived to be so old. Therefore, many Christians simply dismiss these

---

[407] John Sanford, Jim Pamplin, and Christopher Rupe, "Did Noah Live to Be 950 Years Old?" Encouragement for Believers (FMS Foundation, 2014), (https://www.logosra.org/genetic-entropy)

records as mythology. However, the next part of the data is not so easily dismissed...

If we plot the lifespan of Noah and his descendants, we see an abrupt change during Noah's life, followed by an amazingly systematic decline, continuously going to shorter and shorter lifespans. This decline in lifespan began at the time of the Biblical Flood. This is seen in all three of the primary translations of the Old Testament. There are some variations in the data, depending on the translation (Masoretic, Septuagint, or Samaritan). However, these differences do not fundamentally change the shape of the downward curve. More specifically, we can make the following five logical inferences from our analysis of the Biblical data:

1. As noted, the lifespan data strongly supports the historicity and veracity of the Bible, and in particular, the book of Genesis.
2. The lifespan data indicate that the extreme longevity of the early Patriarchs was real, and that the rapid decline of longevity after the Flood was real. This supports the Biblical perspective of on-going degeneration since the Fall. In light of recent scientific findings, the documented decline in longevity is best understood in terms of mutation accumulation and genetic entropy.
3. The smooth decline in longevity indicates there are no major "gaps" in the data. So, the number of generations from Adam to Jesus, as described in Luke chapter 3, is either correct, or very nearly correct. There is simply no room in the curve for hundreds (or even thousands) of missing generations – as some contend.
4. The drastic decline in longevity began very specifically at the time of the Flood. This strongly supports the reality of a supernatural, cataclysmic world-changing flood, not an ordinary or local flood.
5. Since the genealogies and longevity data are tightly linked, the validation of the longevity data strongly supports the genealogy data (i.e., time from father to son, with no major gaps, etc.), so we can reasonably infer that Adam and Eve lived in the relatively recent past contrary to OEC or secular assertions. The declining longevities strongly indicate that evolution is going the wrong way, and that the evolutionary timeline is not viable.[408]

But could there really be only one paternal ancestor for all people? As is the case with Mitochondrial Eve, evolutionists regret that they coined the term

---

[408] Ibid.

"Y-chromosome Adam" and generally avoid it. However, there are interesting points to make for this important part of the human genome.

> We have used SNV (single nucleotide variant) data to analyze the Y chromosomes of several hundred men from multiple modern human populations. [409] That analysis has allowed us to reconstruct the original Y-chromosome Adam sequence, just as we did with Mitochondrial Eve. The Y-chromosome Adam sequence has in turn allowed us to determine how many mutations separate modern men from Adam. Today, the Y chromosomes of modern men are [only about 300 mutations] removed from Y-chromo-some Adam. If the Y chromosome mutates extremely rapidly (to explain the 70% difference between chimp and man), how is it possible that all men have nearly identical Y chromosomes, and are so very similar to Y Chromosome Adam? Even if we assume a normal mutation rate for the Y chromosome (about 1 mutation per chromosome per generation), we would [only need 300 generations (about six thousand years), to get 300 mutations]. This is the most straight-forward application of the 'molecular clock' concept. The numbers are in perfect agreement with the biblical perspective. However, in 100,000 years (the evolutionary/OEC perspective), we would expect about 100,000 mutational differences between modern men and Y Chromosome Adam—about 333-fold more than is actually seen. This calculation assumes a typical human mutation rate. If we assumed that the human Y chromosome actually had an enormously higher mutation rate than for other human chromosomes, the problem would be vastly worse. In terms of the Y chromo-some, the evolution model completely breaks down at all levels.[410]

Similarly, Dr. Nathaniel Jeanson, who holds a PhD from Harvard in cell and developmental biology, confirms Sanford's findings in his book *Replacing Darwin*. Even his critics acknowledge many of his conclusions, which are similar to Sanford's:

> Dr. Jeanson suggests that the current bank of evidence available today is consistent with a view that includes a

---

[409] An SNP or SNV (single nucleotide variation) occurs when a base-pair is changed in relation to the corresponding position on a comparable chromosome.
[410] John C. Sanford and John R. Baumgardner, *Genetic Entropy & the Mystery of the Genome* (Waterloo, NY: FMS Publications, 2008)

designing God; in one of the more gripping discussions, the author shows how the rate of human mutation actually corresponds to a creationist time scale of 6,000 years. The author is a scientist with peer-reviewed publications and a Ph.D. in cell and developmental biology from Harvard University. His knowledge of the material—historical and -—and the rigor of his analysis are unimpeachable.[411]

The biblical timeframe fits perfectly with known human mutations rates and the observed divergence from the Adam sequence. But the evolutionary timeframe would create much more Y— chromosome diversity than is actually seen. The evolutionist's problems get massively worse when they invoke an ultra-high mutation rate for the human Y chromosome, as necessitated by the new chimp/human sequence comparisons. This new data is showing that Y Chromosome Adam very consistently fits the biblical perspective and is not at all compatible with the evolutionary perspective.[412]

Similarly, researchers have calculated the consensus sequence for human mitochondrial Eve DNA using over 800 available sequences. Analysis of this consensus reveals an unexpected lack of diversity within human mtDNA worldwide. Not only is more than 83% of the mitochondrial genome invariant, but in over 99% of the variable positions, the majority allele was found in at least 90% of the individuals. In the remaining 0.22% of the 16,569 positions, which we conservatively refer to as "ambiguous," everyone could be reliably assigned to either a purine or pyrimidine ancestral state. There was only one position where the most common allele had an allele frequency of less than 50%, but this has been shown to be a mutational hot spot. On average, the individuals in most dataset differed from the Eve consensus by 21.6 nucleotides. Sequences derived from sub-Saharan Africa were considerably more divergent than average. Given the high mutation rate within mitochondria and the large geographic separation among the individuals within our dataset, we did not expect to find the original human mitochondrial sequence to be so well preserved within modern populations. With the exception of a very few ambiguous nucleotides, the consensus sequence clearly represents Eves mitochondrial DNA sequence which, like Adam, fits well within a YEC paradigm.[413]

[411] "Replacing Darwin: The New Origin of the Species," *Kirkus*, December 13, 2017, (https://www.kirkusreviews.com/book-reviews/nathaniel-t-jeanson/replacing-darwin/)
[412] John C Sanford and Robert Carter, "God, Family, and Genetics - A Biblical Perspective," Kolbe Center for the Study of Creation, August 27, 2017, (https://kolbecenter.org/god-family-genetics-bible-perspective/)
[413] https://www.icr.org/i/pdf/technical/The-Eve-Mitochondrial-Consensus-Sequence.pdf

YEC theory yet again is not only viable, but consistent with the data. OEC theory will usually be all over the map, as some retreat from secular science while some rightly maintain the necessity of a historic Adam and Eve but keep millions of extra years in the timeline. Again, OEC theory is viable, but it isn't so strong that it makes the YEC case an embarrassment. If anything, it would seem to be the opposite.

Predictability and YEC?

I am amazed at the developments in YEC theory on "Junk DNA" and "Neanderthal DNA" over the last twenty-five years just to name two. During my undergraduate studies in 1996, I was often told by both secular authorities and OEC Christians that science had concluded that most DNA was junk, since it was seemingly unusable, which begged the question, "Why would a designer use such poor design?" This was cited by Francis Collins and noted atheist Richard Dawkins as the proverbial slam-dunk against the creationist perspective. Fast forward to today, and we now know that there is little to no junk DNA. The useful information within DNA continues to grow and is now hovering at 90%, just as YEC scientists have always predicted.[414]

Similarly, it has often been said that the Neanderthal was an obstacle for YEC theory. The cover of *Cell* magazine ran the title: "Neanderthals were not our ancestors" and therefore an apparent obstacle for YEC theory which maintained that Neanderthals were humans in like manner to you and I. Then,

---

[414] Jeffrey Tomkins, "The Junk DNA Myth Takes a Well-Deserved Hit," Creation.com | Creation Ministries International (*Journal of Creation*, December 2011, p.23-27), (https://creation.com/review-wells-junk-dna)

in 2010, researchers announced their completed draft sequence for the Neanderthal genome, which corroborates that Neanderthals interbred with other peoples, just as creation science theorists such as Jack Cuozzo had long predicted.[415] Given the historical accounts of early humanity in the Bible, this idea should not be new to the historical sciences but confirm another YEC theory.[416] As of February 2020, scientists have reluctantly concluded that "all modern humans have Neanderthal DNA," just as YEC theorists like Dr. Cuozzo have long predicted.[417]

The Tower of Babel and genetics

Let's move past Adam and Eve and genetics and explore the next great hurdle for YEC theory—the Tower of Babel account and its plausibility.

The Tower of Babel has been a favorite bedtime story for generations but as I showed in the last chapter it is solidly based within a historic framework. But is it more than just a fairy tale when we test it through the natural sciences? Like the Creation and Flood accounts, there are only a couple of verses that apply to our model of genetics. But, like the others, these verses are as profound as they are simple.

- Now the whole earth had one language and one speech. (Genesis 11:1)
- And they said, "Come, let us build ourselves a city, and a tower whose top is in the heavens; let us make a name for ourselves, lest we be scattered abroad over the face of the whole earth." (Genesis 11:4)
- Come, let Us go down and confuse their language, that they may not understand one another's speech. So the Lord scattered them abroad from there over the face of all the earth, and they ceased building the city. (Genesis 11:7-8)

It sounds like they were in a homogenous culture, but what do people in that situation do? Would you expect them to mix freely? Were language or cultural barriers present that would have prevented the sons of Shem from marrying the daughters of Japheth? Would the daughters of Ham be expected to marry freely with the sons of any of the three men? In Gen 11:4, they knew about

[415] Jack Cuozzo, "Buried Alive - The Startling Truth about Neanderthal Man," Jack Cuozzo, (http://www.jackcuozzo.com/)

[416] Brian Thomas, "Neandertal Genome Confirms Creation Science Predictions," The Institute for Creation Research, May 28, 2010, (https://www.icr.org/article/neandertal-genome-confirms-creation/)

[417] Katherine J. Wu, "Modern Humans May Have More Neanderthal DNA Than Previously Thought," Smithsonian.com (Smithsonian Institution, February 4, 2020), (https://www.smithsonianmag.com/smart-news/new-research-expands-neanderthals-genetic-legacy-modern-humans-180974099/)

the potential for spreading out and getting separated from one another and intentionally did the opposite. However, this was against the express command of God, who had ordered them to spread out (to populate the earth). So, He took matters into His own hands. There are tremendous implications that come from the Babel account. First it explains the amazing cultural connectivity of ancient peoples—like pyramid building, common flood legends, and ancient, non-Christian genealogies that link people back to biblical figures.[418]

> The dramatic rise in world population over the past several decades is a well-known fact. From a biblical perspective, the current human population easily fits into the standard model of population growth using very conservative parameters. In fact, starting with 6 people and doubling the population every 150 years more than accounts for the current human population (a growth rate of less than 0.5% per year). Population size would have increased quickly given the rate at which the post-Flood population reestablished agriculture, animal husbandry, industry and civilization. So, we must ask the question, "Why are there so few people in the world today?" Could the answer be that the world is young and we have only been here maybe 10,000 years?[419]

From the points covered in this section, many of my OEC colleagues have conceded and adopted a YEC point of view on humanity being recently created, though most still maintain their belief in an ancient cosmos.

---

[418] https://answersingenesis.org/tower-of-babel/babel/
[419] https://www.coursehero.com/file/p28jnpd/that-they-knew-about-the-potential-for-spreading-out-and-getting-separated-from (https://ourworldindata.org/world-population-growth)

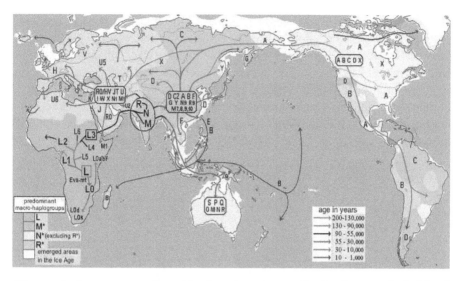

The evolutionary map of world migrations is startlingly close to the biblical account of a single dispersal of people from Babel. The evolutionary "Out of Africa" theory tells us there was a single dispersal of people, centered near and travelling through the Middle East, with three main mitochondrial lineages, with people traveling in small groups into previously uninhabited territory, and that all of this occurred in the recent past. Every item in that list is something directly predicted by the Tower of Babel account in the Bible.[420]

After the Flood

The last remaining significant reference in the Bible that will help us build our model of human genetic history is called the Table of Nations. It is found in Genesis chapters 9 and 10. As discussed in the previous chapter, the Table of Nations is a record of the post-Babel tribes, who they descended from, and where they went. If the Bible is an accurate source of history, one might expect to be able to find a significant amount of evidence for the Table of Nations in genetic data. The truth is not that simple, however, and it is important to keep several things in mind. First, the account was written by a person in the Middle East and from a Middle Eastern perspective. It is incomplete in that there are huge sections of the world that are not discussed (sub-Saharan Africa, Northern Europe, Most of Asia, Australia, the Americas, and Oceania). It also reflects a snapshot in time. It was written after the

[420] Maulucioni, "Hypothesized map of human migration based on mitochondrial DNA," Wikimedia Commons, (Creative Commons—Share Alike 3.0 unported), (Migraciones humanas en haplogrupos mitocondriales.PNG)

dispersion began, but not necessarily before the dispersion was complete. Indeed, much has changed in the intervening years. People groups have migrated, cultures have gone extinct, languages have changed, separate cultures have merged, etc. The history of man has been full of ebb and flow as people mixed or fought, resisted invasion or were conquered. The history of man since Babel is very complicated. Modern genetics can answer some of the big questions, but answers to many of the smaller details may elude us forever.

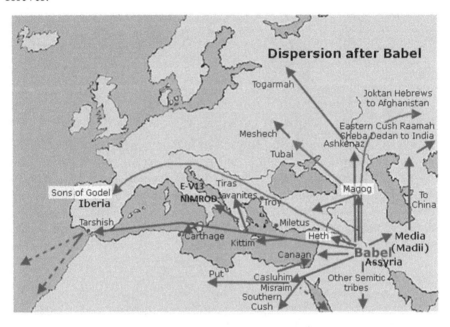

Dispersion after Babel ironically matches the secular map of migration (pictured previously) quite well.[421]

This is an important topic for the creation model. The world does not look at the Bible in a favorable light. In fact, it disparages it, sometimes with open hostility. Attacks are often centered on the claim that the Bible is not reliable on historical grounds, and if the history of the Bible is inaccurate, what about the theology? Think about what Jesus told Nicodemus in John 3:12, "If I have told you earthly things and you do not believe, how will you believe if I tell you heavenly things?" Many OEC theorists have grown to see less history in the Bible as Francis Schaeffer long warned; therefore, the spiritual

---

[421] "Dispersion After Babel: Books of the Bible, Bible History," Pinterest, (https://www.pinterest.com/pin/436356651386887110/)

implications are meaningless to them. What would happen for evangelism if the history of the Bible including YEC turns out to be true after all?[422]

One only need to look at what the Bible has long told us about history and science being corroborated (such as the two maps above or the various archaeological discoveries) to see how valid the biblical model is.

> Given the premise of a miraculously created Adam and Eve, the most coherent, powerful, and compelling explanation for most of the genetic diversity found within the human race is "designed diversity". This is especially true when we consider the various forms of human beauty and the various forms of human gifts and talents. In addition, designed diversity appears to have enabled rapid human adaptation after the flood as well as Babel. These various genetic mechanisms falsify the claim that there is no way two people could give rise to the human allele distribution that we see today.[423]

Though we have only scratched the surface, I hope we have made at least a viable case why many YEC scientists have intellectually sound reasons for maintaining a recent creation position and see no reason at all for jettisoning the historicity of the early chapters of Genesis. What we find is that YEC theory is not only supported by theology and the social sciences but seems to fit natural science data consistently. This doesn't prove YEC theory but shows it to be viable and would force OEC theorists to construct their own consistent model to support these same facts.

What about the science of language and writing? It, too, seems to support YEC theory.

> Secular linguists are puzzled by the existence of twenty or so language families in the world today. The languages within each family (and the people that speak them) have been shown to be genetically related, but few genetic links have been observed between families. This is a problem for secular linguists. If, as they believe, man evolved from an ape-like ancestor, man would at some point have gained the ability to speak. This process of change would actually be superbly

---

[422] Robert W. Carter, "Adam, Eve, and Noah Vs. Modern Genetics," Creation.com | Creation Ministries International, May 11, 2010, (https://creation.com/noah-and-genetics)
[423] John C Sanford et al., "Adam and Eve, Designed Diversity, and Allele Frequencies," in *International Conference on Creationism* (Pittsburgh, 2018), (https://digitalcommons.cedarville.edu/icc_proceedings/vol8/iss1/8/)

dangerous, as they admit. But still, if speech did evolve somewhere, somehow, we would expect to find that all languages are genetically related. They clearly are not. Some have therefore suggested that man evolved speech simultaneously in more than one place. This suggestion is beyond belief, considering the dangers involved in the supposed evolution of speech. So how did the language families come into existence?[424]

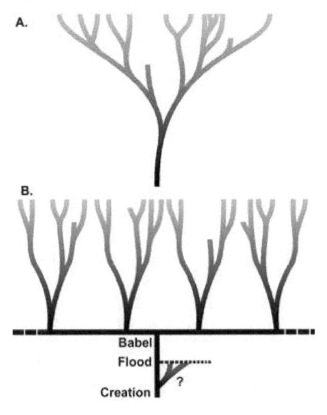

*The conventional view (**A**) and biblical view (**B**) of language development. In the conventional view, language developed from a single 'protolanguage' and diverged into different languages as time progressed. In the biblical model, man was created with language. This was supernaturally changed at Babel, where God confused the languages. Scripture does not tell how many languages arose at Babel.*[425]

---

[424] https://creation.com/the-tower-of-babel-account-affirmed-by-linguistics
[425] Ibid.

Determining whether or not languages share a common ancestor is not easy. A Dutch student learning Hindi might not realize that Hindi is related to Dutch. Yet, both languages have been shown to be part of the Indo-European language family. Steel has previously covered in detail the development of the Indo-European languages, clearly refuting claims that this paralleled biological evolution. Apparently, all languages in this family have developed from a parent language, which no longer exists.

This idea was unknown in the late 18th century, until Sir William Jones suggested that Greek, Latin and Sanskrit had independently sprung from some common source, which, perhaps, no longer exists. He also suggested that other groups of languages, such as the Celtic and Germanic languages, though quite different, might also be related in the same way. Few question his findings today. Comparative and Historical Linguistics have more or less carried on what Jones began. Two centuries have revealed much, and the findings are encouraging for Creationists, who believe the account of the Tower of Babel in Genesis 11 to be a true, historically scientific account of events....

> The Indo-European language family is not the only language family in the world. There are others, which are more difficult to examine. We have many writings of some European languages, covering more than 2,500 years of development. For many other languages, however, there are no writings at all. That makes the study of their development more complicated. The traditional way of comparing languages was to compare the history and grammar structures of two languages, while keeping in mind physical and cultural similarities between the tribes. This method was useful in Europe, but it was time-consuming and proved difficult in Africa. Several decades of hard work at the beginning of this century had uncovered only the tip of the iceberg, as far as all languages in Africa were concerned.[426]

A dramatic breakthrough came in the person of Joseph Greenberg in the middle of last century. Greenberg came up with a new method. He collected lists of words from many African languages and compared them with each other. He noticed clear patterns. Several languages had similar sounding words for similar things, and Greenberg concluded that these languages must

---

[426] Ibid.

therefore be related. His method has become the norm in comparative linguistics.

Greenberg's method is one of two major ways of classifying languages. Typological classification looks at grammatical structures and classifies languages accordingly. However, there may not be a genetic relationship between languages with a similar typological makeup. Since we are interested in genetic relationship, we will now take a brief look at the second method, genetic qualification, to consider its relation to YEC's account of Babel.[427]

Genetic qualification

Genetic qualification prefers to use only "core vocabulary," i.e., words which are said to change little over time. The method aims to see how many of these words are similar in different languages, while keeping in mind how words usually change in pronunciation.

The core vocabulary includes, amongst others, words for body parts, numbers, and personal pronouns. When clear *patterns* of similarities between languages are observed, then those languages are said to be related.

> The word "patterns" in the previous paragraph was carefully chosen, because the core vocabulary between related languages is never identical, but similar, or "cognate". Words are cognate when they are shown to be consistent to the pattern of phonetical change that has taken place in the past. For example, the word *tahi* in Tongan might not look like *kai* in Hawaiian, even though they both mean "sea". But, if you also compare Tongan *tapu* to Hawaiian *kapu* (both meaning "forbidden") and Tongan *tanata* to Hawaiian *kanaka* —meaning "man" — you begin to see a pattern: Where Tongan has an initial "T," Hawaiian has an initial "K", and one begins to see that the words might be related. They are cognate.[428]

Deciding which words are cognate and which words are not is never easy. Different scholars have made different judgements when comparing the same lists. There is no general agreement in all cases. There are, however, a few

---

[427] Ibid.
[428] Terry Crowley, *An Introduction to Historical Linguistics* (Auckland: Oxford University Press, 1997), quoted in Duursma, "The Tower of Babel Account Affirmed by Linguistics," Creation.com | Creation Ministries International, December 2002, (https://creation.com/the-tower-of-babel-account-affirmed-by-linguistics)

rules to go by, as certain phonetical changes are more likely to occur than others. Stronger sounds, for example, may become weaker.

Equally, words may lose initial or final letters, or merge two consonants into one. These changes are fairly common. The opposites of these examples may also happen but are less common. Words easily lose sound; they rarely gain it. "The ultimate question, is," says Ruhlen, "whether all human languages are genetically related,"[429] but the evidence for this is scarce. There are a few words which, he says, are similar in all languages. However, the words he gives in his example do not have the same meaning in every language. The meanings vary from "one" to "finger" and "hand."[430] There are similarities between them, but this is not convincing evidence of genetic relationship between language families.

> It must be pointed out, though, that we cannot go back too far in time. Core vocabulary is stable but does change. In some languages this change has been measured for more than 2,000 years. The result shows that 19.5% of the core vocabulary changes every 1,000 years.[431] If this is the same for all languages, it means that statistically all words in a language should be replaced within a period of about 10,000 years. That would make any research beyond that period of time impossible. This, in turn, makes it impossible to prove that all language families are ultimately related....
>
> [Thus] the history of languages cannot be traced back for more than 10,000 years. We have also seen lack of knowledge regarding the evolution of human speech. It seems that there is little evidence to support the view that all languages evolved from one or more proto-languages. There is, however, another explanation for the existence of the language families in the world today.... [YEC][432]

As I alluded to in *The Philosophy of History,* the facts we observe today are consistent with the Tower of Babel account in Genesis 11, but this does not prove the correctness of the account absolutely of course. Since the history of languages cannot be reconstructed

---

[429] Merritt Ruhlen, *A Guide to the Worlds Languages* (Stanford: Stanford university, 1987), quoted in Duursma, "The Tower of Babel Account Affirmed by Linguistics," Creation.com | Creation Ministries International, December 2002, (https://creation.com/the-tower-of-babel-account-affirmed-by-linguistics)
[430] Ibid.
[431] Ibid.
[432] Ibid.

beyond 10,000 years, evidence for (and against) alternative views is limited.

However, if we take an objective look at the facts at our disposal, we cannot but draw the conclusion that the Bible account has far more going for it than the alternatives, for which there is little, if any, evidence. We therefore wholeheartedly believe that the findings of historical and comparative linguistics have served indeed to affirm the Tower of Babel account recorded in Genesis 11, beyond reasonable doubt. Believing this account, however, requires believing in God, and the denial of the evolution theory, which suggests that all animals, humans, and even human language, arose by chance. For many, this might prove too big a price to pay, despite the evidence but for the Christian I am not sure why the reluctance to accept a YEC interpretation.[433]

Whether we look at the origins of human genetics, Adam and Eve, or the feasibility of the genetics associated with the Tower of Babel, YEC theory is at the very least coherent. Moreover, secular and non-secular theorists alike agree that we are winding down genetically. This is why mainstream science asks, "Why are we not dead 100 times over?"[434] If we really were mutating at the same rate we are now, as Dr. Sanford and others have shown, it makes sense why we might only have been around 10,000 years. If, on the other hand, we are tens (if not hundreds) of thousands of years old, as OEC theorists assert, then we have no choice but to assume the degeneration of our genes was much slower in the past. Theology, the social sciences, and the natural sciences fit well with YEC theory that includes a historical Adam and Eve and a dispersion around five thousand years ago.[435]

Let's turn our attention to Noah and a global flood to see where the evidence lies as far as the "created kinds" of animals that repopulated the earth after the Flood. YEC circles often treat *kinds* as a fact with little or no explanation, while OEC theorists rightly critique this component as weak or wrong. Perhaps both sides are wrong, or at least mislead.

---

[433] K.J. Duursma, "The Tower of Babel Account Affirmed by Linguistics," Creation.com | Creation Ministries International, December 2002, (https://creation.com/the-tower-of-babel-account-affirmed-by-linguistics)

[434] Kondrashov, "Contamination of the Genome," (https://www.ncbi.nlm.nih.gov/pubmed/7475094)

[435] Harvard PhD cell biologist Nathaniel Jeanson just finished (May 2020) a 12-part (over 6-hour) video series confirming the genetic accuracy associated with the biblical account post-Babel (highly recommended). Providing further predictability of the YEC biblical account: https://www.youtube.com/playlist?list=PL1v9pqs4w1mwrGlCET76Rs99Fx0EfJXE4

Is the prediction of created kinds viable from a YEC perspective?

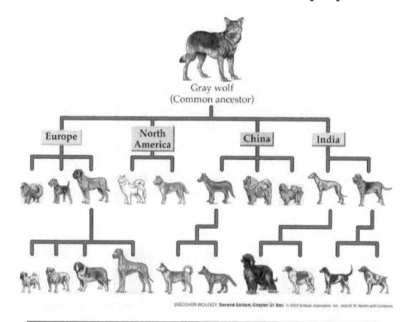

A Definition of Created Kinds

- A recognizable base form and structure that does not change over time
- Limited variation in surface features over time
- Reproductive discontinuity between kinds; Reproductive continuity within a kind.
- Created Kinds appeared approximately 6,000 years ago
- Taxonomic comparison averages near the Family level

Even secular publications such as Discovery Biology agree (more or less) with the concept of biblical kinds, though they extrapolate well beyond the science to assert that the dog kind, for example, came from a non-dog at some point in the past.[436]

---

[436] Michael L Cain et al., *Discover Biology*, 2nd ed. (WW Norton and Co., 2002)

One objection I often hear is what the "created kinds" referenced in Genesis means. This is a good question and one that most creationists have not spent enough time on.[437] Similarly, I can ask an OEC or secular colleague what constitutes a *species*, and not get a consistent answer either. A recent article by Henry Taylor of the University of Birmingham described why we cannot define a species and why it's likely to get worse. He said, "There is absolutely no agreement among biologists about how we should understand the species, and this is only the tip of a deep and confusing iceberg."[438] He showed that many have sought to end the classification all together. The article even referred to the German biologist Willi Hennig, who suggested in the 1960s that we think about a species in terms of its ancestry. This is a unique question that fits well with the created kinds mentioned in Genesis, sometimes referred to as baraminology. Roger Patterson gave a good breakdown of the modern classification system, as well as a brief introduction of baraminology in a 2007 article:

> Genesis records that God created the animals and plants according to their kind. Genesis explains that God created specific kinds of animals. These kinds were able to breed and reproduce more of the same kind with a great variety of traits. It is not absolutely clear what the boundaries of the original kinds were, but it is clear from Genesis that the different animals and plants did not evolve from one another. The current system of classification is based on the pioneering work of the creation scientist Carolus Linnaeus. Linnaeus developed a classification system that was based on physical characteristics. Linnaeus is credited with popularizing the use of hierarchies and binomial nomenclature—the two-name system used for names in science today. Linnaeus called man *Homo diurnis* (man of the day) and grouped him in the primate group based on physical traits. Today, humans are called *Homo sapiens* (wise man). Classifying humans based on physical traits alone does not reflect the biblical idea of being created in the image of God. While it is true that humans share the physical traits attributed to mammals, humans have a spirit that distinguishes them from animals. Despite the fact that we share many traits with the primates,

---

[437] https://www.huecotanks.com/debunk/kinds.htm
[438] Henry Taylor, "We Don't Really Know What 'Species' Are. Here's Why," The Wire Science, July 23, 2019, (https://science.thewire.in/the-sciences/species-biology-biological-taxonomy/)

humans are not simply highly evolved apes; we were specially created in the image of God.[439]

Linnaeus based his work on natural theology, the idea that God had created order in the universe and man could understand that Divine Order by studying the creation. He wrote in a preface to *Systema Naturae*, "The Earth's creation is the glory of God, as seen from the works of Nature by Man alone." Linnaeus believed in "fixity of species" (the idea that organisms do not change over time) early in his life, but his plant-breeding experiments showed that hybrids were evidence against the idea that species have remained the same since they were created. Linnaeus found that hybridization could happen above the species level and that organisms in nature were in a state of competition. He explained this as the struggle for nature to maintain the balance that God had instilled in it at creation. New organisms that arose were all derived from the primae speciei (original kinds) and were a part of God's original plan because He placed the potential for variation in the original creation. Modern biblical creationists still use the concept of the created kind as a basis for classification and the limit of variation.[440]

> A group of creation scientists called the Biology Study Group is currently attempting to classify animals within created kinds, or baramins (from the Hebrew bara—create and min—kind), based on several criteria, including genetic information and breeding studies. The created kinds roughly correspond to the current classification at the **family level**. However, some kinds may extend up to the order or down to the genus level, since the current system of classification does not take the idea of special creation into account. Any organisms that can interbreed are considered part of the same kind, but those that can't, may or may not be. Further research is needed to understand which organisms, both living and extinct, belong to each created kind....
>
> Creationists disagree with the idea of a "tree of life" as evolutionists see it—all life originating from a single, unknown, common ancestor. If we consider the created kinds from Genesis, the picture of life would look more like an orchard—distinct groups of animals showing variety within a kind. The trees in this orchard do not overlap one another or cross one another, representing the limits of variety within

---

[439] https://answersingenesis.org/creation-science/baraminology/classifying-life/
[440] https://nwcreation.net/biblicalkinds.html

the DNA of the created kinds. This view (developed by Dr. Kurt Wise) is confirmed by the evidence from operational science.

While new species have been observed to arise, it is always within the limits of the created kinds. The study of this variability and the relationships of animals within the original created kinds is called baraminology. This approach to classifying life is fundamentally opposed to the tree of life. This does not mean that creationists reject the majority of classifications by evolutionary biologists but that the evolutionary history associated with the classifications is rejected. More research is needed in the field of baraminology to understand the relationships within the created kinds. This field of research can make specific predictions about the relationships of organisms based on breeding experiments and improve the current understanding of God's divine order.[441]

The variety of dog breeds provides an excellent example of the genetic diversity God gave to the original created "kinds."[442]

One thing to remember is that diversification and adaptation is limited to the information within the created kind. In other words, this is not Darwinism in the neo-Darwinian term. A cat will not adapt to have gills for underwater breathing or wings for flying, but a cat population can change quickly to include a large variety of cats within a small population. More work should

[441]Roger Patterson, "Classifying Life," Answers in Genesis, March 1, 2007, (https://answersingenesis.org/creation-science/baraminology/classifying-life/)
[442] "Dog," Wikipedia pictures (Wikimedia Foundation, last mod. April 6, 2020), (https://en.wikipedia.org/wiki/Dog)

be done on how small this population needs to be. Is it four pair of cat kinds? Ten pair?

Since Genesis does not give us exact details on the morphology, YEC scientists need a little more humility coupled with robust scientific assessment so that they can coherently address this topic. My colleagues from Logos Research Associates, like microbiologist Andrew Fabich, have been working on elements of this topic in the eKINDS initiative from CRS (Creation Research Society).[443] I had the opportunity to attend a talk with Kurt Wise in St. Louis in July 2020 and he readily acknowledged much more research was needed within baraminology. He also made the good point that this scientific discipline was created specifically by creation scientist (for better or worse). So let's critique baraminology on an academic level, based on a 2006 article by Todd Wood in *Creation Research Society* and see how it holds up as a scientific discipline.[444] (To read the whole article, please reference the footnotes). Is baraminology a serious scientific interpretation of the facts? Is it possible that all the species we see today came from a group of ancestral "kinds" from Noah's Ark less than 10,000 years ago?

> The creationist bio-systematic method of baraminology has grown significantly in the past decade. Its conceptual foundations were discussed in the evolution/creation debates of the nineteenth century, long before Frank Lewis Marsh coined the term baramin in 1941. Currently, baraminology has been applied to dozens of groups, and the results of 66 baraminology studies are summarized and evaluated here. Though bias in group and character selection prevents firm conclusions, it appears at this time that Price's suggestion that the family is an approximation of the "created kind" may be correct. Criticisms of baraminology from evolutionists and creationists alike can be resolved with further research. Whatever its future, baraminology is at present a useful tool for investigating God's biological creation....
>
> Early in the twentieth century, models of limited evolution began to appear in creationist writings. These models were new formulations of old ideas, but the creationists proposing them seemed unaware of their predecessors. Seventh-day

---

[443] J O'Micks, "EKINDS – Examination of Kinds in Natural Diversification and Speciation," Creation Research Society, 2017, (https://www.creationresearch.org/ekinds-examination-kinds-natural-diversification-speciation/?hilite='ekinds')

[444] Todd C Wood, "The Current Status of Baraminology," Creation Research Society, December 2006, (https://www.creationresearch.org/current-status-baraminology/)

Adventist creationist George McCready Price proposed as early as 1924 that the "created unit" was the family, not the species.[445] He repeated his proposal in 1938 and 1942. Dudley Joseph Whitney (1928) and Harold W. Clark (1940) also accepted wide variation, although neither set specific limits on the variation. Even Byron C. Nelson (1927), who advocated a type of species fixity, allowed for wide genetic and phenotypic variation.[446]

Summary of Baraminology Results

Creation science has been able to account for 83.3% of all animal groups from a created kind and 81.8% of all plant groups.[447] Though some can say this is not good enough, over 80% of all creation can be accounted for by a primitive classification (close to the family level) and from dating Noah's Ark to approximately 4500 years ago. This is impressive, since most OEC theorists would say you can't get close to accounting for all the created kinds in the world. If you date the Flood at approximately 3300 BC (not 2500 BC), then we get over 90% accounted for. More work is needed, but to say OEC theorists have it figured out is laughable. The fact that we can get over 90% accounted for is impressive and keeps these models viable, especially if you add the credibility's of the social sciences and biblical exegesis as we have already covered. I continue to invest financially in the eKinds initiative to see how far one can take the created kinds in accounting for the life we see today. Is it at the genus or family level, or somewhere in between? Time will tell. So far, testing and analyses seem consistent with Price's suggestion that families were approximately equivalent to created kinds, but it probably should not be considered a confirmation of his idea.[448]

> The approximate equivalence of families and kinds has been suggested repeatedly by creationists, and Wood and Murray recommend using the family as a starting point for baraminology.[449] These ideas may have biased the search for

[445] George McCready Price, *The Phantom of Organic Evolution* (New York: Fleming H. Revell Company, 1925), quoted in Wood, "Current Status," (https://www.creationresearch.org/current-status-baraminology/)

[446] M Adler, *Merkmalsausbildung und Hybridisierung bei Funariaceen* (Bryophyta, Musci, 1993), In Scherer, S. (editor), Typen des Lebens, (Pascal-Verlag, Berlin, Germany), quoted in Wood, "Current Status," (https://www.creationresearch.org/current-status-baraminology/)

[447] Wood, "Current Status," (https://www.creationresearch.org/current-status-baraminology/)

[448] GM Price, "Nature's two hundred families," *Signs of the Times*, 1938, 65(37):11, 14–15.

[449] John Woodmorappe, *Noah's Ark: a Feasibility Study* (Santee, CA: Institute for Creation Research, 1996)), quoted in Wood, "Current Status," (https://www.creationresearch.org/current-status-baraminology/)

baramins. Using a more restricted sample of 11 groups, Wood examined the utility of baraminic distance correlation and MDS....[450] Here, [we] can expand the sample by adding the results of Mace and Wood's analysis of extant cetaceans.[451] These twelve datasets [see diagram below] have been studied using both baraminic distance and MDS. The sample is at least as biased as the full set of studies, but it has the advantage of the same baraminological methods used in each case. Three of the datasets included taxa only from the taxonomic rank of tribe (or multiple tribes). Six datasets include taxa from the rank of family and at least one extra-familial outgroup. One dataset (Equidae) is a single family with no outgroup. Two datasets include more than one family. Of the four datasets that include no extra-familial outgroup, none were interpreted to show evidence of discontinuity. Of the remaining eight datasets, five were interpreted as showing discontinuities, and three were inconclusive. Even though this is a very limited sample, the results of the survey suggest that Price may have been correct, in that discontinuity is not found below the rank of family.... Baraminic distance correlation showed that all taxa were connected by significant, positive correlation, but there was no evidence of significant, negative correlation defining a group.[452]

[450]Todd Charles Wood, "[PDF] Visualizing Baraminic Distances Using Classical Multidimensional Scaling," [PDF] Semantic Scholar, January 1, 1970, (https://www.semanticscholar.org/paper/VISUALIZING-BARAMINIC-DISTANCES-USING-CLASSICAL-Wood/7569d349c15d1698d902607bce20c55162c853f2) quoted in Wood, "Current Status," (https://www.creationresearch.org/current-status-baraminology/)
[451] SR Mace and TC Wood, "Statistical evidence for five whale holobaramins" (Mammalia: Cetacea), 2015, Occasional Papers of the BSG5, quoted in Wood, "Current Status," (https://www.creationresearch.org/current-status-baraminology/)
[452] https://www.creationresearch.org/current-status-baraminology/

Dataset	Rank	Taxa	Relevance Cutoff	Characters after Relevance Filtering	Nonfamilial Outgroup	Discontinuity	Reference
Astereae	tribe	25	0.95	23	no	no	Wood 2005a
Tropidurus	tribe	27	0.95	66	no	no	Wood 2005a
Heliantheae s.l.	tribe	98	0.95	139	no	no	Cavanaugh and Wood 2002
Phalacrocoracidae	genus/family	35	0.95	136	yes	?	Wood 2005a
Sulidae	family	10	0.95	109	yes	?	Wood 2005a
Curculionidae	family	103	0.95	106	yes	?	Wood 2005a
Equidae	family	19	0.95	33	no	no	Cavanaugh et al. 2003; Wood 2005b
Poaceae	family	66	0.95	32	yes	yes	Wood 2002a, 2005b
Spheniscidae	family	30	0.95	33	yes	yes	Wood 2005a
Iguanidae	family/order	35	0.9	57	yes	yes	Wood 2005a
Testudines	order	30	0.9	93	yes	yes	Wood 2005a
Cetacea	order	72	0.95	121	yes	yes	Mace and Wood 2005

Summary of datasets analyzed by Baraminic Distance Correlation and Multidimensional Scaling.[453]

[453] Ibid.

Criticisms of Baraminology

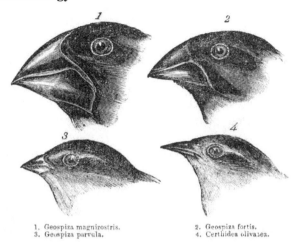

1. Geospiza magnirostris.
3. Geospiza parvula.
2. Geospiza fortis.
4. Certhidea olivasea.

Harvard PhD (cell biology) Nathaniel Jeanson has carefully articulated in his book Replacing Darwin why the YEC explanation not only accurately predicts that species should still be forming right now but if we apply these calculations to birds (for example) we can predict the rate at which new species should form. If birds formed new species at a constant rate over 4,500 years, then on average about 2.4 new species should form every year and this aligns precisely with the 11,000 recognized bird species today.[454]

As I discuss baraminology, a variety of questions, objections, and criticisms arise, often repeatedly. Some of these criticisms have not been published, but some have. Some come from evolutionists and some from fellow creationists.... Often, baraminology is dismissed as the anti-evolution argument "this structure is too complex to evolve" repackaged in formal terminology. While I believe holobaramins had separate origins by God's direct creation, I personally do not use baraminology to argue that an organism or group of organisms could not have evolved. Rather, I interpret holobaramins as separate creations of God. It is possible that a macroevolutionary theory could be devised to account for the discontinuity between holobaramins. It is also possible that baraminology could become a

---

[454] Nathaniel T. Jeanson, Replacing Darwin (Green Forest, AR: Master Books, 2017), 160.

"too-complex-to-evolve" argument if used as an apologetic rather than as a technique to understand organisms.[455]

Another argument repeatedly made against baraminology is that it limits evolution with arbitrary criteria and at arbitrary classification ranks. Statistical methods developed for baraminology would render this objection invalid. The success of statistical methods is especially apparent when examining the results of baraminic distance correlation and MDS (above table), which seem to reveal a consistent pattern of discontinuity around the rank of family. If discontinuity were arbitrarily assigned, we might expect more examples of inconclusive datasets, or datasets that reveal discontinuity within families. While it is possible that future research will find that baraminological methods are not consistent, the present evidence does not warrant that conclusion.

> Evolutionists and fellow creationists have sometimes complained that the terminology is confusing or unnecessary. It is hard for me to appreciate this objection when baraminologists use only three special terms (apobaramin, holobaramin, and monobaramin). Although additional terminology has been proposed (e.g. archaebaramin, potentiality region), these terms have limited use and are not common in the baraminology literature.[456]

> Furthermore, apobaramin, holobaramin, and monobaramin have meaning and utility only to creationists. Because evolutionists and many OEC do not recognize discontinuity (or minimize it when they do), their terminology is not adaptable to baraminology. Ultimately, history will decide the value of the baraminological terms, but in the meantime, the few special terms provide a convenient and precise way to describe the results of baraminological research.[457]

I have found baraminology to be much more credible, though it's in its infancy, than many OEC theorists will admit. Keep in mind that no secularist can even define what a species is, so be cautious about throwing too many stones in this glass house we call academia. As Williams noted, character

---

[455] SR Mace and TC Wood, "Statistical evidence for five whale holobaramins" (Mammalia: Cetacea), 2015, Occasional Papers of the BSG5, quoted in Wood, "Current Status," (https://www.creationresearch.org/current-status-baraminology/)

[456] KP Wise, "Practical baraminology," *Creation Ex Nihilo Technical Journal*, 1992, quoted in Wood, "Current Status," (https://www.creationresearch.org/current-status-baraminology/)

[457] Ibid.

selection was a serious problem for phenetics.[458] This is an obvious problem in baraminology in the analysis of sulids, phalacrocoracids, and curculionids.[459] Future research projects need to address this issue. Some of these future projects will involve studying the datasets already analyzed by baraminological techniques. Other projects must focus on analyzing additional datasets to expand the pool of baraminological studies that can be evaluated. Projects on fossil and extant cetaceans, Hyracotherium, snakes, and chickens have already been initiated. Since there are so few baraminological studies published, the field is wide open for future contributions.

Similarly I am ecstatic to see Nathaniel Jeanson, a Harvard PhD, not only advance the credibility of YEC but provide a series of testable predictions[460] in relation to both the genetics of Babel but of baraminology as well:

> Natural selection has dominated the discussion of the origin of species for 150 years [and even evolutionists as of 2016 at Kings College recognize this is no longer tenable]. In contrast, genetic drift has remained obscure and unknown to the vast majority of people. In short, genetic drift is the application of statistics to genetics. But never fear: the math is fairly easy to follow—and has remarkable relevance to the origin of species. One of the keys to understanding the origin of species is genetic drift—the simple application of statistics to basic genetics. If Noah brought heterozygous ancestors on board the Ark, then the formation of new species—at a rapid pace—was virtually guaranteed. And if this process was virtually guaranteed, then creationists are sitting in the driver's seat when it comes to the central question in the creation/evolution debate.[461]

Similarly, Dr. Jeanson breaks down in detail each element of human genetics and genetic drift to account for baraminology. He does this both qualitatively and quantitatively which is something almost rarely done by either Darwinists

---

[458] A Williams, "Baraminology, biology and the Bible," *TJ*, 2004, quoted in Wood, "Current Status," (https://www.creationresearch.org/current-status-baraminology/)

[459] TC Wood, "A creationist review of the history, geology, climate, and biology of the Galápagos Islands." *CORE Issues in Creation* 1, 2005, quoted in Wood, "Current Status," (https://www.creationresearch.org/current-status-baraminology/)

[460] Y Chromosome molecular clock, population curves, and how genetic drift does account for predictable models in favor of YEC hypotheses.

[461] https://answersingenesis.org/natural-selection/secrets-to-the-origin-species-demystifying-genetic-drift/

or OEC.[462] YEC theorists really needed to step up their research in this area and there are subtle signs like the work of Dr. Jeanson and others, that they are doing just that.[463] Imagine how much further they could go if they had a fraction of the funding and equipment that the microbiology laboratory at the University of Arkansas (where I worked for 3 years) has. It remains apparent that from what we know today, a dog has always come from a dog-type animal and likely will only produce dog-type animals in the future (micro-evolution/adaptation/speciation), and this fits well with the understanding of what Genesis means by "created kinds." The antithesis of this would be that dogs came from a non-dog kind if we traced history back far enough; similarly, it may eventually give rise to a non-dog kind in the future (macro-evolution). We know that domestication can happen very quickly, as we have been able to raise domesticated foxes in less than fifty years, and we know that not all hybrids are sterile, since fertility is dependent on chromosomes:

> Species were once thought to keep to themselves. Now, hybrids are turning up everywhere, challenging evolutionary thinking. All these data belie the common idea that animal species can't hybridize or, if they do, will produce inferior or infertile offspring – think mules. Such reproductive isolation is part of the classic definition of a species. But many animals, it is now clear, violate that rule: Not only do they mate with related species, but hybrid descendants are fertile enough to contribute DNA back to a parental species.[464]

What we know today heavily favors YEC theory, since anything outside of small changes and adaptations goes beyond what we know and can test. Most OEC theorists usually accept their naturalist colleagues' version of facts or acknowledge that most elements of Darwinism are either false or questionable, while at the same time denying a global flood or created kinds repopulating the earth, with only an ad hoc assertion that "we need more time," similar to their naturalist cousins. Let us hope work continues for the secular and OEC world to better understand what they mean by species;

---

[462] Nathaniel T. Jeanson, Replacing Darwin (Green Forest, AR: Masters Books, 2017)
[463] May 2020 – some exciting news based on the 15-part series showing how human history and genetics post our unraveling of the human genome point increasingly to the YEC position concerning genetics, history and mankind (outside of cosmogony). [https://answersingenesis.org/theory-of-evolution/molecular-clock/young-earth-y-chromosome-clocks/]
[464] Elizabeth Pennisi, "Shaking Up the Tree of Life," Science. Nov. 2016.

likewise, let's hope that YEC theorists make inroads into the concept of kinds and the limits found within baraminology.[465]

As I was editing this work, I noticed a new headline that seemed to add credence to the YEC position on created kinds. *Inverse* publication ran an article in December 2019: "Ancient Humans procreated with at least four other species"—Neanderthals, Denisovans, and two unnamed species.[466] Of course, what they call "species" is what baraminologists would call "kinds." The article mostly substantiates the belief that each of us are at least 2% Neanderthal (just as YEC scientist Jack Cuozzo predicted decades earlier).[467] These hominids were the same basic kind and could interbreed. In like fashion, *Live Science* recently acknowledged that ancient wolves seemed to be a common ancestor to most dogs.[468] OEC theory cannot always have its cake and eat it, too, as these secular articles beautifully articulate.

---

[465] I plan to maintain moderate financial support to this endeavor going forward, as I feel this is an area of YEC theory that should be stronger than it is; on the flip side, I'm appalled that secularists cannot tell me what a "species" is. Any articles in *Science* simply mock creation science but do nothing to disprove their theories. Similarly any published OEC criticisms I found resorted to mere hand-waving dismissals.

[466] Sarah Sloat, "Ancient Humans Procreated with at Least Four Other Species," *Inverse* (*Inverse*, December 29, 2019), (https://www.inverse.com/article/61940-ancient-human-four-species-mating-mixing)

[467] Jack Cuozzo, "Buried Alive - The Startling Truth about Neanderthal Man," Jack Cuozzo, (http://www.jackcuozzo.com/)

[468] Becky Oskin, "Ancient Wolf DNA Could Solve Dog Origin Mystery," LiveScience (Purch, May 21, 2015), (https://www.livescience.com/50928-wolf-genome-dog-ancient-ancestor.html)

Conclusions

May my heart always be open to little birds who are the secrets of living whatever they sing is better than to know and if men should not hear them men are too old. – E. E. Cummings

Dr. Humphreys, Dr. Baumgardner (pictured above) and Dr. John Sanford are set to host a small university tour in Summer 2020 and further test their theories and many of the concepts described in this book to the physics, astronomy, genetics, and geology departments of several secular universities. Dr. Sanford taught at Cornell for over thirty years and has been responsible for innovations within the field of genetics (including the invention of the gene gun). Dr. Humphreys has been a nuclear physicist for most of his career and has successfully described the magnetic fields of Uranus and Neptune (against NASA's expectations) based on a YEC perspective. Dr. Baumgardner was described as "one of the best geophysicists in the world today." But when I asked William Lane Craig (or countless other OEC I have worked with over the years) if they had ever met with, read or interacted with any of these scholars I was told: "No." (One hope I have from the project in which this book is a small part is to see OEC/YEC working together more; I'd love to see William Craig taking part on a trip perhaps to Mt. St. Helens with Steve Austin, or an astronomical conference with Humphreys, a genetic debate with John Sanford or a tour of the Grand Canyon with Walt Brown. From my various interactions with William Craig I would guess that he has not really worked with any of the topics I have merely touched upon here so for him to label all YEC as an "embarrassment" is certainly unwarranted and seemingly unjust.

I have always found the concept of *time* fascinating. Whether it is the Egyptian diagonal calendar the Gregorian or understanding time dilation and how it can react to gravity, I remain in awe of time. We have only begun to scratch the surface of what *time* is and how it operates within the confines of space and gravity. In this book, we have hopefully cleared away some of the mud to show that YEC theory is not as farfetched as many assert. Although we are inundated with stories of millions and billions of years from the media and scientific community, the empirical evidence is lacking.

I've spent years studying ancient history and the last few years in classes by Schumacher, Wolfson, and Wysession refining my knowledge of space and earth sciences while defending many of the points I cover in this book to a hostile, critical audience. When we interpret Scripture to line up with the latest thinking in science, we are actually playing science as authority over the Bible and can never be quite sure if what we believe today will still be true tomorrow. We are also constantly trying to convince others that we are justified in believing that the new scientific theory proves the Bible, too. This could continue as long as science keeps discovering "new truths." What kind of credibility would we have in the eyes of the non-Christian world? Who would take us seriously? While our eternal destiny is not dependent upon our belief in the age of the Earth, a careful study of the Bible warrants us not being too quick to adopt secular thoughts in geology and astronomy, especially when they appear to oppose God's Word. In the end, both options are possible. I hope one can see why I hold that YEC theory is just as credible as OEC theory while I remain an agnostic on the exact dating therein.[469]

In *How Not To Be Secular*, professor of philosophy James K.A. Smith suggests that we become less disenchanted with our modern self (presentism) and the notion that we have it all figured out, but he also encourages Christians to abandon their notion of the Bible + the Enlightenment, since most of the science of the Enlightenment is false (think positivism). He challenges Christians to understand just how far the transcendent, biblical God is above our comprehension.[470] This echoes the points I have attempted to show throughout this book, and I encourage you to push yourselves past such preconceived notions.

In the words of William Lane Craig, "What I mean by a good argument is one that makes its conclusions more likely than not. A good argument does not need to make its conclusion certain but instead just to be more probable than its opposite or opposing view."[471] With this understanding, coupled with

---

[469] Jay Seegert. *The Age of the Earth*. P. 18-9. 2013.
(https://www.thestartingpointproject.com/)
[470] James K. A. Smith, *How (Not) to Be Secular: Reading Charles Taylor* (Grand Rapids, MI: William B. Eerdmans Publishing Company, 2015)
[471] Craig's opening argument in his debate with Francisco Ayala on: "Is Intelligent Design Viable?"

my discussion on the notion of common science and intuition from Douglas Axe, and the criteria for establishing an inference to the best explanation via McCullagh, my first two premises concerning biblical exegesis and the social sciences are at least 51%+ more probable than OEC theory's negation in these areas which would mean YEC is more likely true than OEC (assuming you're a Christian and not a follower of scientism of course).

If the viability of YEC theory received at least one check for being the inference to the best explanation on your notepad for the three areas we covered, it stands that it should be a viable option for students.[472] Naturalism is all but dead, like positivism a century ago, so what better time to rereview YEC theory?

There is no reason to limit yourself to groups like AIG or ICR when considering YEC theory. We should look at groups like Logos Research Associates, who are an independent conglomerate of open-minded and accredited persons that are also YEC.[473] I can think of no better way to end this book than by quoting their mission statement as you consider what we have covered in this short book:

- Since its inception, Logos Research Associates has been committed both to a high view of Scripture and to a high view of science. We contend, contrary to popular perception, that good science strongly and consistently affirms Scripture. We acknowledge that this view is rejected in most academic circles today, and even within many Christian circles. While we earnestly seek to contend for the faith, we are at the same time committed to demonstrating respect toward fellow Christian believers who do not agree with us. This motivates us to find ways to defend what we believe to be true while not offending or denigrating other earnest Christians. We humbly look to God for the wisdom and grace to help us be faithful on both counts.

- We at Logos Research Associates are convinced that the first 11 chapters of Genesis are foundational to the coherence of the rest of the Scripture, and so we cannot in good faith minimize their face-value meaning – as so many urge us to do. In humility we are convinced that good science allows us to defend Genesis 1-11 as

---

[472] For me, YEC theory receives 2 out of 3 marks in its favor and OEC theory, 1 out of 3.
[473] I am working to develop a nine-day YEC seminar similar to the Discovery Institute's in Seattle on intelligent design theory with Logos Research Associates: www.LogosResearchAssociates.org

genuine history. There are four prominent rea-sons we view these chapters as so foundational.

- First, we are persuaded that Scripture clearly describes and builds upon a miraculous and perfect creation which originally was free of sin, death, suffering, disease, parasitism, and predation. The perfect creation described in Genesis 1 and 2 is a fundamental reflection of God's own perfect character. The perfect nature of the pre-Fall world is in fact a powerful picture of the heavenly state which is the eager expectation of every true Christian. To reject a perfect and miraculous creation calls the character of God into question, undermines the veracity of Scripture, and diminishes the glimpses Scripture gives us into the reality of heaven

- Secondly, we are persuaded that the description of a literal Fall in Genesis 3 provides the only coherent explanation today for the origin of natural evil, human sin, suffering, disease, parasitism, and predation. Most of the rest of Scripture reveals the mind-numbing consequences of the Fall as well as the nature of the spiritual war which still rages around us. Rejecting a literal Fall not only brings the character of God into question (is God the author of evil?) but leaves the origin of death and suffering entirely unanswered. More importantly, if in reality there was no Fall, and the human race did not in reality acquire a sin nature as a result, then the proposition that we actually can and do commit acts of rebellion against God is undermined. If our actions are only natural impulses, then there is no basis for judgment, we do not need to be saved, and Christ had no reason to go to the cross.

- Thirdly, catastrophic judgment in the form of a global Flood (Genesis 6-9) is foundational to understanding the Scriptural themes of God's holiness, His unconditional requirement for justice, and His need to purge away evil. It is only in this light that we can understand the need for the Mosaic Law, for atoning sacrifice for sin, and for the substitutionary work of Christ on the cross. To reject the Flood blurs the certain reality of the coming final judgment. It calls into question Christ's description of the world conditions just prior to His return, which He likens to the time just prior to the Flood of Genesis (Mat 24:37-39).

- Lastly, if there was no Flood then there was no Tower of Babel event (Genesis 10-11), and therefore no adequate explanation for the astonishing diversity of ethnic groups and languages we observe in the human population today.

- For nearly 2000 years, these basic truth claims concerning the history of the world (a perfect original Creation, the Fall, and a global Flood judgment) have been foundational to our understanding of the Gospel. However, in light of modern interpretations of certain scientific evidences, some now say that believing such things is simply no longer possible. Many good, intelligent, honest, Christian believers say the scientific evidence now demands that we must set aside the face-value meaning of Genesis 1-11 (and many other parts of Scripture) to accommodate certain modern scientific findings. The following article tries to explain, in good faith and with Christian love, why those Scriptures are simply too important to dismiss, and why good science allows, and sometimes even seems to require, a Genesis 1-11 understanding of world history.

- To our brethren who are committed to the "old earth" perspective, we wish to re-affirm that we consider you our brothers and sisters in Christ, we respect your differing perspective, and we understand the complexity of the scientific issues being debated.[474]

Please visit me at our Creation History Museum:
(www.NWABibleMuseum.org), our coffee shop and art gallery (Reverie), or email me at CreationHistory@yahoo.com.
I hope this work has offended dogmatic YEC groups and equally dogmatic OEC groups and caused them to dig deeper into their Bibles as well as science, history, philosophy, and the arts. If I am wrong, I do look forward to my OEC & YEC colleagues showing me where I am in error; point by point and page by page.[475]

"Who has put wisdom in the inward parts or given understanding to the mind?" (Job 38:36)

"Let God be true, and every man a liar." (Romans 3:4)

---

[474] "Convictions," Logos Researchers, (https://www.logosresearchassociates.org/convictions)
[475] Naturalism (thus atheism) has no answers as I have thoroughly discussed in The Philosophy of History, and all religions outside of the Bible are built outside of history; so the thinking person should not only take Christianity seriously but also relook at YEC and what it is and what it is not especially in this time of Coronavirus. What if the next plague is many times worse? Is your God the one of the Bible or the one of the 20th century West?

Appendix A: Theistic Evolution and Intelligent Design

"Evolution is not a fact. It doesn't even qualify as a theory or hypothesis. It is a metaphysical research program, and it is not really testable science."

– Karl Popper

Did you know almost every "fact" in the Scopes Trial (looked at historically in a pro-Darwinian manner) has been shown false? Did you know that Darwinian hypotheses has done nothing but grow weaker overtime? Did you know with the Royal Society meeting (at Kings College) in 2016 that all the pro-Darwin groups were at a loss on how to advance the seemingly bankrupt theory? They did recognize that mutations and natural selection were not enough for anything above micro-evolution (speciation/adaptation) to be true; unfortunately since they could not find anything naturalistic to replace the theory they decided to double-down on continuing to teach lies (for lack of a better word) in our students' textbooks.

I have shown why Neo-Darwinism (and moreover naturalism) is false in *The Philosophy of History*, and while I could write an entire book refuting Darwinism, I was pleased to see the Discovery Institute producing a 1000 page book refuting the concept of "theistic evolution" (recently rebranded evolutionary creationism) titled: *Theistic Evolution: A Scientific, Philosophical and Theological Critique*. With so many great minds contributing to such a momentous work, I could not hope to produce anything better so I will simply reference you to this book. With Darwinism in such a weak intellectual state in 2020, I am dumbfounded to see Christians attempting to endorse Darwinism with a pseudo-form of Christianity in front of it. What I have found of late is these *Christians* know little to nothing about the theory of Darwinism and even less about Christianity (theistic evolutionists seem to be more kin to the Gnostics of long ago). While so much more could be said, I have found that this 1000-page book should hopefully serve to be the proverbial *nail in the coffin* to the Christian heresy known as "theistic evolutionism" (though groups like "Capturing Christianity" lead by the WLC devotee Cameron Bertuzzi as well as Bill Craig himself will refuse to read it or argue through it).

People often ask: "So is it conspiracy or are the majority of scientists who believe in Darwin just stupid?" As my friend and Harvard doctorate Nathaniel Jeanson has said: "It's neither. Not a conspiracy and not stupidity. It's simply ignorance." I have lost count of how many Christians and non-Christians alike refuse to even read a book on Intelligent Design or one critical of Darwinian thought let alone a Creation Science book. I have sat down with instructors at the university, college and high school level time and time again and been aghast that they do not even know there is another side to the argument. Once I ask them just a few questions and we start talking they will almost always say something like: "I had never thought about that."

Günter Bechly, a renowned paleo-entomologist, is a perfect example of this. At the bicentennial of Darwin's birth, Bechly directed the Darwin Day exhibit at the prestigious State Museum of Natural History in Stuttgart, Germany. Attracting over 100,000 visitors, the event was one of the largest celebrations in Germany of Darwin's birth year. Bechly created an exhibit to demonstrate refutation of intelligent design. It featured both Darwin's Origin of Species and some books by intelligent design theorists. But Bechly happened to read some of the pro-intelligent design books. He noted, "What I recognized to my surprise is that the arguments I found in those books were totally different from what I heard either from colleagues, or when you watch YouTube videos where the discussion is around intelligent design versus neo-Darwinian evolution. And I had the impression that on one side those people are mistreated, their position is misrepresented, and on the other hand that these arguments are not really receiving an appropriate response and they have merit."[476]

He was promptly dismissed (see the wonderful documentary *Expelled: No Intelligence Allowed*); and similar stories go on and on and on. So too it is with YEC. I highly encourage more Christians to look at the Discovery Institute: Center for Science and Culture as being a much better fit than any form of Darwinism for the Christian. I just returned from a meeting with Drs. Meyer/Axe/Behe/West in Dallas (January 2020) and we discussed further advancement of their critique against theistic evolution so I can do no better than point you to this wonderful and holistic book that provides a comprehensive rebuttal of theistic evolution or evolutionary creation on practically every front:

---

[476] https://freescience.today/story/gunter-bechly/

https://www.discovery.org/store/product/theistic-evolution/

Edited by J. P. Moreland, Stephen Meyer, Christopher Shaw, Ann Gauger, and Wayne Grudem and featuring contributions from two dozen highly credentialed scientists, philosophers, and theologians from Europe and North America, Theistic Evolution: A Scientific, Philosophical, and Theological Critique provides the most comprehensive critique of theistic evolution yet produced (almost 1,000 pages). It documents evidential, logical, and theological problems with theistic evolution, opening the door to scientific and theological alternatives—making the book essential reading for understanding this worldview-shaping issue.[477]

---

[477] https://www.discovery.org/store/product/theistic-evolution/

Appendix B: Dinosaurs – Just for Fun

"Education is not merely neglected in many of our schools today but is replaced to a great extent by ideological indoctrination. "
— Thomas Sowell, (*Inside American Education*)

If I look at the random headlines over the last 2 months I see: *time-stopping Paradox and black holes, Shark bones in land-locked Kentucky, we all are Neanderthal, Human growth population, how DNA has decode our origins, 95% of the Human Genome cannot evolve, more soft tissue inside dinosaur bones found,* etc. Now – "if" YEC is true then it would easily explain all these headlines it would seem. OEC and especially theistic evolution and naturalism have to go to extreme lengths to attempt to *concoct* a story that can attempt to fit the data. It is for reasons like this that I really began to pay more attention starting around 2005 to how a YEC mindset does seem to provide more readily assessable answers to these various dilemmas (especially as a Christian) than the secular models that I have spent so much time immersed in as well as those from my OEC colleagues.

With that being said one of my editors asked if I would be addressing dinosaurs? So just for fun, with the above reoccurring headlines in mind, I decided to add this appendix.

Dinosaurs and Baraminology

It's funny – not my cup of tea at all but it is kind of ironic of developments of late. In the past I have always pointed people to four documentaries on dinosaurs. The first is your typical National Geographic special and the one that is propagated throughout textbooks and museums assuming a naturalistic ontology. The second one (my favorite) was hosted by the late Leonard Nimoy *Ancient Mysteries* (A&E) in 1997, where by agnostically looking at all the evidence they conclude that dinosaurs must have been seen by ancient man even if the dinosaurs dated back to 65M years ago. Lastly was a DVD on the possibility of dinosaurs, historically known as dragons, being mostly killed off during Noah's Flood. (Just for fun I include a copy of the 2012 *Ancient Aliens* from the History channel where they purport "aliens" were the reasons behind the dinosaur extinction (of course) but some did live to coincide with the timeline of mankind). Oddly 3 of the 4 support the position of humans and dinosaurs being contemporaries which begs the question "why?"

Again – I do not have a horse in the race when it comes to dinosaurs, but what I try and encourage to all sides to do is simply "think critically" and not just

260

accept the dubious and spoon-fed answer given to us by the naturalists as well as the OEC side. I have no problem with dinosaurs being 65M+ years old but I find the growing line of evidences within this area from the social sciences and theology to not strongly support this line of thinking; nor does the natural sciences support this inference without some very strong extrapolations of the data. Like Francis Schaeffer, I can say simply: "I do not know." But I say this as a very informed person on all sides of the data, not just a simple shrugging of the shoulders. Dinosaurs are fun, but they are not as important biblically speaking as the areas I have already covered concerning creation, Adam/Eve, Noah's Flood, Tower of Babel, that are each covered in detail in Genesis 1-11.

Part of what's fun with something like dinosaurs, is that there is so much mystery behind them. For example, the wooly mammoth was once described as living tens of thousands of years before mankind until it became undeniable that they were hunted and killed by ancient man. The evidence continued to pour in however, that the mammoth was not that ancient; so now, even unfriendly to creation or intelligent design sites like Wikipedia recognize that the mammoth was alive as recent as 2000 BC.[478] Think about the margin of error from a science textbook 75 years ago to today. The majority of the science section of that textbook is now known as false whereas the history and philosophy of history of the bible has done nothing but grow in strength and explanatory power through today. With that being said, all I am calling for on the topic of dinosaurs is a little bit of humility. Some YEC groups make dubious extrapolations such as man perhaps riding dinosaurs, but this is a minor extrapolation compared to the naturalistic concept of dinosaurs *evolving* from Eoraptor or a type of Archosauriaas.

OEC groups offer almost nothing to the debate aside from always taking the side of the natural/secular scientists including when they are shown fallacious (which is most of the time). For example, when William Lane Craig was asked about dinosaurs in his 2016 speaking trip to Singapore he was asked about dinosaurs. Instead of addressing the question, he did a quick *dodge* which is quite characteristic of my OEC colleagues. Instead of simply saying: "I don't know" he made a random comment about how he has seen books with Tyrannosaurus Rex eggs on Noah's Ark and then he reassured the audience he was not retreating in light of modern-science, but that if one reads Genesis carefully (alluding to the Framework hypothesis we already critiqued in chapter one) then we are able to read in eons of time in which the dinosaurs lived over *55 million* years before mankind came onto the scene. Again these are those "weak" type responses that OEC throw out there that not only makes

---

[478] https://en.wikipedia.org/wiki/Woolly_mammoth

them appear to not have thought through these questions and therefore look somewhat non-intellectual; or worse yet, they appear to be dismissing the Bible as mostly myth while reminding the audience these things are simply not important as long as they "believe in Jesus"! I would have said to the same question: "I don't know." And then I would have given them the three most relevant theories and encouraged them to research on their own and then come back and tell me perhaps? Dr. Craig's hubris leaked through when he commented at the end of the above-mentioned question that "certainly most *academics* don't believe in dinosaurs and the bible." As mentioned earlier, I have had to remind Dr. Craig on three different occasions that most *academics* do not believe in the virgin birth either, walking on water, water into wine, etc. So, is there any more credible answer than Dr. Craig's response above to dinosaurs and the bible?

The 110M year-old ankylosaur, what many including national geographic are dubbing a *new* species aka "nodosaur", was found almost completely intact/mummified for 110M years in 2017 (ironically without any good explanation of "how"). I am hopefully going to be able to inspect this specimen much closer this year, but for now I find it quite ironic that even National Geographic acknowledges this beast was preserved beautifully in a "great flood" sometime around 110M years ago.[479]

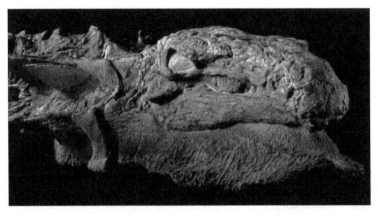

Similarly, it is now accepted by even the most ardent naturalistic scientist (as well as the OEC scientists clinging to their heels) that dinosaur soft tissue is present in many fossilized dinosaur bones. It's not just dinosaur soft tissue

---

[479] https://www.nationalgeographic.com/magazine/2017/06/dinosaur-nodosaur-fossil-discovery/

either, but the presence of detectable proteins such as collagen, hemoglobin, osteocalcin, actin, and tubulin that they must account for.[480]

> *National Geographic's* article titled, "Many dino fossils could have soft tissue inside"[9] reveals that the scientific community is expecting many more examples of dinosaur soft tissue in the future. These facts have been a thorn in their side for several years now as they are incredibly difficult to explain within an evolutionary (millions of years) timeframe. Needless to say, they fit beautifully within a biblical (young earth) timescale; these are almost certainly the remains of creatures that were buried during the Genesis Flood, approximately 5,400 years ago.[481]

Of course, the naturalistic (and thus OEC) community is frantically trying to keep their cool, by suggesting that iron may be what has helped preserve this tissue over 65M years so every naturalistic (and OEC) scientist has jumped on this dubious response as they have quickly swept the story under the rug.

In February 2019 Mary Schweitzer's idea that iron generated free hydroxyl (OH) radicals (called the *Fenton Reaction*) causing preservation of the proteins was challenged. Free radicals are far more likely to help degrade proteins and other organic matter. Indeed, the reaction is used to destroy organic compounds. It also requires that the hydroxyl radicals are transported by water. However, water would have caused hydrolysis of the peptide bonds, and very fast deamidation of the amino acids residues asparagine and glutamine. Aspartyl residues should also have isomerized to isoaspartyl residue if exposed to water. Tyrosine, methionine and histidine would have been oxidized under Schweitzer's proposed conditions. But the dino proteins show that these unstable residues are still present:

> The dilemma is this: how did the fragment successfully become cross-linked through aqueous hydroxyl free radical attack apparently explaining peptide survival while hydrolytically unstable moieties such as Asn avoid contact with the aqueous medium—for 68 million years? If we are to accept the benefits of random aqueous hydroxyl radicals cross-linking the peptide matrix in an undefined chemical

---

[480] Other researchers had found osteocalcin 'dated' to 120 Ma: Embery G. and six others, Identification of proteinaceous material in the bone of the dinosaur *Iguanodon, Connective Tissue Res.* 44 Suppl 1:41–6, 2003. The abstract says: "an early eluting fraction was immunoreactive with an antibody against osteocalcin."
[481] https://creation.com/dinosaur-soft-tissue

bonding, we should also accept the cost—peptide and amino acid hydrolysis.[482]

It's quite ironic, and a bit comical, that Bill Craig and other OEC usually give the typical *hand-wave* against YEC arguments with gusto; for example even when it was being led by secular scientists on potential problems with the speed of light's consistency or dinosaur soft-tissue, Craig was quick to say: "Sounds like some type of YEC argument to me!"[483] Thus committing the most elementary logical fallacy (genetic) while providing no substance to these type responses (typical of his deistic form of *post-foundational realism*). Equally ironic is when Jack Horner, one of the best known paleontologists in the United States, has inferred that at least one-third of all dinosaurs we thought we knew never even existed![484] No need to go into minute detail here, but suffice it to say, Horner has put together a quite convincing theory that the majority of dinosaurs that we thought were sub-species (ex: Triceratops) were in reality just shape-shifting dinosaurs. How could scientists have been so confused on this topic? In Jack Horner's words, "Scientists like to name dinosaurs."[485] So while this opens a plethora of new questions, Horner's views have largely been accepted by secular scientific journals which makes sense from a YEC vantage point. To me it is a call to remain humble before shutting the door on critical thinking as both Ken Ham and Bill Craig have done in many areas.

[482] DeMassa, J.M. and Boudreaux, E., Dinosaur peptide preservation and degradation, *Creation Research Society Quarterly* 51:268–285, 2015. Thomas, B., Does the toast model explain fossil protein persistence? *Acts & Facts (Impact)*, 48(3) March 2019.

[483] https://calvaryoxnard.org/old-earth-young-earth-resources/; https://answersingenesis.org/astronomy/cosmology/photon-reference-frame-and-distant-starlight-analyzing-ideas-gerald-l-schroeders-i-science-godi/

[484] https://www.newscientist.com/article/mg20727713-500-morphosaurs-how-shape-shifting-dinosaurs-deceived-us/

[485] Ibid.

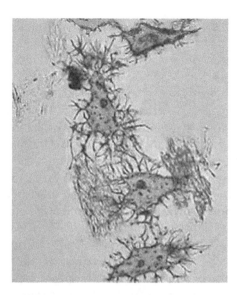

Bone cells discovered by Schweitzer, showing classic appearances including nuclei and connecting fibrils—from a Brachylophosaurus *allegedly 80 million years old.*[486]

Lastly, I just received and read through a copy of Brian Thomas' doctoral dissertation from the University of Liverpool (England) in the Fall of 2019 on this very topic:

> This thesis describes the novel application of second-harmonic generation (SHG) imaging, and established technique in biomedical science, to ancient bone. In this study, four separate and independent techniques confirmed that SHG reliably detects trace amounts of collagen protein in certain medieval and ice age bone samples. The soft-tissues found in these dinosaur bones present a poor fit with deep time. If the Noahic Flood deposited those fossils only thousands of years ago, there it is no wonder they still have these proteins including bone collagen and levels of radiocarbon well above AMS detection thresholds. The inability of pMC values to distinguish between Jurassic and Cretaceous sample sources conforms to this model.[487]

---

[486] https://creation.com/dinosaur-soft-tissue
[487] Brian Thomas. *Ancient and Fossil Bone Collagen Remnants.* October 2019. Pp. 131-4.

What is refreshing about this is that a creation scientist is literally doing a doctoral dissertation at a secular university on such a topic. We're not talking pseudo-science with various and alleged dinosaur tracks or big-foot sightings as was the case 40 years ago with YEC; we're literally talking about good/solid research that is pushing the evidence in a new direction. Whether Dr. Thomas' findings are eventually overturned or not, it seems his YEC model, along with what we have reviewed on YEC based cosmology, Noah's Flood, baraminology, and Adam & Eve, are all quite "viable" and worthy of further exploration. Compared to the OEC side who just "punts to the naturalistic scientists" the YEC side seems to be, in some ways, the more scientific of the two groups over the last few decades at least. All jokes aside, I do hope to see more critical thinking by both YEC and OEC groups, but I do encourage all sides to begin holding the OEC side more accountable to give some good, logically consistent and biblically sound answers when asked a question about a topic (not just hand-waving or a faulty appeal to authority (an "authority" that would burn them at the stake as quickly as it would the YEC side if they had their way)). While Dr. Craig is quite ingenious in defending the Resurrection, his and other OEC's simple hand-waving dismissal of parts of the Bible they cannot explain naturalistically calls into question the credibility of Scripture. As we have already seen, many of the OEC's appeal to the natural sciences as being on their side are either spurious or inconclusive at best.

Appendix C – Theoretical Modeling

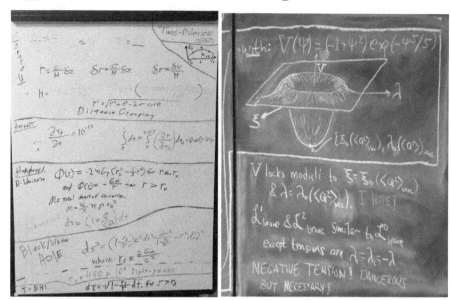

To the left you will see what I had first written out on a dry erase board when testing some of the math that goes into time dilation modeling. To the right you will see similar writings on a chalkboard from the movie *Interstellar* when they use the same beginning point to see if a theory holds up on paper. This is normal in theoretical physics. For example, when physicists detected the Higgs Boson a few years ago using the Hadron Collider, they were able to substantiate what we already knew on paper. We start with theoretical physics and see if the theory is sound on paper then we normally never have the opportunity to substantiate it. The Hadron Collider costs about $5B and still is not nearly powerful enough to substantiate something like the physics behind a blackhole but we were able to substantiate the existence of this elementary particle in the standard model of particle physics.

The reason I am describing this briefly is to show for example that what I have discussed in this short work holds up for the most part "on paper" which is an important first step. Obviously on paper and through computer simulation is about as technical as I can get since I do not have an extra $5B lying around to construct my own collider or the $1.6B for the Galileo Probe. This is no real surprise since the vast majority of theories for space cannot be substantiated at this time. Nonetheless, the physics behind the theories I touched on holds up well as do computer modeling of each but I will leave it to others (both OEC and YEC) to hopefully build upon and expand the hypotheses within their own respective work.

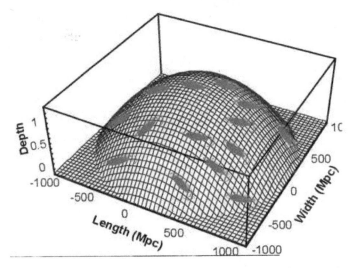

Dr. John Hartnett prematurely (in my opinion) abandoned many elements of his Carmeli Cosmology which had some holes in it, but nonetheless remains a solid theory on paper utilizing the 5th dimension described earlier.

As far as the geology models, I was able to utilize both computer and physical modeling. Some local construction sites that had to stockade different types of sand and gravel for an extended amount of time were more than happy for me to take periodic measurements and simulate tests and then compare them to what we see within an augmentation box and them compare it to what we see compared to somewhere like St. George Utah or the Grand Canyon. Similarly, I was able to utilize cementing agents in a controlled environment to run similar models. Granted all of these are somewhat primitive and inconclusive in many ways, but at the same time I was able to substantiate the degree of cutoff that happens underwater vs. the wind and similarly put these measurements into a simulation (ex: PaleoGIS) to see what it could look like a century or millennia later. This is not to show that my conclusions are final of course, but it is to show that I not only did the due diligence to test what I was looking at but also give a small glimpse what many (though certainly not all) creation scientists do on a much larger scale that I simply meddled with.

One disclaimer for most computer simulations is that if you "fudge" the physics enough you can almost get whatever conclusion you want. For example, if I precluded the early fountains of the deep in Walt Brown's Hydroplate model then most of his model holds up quite well. However, the supercritical water portion is somewhat complicated as it is difficult to ascertain exactly what the pressure would be.

One thing that was interesting is that I really had to manipulate the simulation in order to get subduction to occur whether on the standard PT model or CPT. Of course, I could have been off on some of my calculations, but it appears Bryan Nickel ran into the same problem as shown below.[488]

488

https://www.youtube.com/watch?v=dhDEkM30xZ8&list=PLvTah6tEcChwZjUyG6X_5_zw VDAalSJHI&index=4&frags=pl%2Cwn

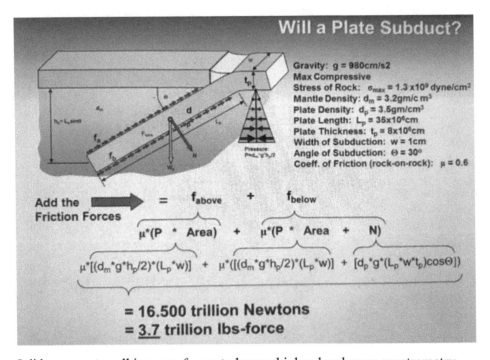

Will a Plate Subduct?

Gravity: $g = 980 cm/s2$
Max Compressive
Stress of Rock: $\sigma_{max} = 1.3 \times 10^9$ dyne/cm²
Mantle Density: $d_m = 3.2 gm/c m^3$
Plate Density: $d_p = 3.5 gm/cm^3$
Plate Length: $L_p = 35 \times 10^6 cm$
Plate Thickness: $t_p = 8 \times 10^6 cm$
Width of Subduction: $w = 1 cm$
Angle of Subduction: $\Theta = 30°$
Coeff. of Friction (rock-on-rock): $\mu = 0.6$

Add the **⟶** Friction Forces $= f_{above} + f_{below}$

$\mu^*(P * Area) + \mu^*(P * Area + N)$

$\mu^*[(d_m{}^*g^*h_p/2)^*(L_p{}^*w)] + \mu^*([(d_m{}^*g^*h_p/2)^*(L_p{}^*w)] + [d_p{}^*g^*(L_p{}^*w^*t_p)cos\Theta])$

$= 16.500$ trillion Newtons
$= \underline{3.7}$ trillion lbs-force

I did manage to call in some *favors* to have a higher-level mass spectrometry technique to compare/confirm some of the protein composition (genetically) discussed earlier so this is anything but pseudoscience. Obviously, all of these examples are crude and subject to error but the YEC work I have seen at a much higher caliber than I have done here is legitimate and testable science; and in my humble opinion just as legitimate if not more than any *naturalism of the gaps* or *time of the gaps* I have seen from the other side over the last two decades of study. From what I have seen throughout the last few years of this project is that creation science is just as much *science* as the secular world partakes. One side assumes God and the Bible and the other naturalism; both have their own starting points.

Secular scholars Fowler and Kuebler seem to agree with me in their 2007 book *The Evolution Controversy*, where they take a stab at competing theories from intelligent design, OEC and YEC and come to the conclusion that all of these theories are strong enough (including YEC) to merit being taught in the public school systems. Though they do not advocate teaching equal time to each, they do find enough strength in their position to conclude it is unwarranted and dishonest to hide this from students in the name of critical thinking.[489]

---

[489] Fowler, Thomas B. and Kuebler. *The Evolution Controversy*. Baker Academic. p. 357